SPLENDORS OF MEIJI

SPLENDORS OF MEIJI
TREASURES OF IMPERIAL JAPAN

MASTERPIECES FROM THE KHALILI COLLECTION

JOE EARLE

BROUGHTON INTERNATIONAL PUBLICATIONS

A Broughton International Publication

ISBN 1-874780-13-7 (hardback)

© 1999 Broughton International Inc.
© 1999 The Khalili Family Trust

General Editor: Joe Earle
Photography: Alfie Barnes and Christopher Phillips
Design: Martin Bragg Associates and Ivor Claydon
Copy Editor: Anke Cross
Production: Martin Bragg

First published in 1999 by Broughton International Inc.
St. Petersburg, Florida
USA

http://www.broughtonmasterpiece.com

Library of Congress Catalog Card Number: 208-798-5553

Printed and bound in China

Frontispiece: Incense Burner, Catalogue number 1

CONTENTS

CONTENTS (CONTINUED)

ACKNOWLEDGMENT

Throughout history, man's artistic accomplishments have served him well as a provocative and powerful universal language. What he has conceived, he has fashioned with his hands, thus conveying his heritage, his hopes, and his heart.

As the nineteenth century came to a close and Japan emerged from centuries of isolation, it was through the creative genius of her artists and craftsmen that she revealed herself to a waiting world. It is now through these magnificent "enlightened" works of art that we present "*Splendors of Meiji: Treasures of Imperial Japan*".

All who view this Exhibition or peruse the pages of this catalogue are indebted to Dr. David Khalili, whose passion for collecting and preserving these wonderful works of art is second only to the fervor of the artists who created them.

We also want to express sincere gratitude to Andrew Keelan whose administrative abilities have served Dr. Khalili and his collection so well through the years and whose kind demeanor has made this Exhibition such a pleasant experience. Our thanks also go to Sue Bond for her most professional and meaningful advice and consultation.

To Joe Earle, our guest Exhibition curator and author of this catalogue, and to our own Dr. Robert Bianchi go our heartfelt thanks and appreciation for guiding and molding this project over these many months. We are all richer because they have shared their great wealth of knowledge.

We want to also acknowledge the contributions of Dr. Oliver Impey and Malcolm Fairley to the research associated with this collection. It is through their efforts that we gained the necessary insight to bring the Exhibition to fruition.

Our sincere thanks go to all of the wonderful volunteers who work tirelessly to assure the enjoyment of all those who visit the Exhibition. They are true "ambassadors" and we are better because they serve.

Finally, to all of those at Broughton International who work so hard and with such great dedication and devotion so that others may enjoy the world and its people, we sincerely thank you for creating another Broughton Masterpiece Presentation. Only you know the effort required and only you can fully savor the results.

JAMES E. BROUGHTON
President
Broughton International Inc.

FOREWORD

Over the last three decades I have been assembling collections under the auspices of the Khalili Family Trust in a number of different fields, from Spanish metalwork and the arts of the Islamic world to Indian and Swedish textiles. In the course of collecting I came across several examples of Japanese decorative arts of the Meiji Era and was enthralled by their technical excellence and striking designs. Surprised that so little information was available on the art of the period, I decided that I would build up a comprehensive collection covering the forty-four years of imperial rule from 1868 to 1912.

The Meiji Era was a time of astonishingly rapid change, but throughout its four decades the Japanese people continued to nurture and develop their historic art and craft traditions. The collection features works of a beauty and artistic quality which could never be replicated today, many of them created by individuals who attained the honor of admission to the rank of Artist to the Imperial Household. It is my hope that audiences around the world will come to share my view that they represent a level of artistic accomplishment and technical mastery which has never been surpassed.

It is particularly appropriate that my collection of the art of the Meiji Era, selections from which have already been displayed in three British capitals – at the British Museum in London, the National Museum of Wales in Cardiff, and at the National Museums of Scotland in Edinburgh – should now be exhibited in the United States. It was the young American nation, and not the great powers of Europe, that in 1854 took the decisive steps leading to Japan's opening up to the outside world. It was at the Philadelphia Centennial Exhibition, held in 1876, that the Japanese government displayed thirty thousand items from all over Japan. The ten million visitors to that extraordinary international event, which covered some 236 acres and included around 250 buildings, were deeply impressed by the Japanese contribution. One of them called the Japanese bronzes on display "the most marvelous objects here" and another American critic wrote that:

... we found here abundant evidences that Japan outshines the most cultivated nations of Europe in arts which are their pride and glory ...

I am confident that visitors to *Splendors of Meiji: Treasures of Imperial Japan* will experience the same sense of wonder and delight, and will agree with one of the 27 million visitors to the Chicago World's Fair in 1893 that:

...the European or American who enters these [Japanese] galleries ... recognizes at once a new order of things and a new world ... an air of having come from behind the stars ...

I should like to thank Mr. James E. Broughton, President of Broughton International Incorporated, and his wonderful team for all their encouragement and support in realizing my dream of bringing this exhibition before the American public. To my own team in the United Kingdom who have also worked tirelessly towards this end, I am eternally grateful.

DR. NASSER D. KHALILI

PREFACE

One of the characteristics of a true connoisseur and great art collector is what we in the museum world term "an inner eye", capable of recognizing aesthetic achievement where others see nothing. Dr. Nasser D. Khalili possesses such an eye. At a time when the academic community in general and collectors of Asian art in particular were put off by the very exuberance of the arts of the Meiji Era, Dr. Khalili was attracted by the sheer technical bravura and retinally-stimulating beauty inherent in these consummate masterpieces. Gradually he was able to assemble a collection of Meiji decorative art which is today virtually without rival in its scope, breadth, and number of pieces signed by known masters, many of whom gained the singular distinction of being appointed Artists to the Imperial Household. This presentation of over four hundred objects from Dr. Khalili's collection marks the first time in recent memory that the artistic achievements of the Meiji Era have been shown in such encyclopedic and systematic fashion.

Technically accomplished and aesthetically pleasing as these masterpieces are, they also bring to life a formative stage in the development of the United States. The theme parks and shopping malls that dot our national landscape can be profitably regarded as the descendants of the World's Fairs held at the turn of the century in Philadelphia, Chicago, and St. Louis. These great American events, which attracted enormous audiences, not only fostered a sense of nationhood and a spirit of optimism towards the future but also helped define our cultural personality and shopping habits.

I am, therefore, extremely pleased to be associated with this endeavor which is unique in providing our audience with beautiful objects to behold and admire, while simultaneously reminding us of an almost forgotten chapter from the pages of our own history.

DR. ROBERT STEVEN BIANCHI
Director of Academic and
Curatorial Affairs
Broughton International Inc.

INTRODUCTION

Between 1868 and 1912, Japan's leaders built a constitutional nation-state, developed an up-to-date industrial infrastructure, and won major wars against China and Russia. They also preserved and nurtured their country's art and craft traditions, inspiring the creation of works whose beauty and quality astonished the nations of the civilized world. From 1873 onwards, Japan's ceramics, metalwork, enamels, lacquer, and other decorative arts were presented at domestic and international expositions. In the United States, remarkable objects like those in the collection of Dr. Nasser D. Khalili helped define the American image of Japan's national character at a formative time in the history of both countries.

The three largest expositions held here during Japan's Meiji Era (1868–1912) were the Centennial Exhibition at Philadelphia in 1876, the World's Columbian Exposition at Chicago in 1893, and the Louisiana Purchase Exposition at St. Louis in 1904. They were seen by Japanese administrators and workmasters alike as unmissable opportunities for the promotion of their country's achievements. On each occasion, established foreign powers such as France, Germany, and Great Britain were matched or outstripped by the Japanese in money, effort, and organization. Thanks to the technical and aesthetic brilliance of the goods on show, as well as the sheer novelty of all things Japanese, Japan's displays

attracted more favorable comment than those of any other country.

This catalogue is organized along the same lines as the exhibition it documents, with the addition of special sections on the different media: Metalwork, "Satsuma" ware, Lacquer, Enamels, and Porcelain. Although we have included many items which have been acquired during the last five years, much of the text draws heavily upon the official catalogue of the Khalili Collection, completed in 1995. I should therefore like to take this opportunity to acknowledge my indebtedness to the many scholars who contributed to those ground-breaking volumes and in particular to the two principal editors, Malcolm Fairley and Dr. Oliver Impey.

JOE EARLE
Guest Curator

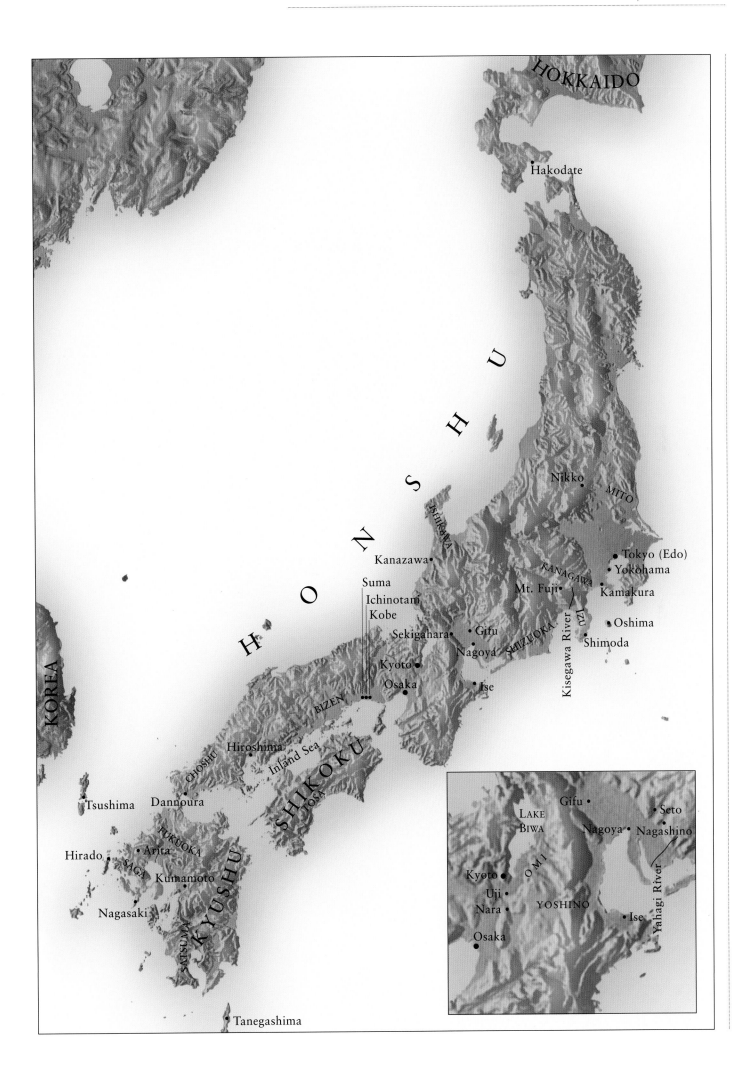

HOKKAIDO

• Hakodate

HONSHU

Nikko• MITO

Kanazawa•

ISHIKAWA

Suma
Ichinotani
Kobe

Sekigahara•   •Gifu

Kyoto•
Osaka•

• Ise

Nagoya•

SHIZUOKA

Mt. Fuji•

KANAGAWA

• Tokyo (Edo)
• Yokohama

• Kamakura

IZU

• Oshima

Shimoda

Kisegawa River

BIZEN

Hiroshima•

CHOSHU

Inland Sea

SHIKOKU

TOSA

Tsushima•

Dannoura•

FUKUOKA

Hirado•   • Arita

SAGA

Kumamoto•

Nagasaki•

SATSUMA   KYUSHU

KOREA

• Tanegashima

LAKE
BIWA

Gifu •

Seto •

Nagoya • Nagashino

Kyoto •

OMI

Uji •

Nara •

YOSHINO

Osaka •

• Ise

Yahagi River

Urban Japan on the brink of the modern age: Utagawa
Hiroshige (1797–1858), *Ohashi Atake no yudachi*
[Sudden shower at the great bridge, Atake] from the
series *Meisho Edo hyakkei* [One hundred views of Edo].
Color print from woodblocks, signed *Hiroshige ga*
[painted by Hiroshige]; 1857. Courtesy of the Honolulu
Academy of Arts, Gift of James A. Michener, 1991.

Urban Japan on the brink of the modern age: Utagawa
Hiroshige (1797–1858), *Saruwaka-cho yoru no kei*
[Night view of Saruwaka Street] from the series *Meisho
Edo hyakkei* [One hundred views of Edo]. Color print
from woodblocks, signed *Hiroshige ga* [painted by
Hiroshige]; 1856. Courtesy of the Honolulu Academy
of Arts, Gift of James A. Michener, 1991.

JAPANESE HISTORY 50,000 B.C.–A.D. 1868: AN OUTLINE

50,000–10,000 B.C. PALEOLITHIC PERIOD.

Japan is occupied by hunter-gatherers using stone tools.

10,000–300 B.C. JOMON PERIOD.

A more settled society of hunter-gatherers starts to live in communities, making the earliest pottery found anywhere in the world. Towards the end of the period, peoples from South China and North-East Asia, the first of several waves of immigrants until about A.D. 500, enter Japan by way of Korea, and rice is grown for the first time.

300 B.C.–A.D. 300 YAYOI PERIOD.

A fully agricultural society develops, bronze and iron are introduced from the Asian continent, and towards the end of the period contact is made with Chinese dynasties.

A.D. 300–710 KOFUN PERIOD.

Political leaders are buried in huge tombs filled with sophisticated luxury goods in a range of materials, many of them made by immigrant craftspeople from Korea. The Yamato state is formed in the western part of Honshu, Japan's main island. Later, the government is reformed along the lines of the Tang Dynasty in China. Under the influence of Prince Shotoku (574–622), the Buddhist religion is introduced to Japan and Buddhist temples are built.

710–794 NARA PERIOD.

The capital is moved from Asuka to Nara, between Kyoto and Osaka. Political and religious reforms culminate in the casting of the Daibutsu [Great Buddha] on the orders of the Emperor Shomu. Contact with Tang Dynasty China is strengthened and many foreign luxury goods are imported. The first works of Japanese literature are written.

794–1185 HEIAN PERIOD.

The capital is moved to Heiankyo (present-day Kyoto), which remains the imperial capital of Japan until 1868. The Heian Period sees the first flowering of Japanese court culture, manifested in romantic literature, Buddhist architecture and sculpture, and masterpieces of lacquer, metalwork and other crafts. Political power passes from the Imperial family to the Fujiwara clan, whose members rule as "regents", but in time regional warrior families assume control over much of the country. From 1156 to 1185, two of these families, the Taira and the Minamoto, struggle for supremacy. The Minamoto are ultimately victorious.

1185–1333 KAMAKURA PERIOD.

Minamoto no Yoritomo takes the title of shogun and sets up a military capital at Kamakura (near present-day Tokyo). In 1274 and 1281, Japan successfully beats off the invading Mongols. From this time until 1868, a series of shoguns, based in Kamakura, Kyoto, and finally Edo (Tokyo), rule in the name of the Emperor. However, until the country is unified in the early 1600s, real power passes to regional feudal lords. Several new sects of Buddhism emerge, among them Zen Buddhism, the religion of the warrior elite.

1333–1568 MUROMACHI PERIOD.

The Emperor succeeds in overthrowing the shoguns but is soon deposed. During the following two centuries Japan is in a state of almost ceaseless civil war, but this is also a time of rapid expansion which sees the emergence of towns, the introduction of a money economy, and the development of some of Japan's best-known traditional arts including ink painting, garden design, the tea ceremony, flower arrangement, and the No theater. In 1543, Japan first encounters the West when three Portuguese sailors are shipwrecked on Tanegashima Island.

1568–1615 MOMOYAMA PERIOD.

Three military leaders, Oda Nobunaga, Toyotomi Hideyoshi, and Tokugawa Ieyasu reunite Japan. The arts flourish under Hideyoshi's patronage, setting the scene for the development of sophisticated urban craft workshops that will remain active into the Meiji Era. After a period of widespread contact with the Portuguese and Dutch, including a Japanese mission to Europe from 1582 to 1590, there is an increasingly hostile attitude towards foreigners in general, and Christianity in particular.

1600

Battle of Sekigahara. Tokugawa Ieyasu defeats his rival warlords, and in 1603 establishes the Tokugawa shogunate, with its capital at Edo.

1615

The siege of Osaka castle sets the seal on Ieyasu's conquest of Japan.

1615–1868 EDO OR TOKUGAWA PERIOD.

The Tokugawa shoguns establish a system of military government based at Edo (later renamed Tokyo). Japan enjoys two and a half centuries of relative peace, but remains largely cut off from the outside world. During the Edo Period, a thriving urban culture develops and, with more than a million inhabitants, Edo is the largest city in the world by the end of the eighteenth century. Despite frequent earthquakes, famines and fires, the Japanese economy grows rapidly and although the country is still nominally controlled by the samurai, a new and wealthy urban merchant class emerges. Thanks to the patronage of the merchants and richer samurai, there is a great flowering of literature and the arts, and the crafts of metalwork, lacquer, ceramics, textiles, and carving flourish as never before.

1641

Following a period of persecution of Christianity, the shoguns' seclusion policy is completed with the move of the Dutch trading post to the small island of Deshima in Nagasaki Harbor.

ABOUT 1620–1700

Exported Japanese lacquer and porcelain are popular in Europe for a time, until Chinese products begin to dominate the Western market in the late 1600s.

1716–ABOUT 1800

Controls on foreign goods are relaxed and limited quantities of Western (particularly Dutch) books and scientific instruments begin to be imported. A few Japanese start to take an interest in so-called "Dutch studies" and some of them begin to warn of the need to protect Japan against foreign invasion.

ABOUT 1800–1868

Sporadic Japanese contact with Western countries, and the westward expansion of the United States, culminate in Commodore Perry's 1853–4 mission. Under pressure from the United States and other Western powers, Japan signs trade agreements and allows limited access to foreign trade and diplomacy. There is growing conflict within Japan about the best way to counter the foreign threat, but eventually a group of reforming samurai deposes the shogun and establishes a new government. Japanese craft goods are exhibited in Europe for the first time.

ABOUT 1800–1841

Growth of the North Pacific whaling industry leads to occasional contacts between Western ships and survivors from Japanese wrecks. In 1837 the *U.S.S. Morrison* unsuccessfully tries to land Japanese castaways near Edo, and in 1841 a shipwrecked young Japanese whaler, John Manjiro, is rescued up by an American ship, eventually reaching New Bedford, Massachusetts and not returning to Japan until 1851.

842

Great Britain's easy victory over China in the First Opium War alerts Japan to the dangers of encroachment by the Western powers.

1846

Commodore James Biddle leads the first, unsuccessful U.S. diplomatic mission to Japan. A second mission in 1849, by Commander James Glynn, is also unsuccessful.

1848

California achieves independence from Mexico and enters the Union.

1849

The Californian Gold Rush.

1853

Commodore Matthew C. Perry visits Japan with the largest United States fleet ever seen in the Pacific and demands that Japan establishes trading and diplomatic relations.

1854

Commodore Perry opens up Japan. Japan and the United States sign a Treaty of Peace and Amity (the Treaty of Kanagawa) on March 31. Japanese artifacts are exhibited in London for the first time.

1856

Townsend Harris arrives in Japan as the first United States Consul-General.

1858

The United States and Japan sign a Treaty of Amity and Commerce (the Harris Treaty) despite court disapproval. Japan signs similar "unequal" treaties with Great Britain, France, Russia, and the Netherlands.

1859

Yokohama is officially opened to foreign residents.

1860

Ii Naosuke, a leading advocate of treaties with foreign powers, is assassinated by an anti-foreign fanatic; similar assassinations follow throughout the rest of the century. The Tokugawa shogunate sends its first mission to the United States.

1861

The Takenouchi diplomatic mission is sent to Europe.

1862

The British Minister Sir Rutherford Alcock organizes a Japanese display at the Second International Exhibition in London.

1866

Japan signs tariff agreements with the United States, Great Britain, France, and the Netherlands.

1867–8

Civil war: forces of the Satsuma, Choshu, Hizen, and Tosa domains are victorious over the forces of the Tokugawa shoguns.

1867

Both the shogunate and the domains of Satsuma and Saga participate in the Paris Universal Exposition at the invitation of the French government, sending more than 300 objects.

1867

The Emperor Komei dies in January. The last shogun, Tokugawa Keiki, tenders his resignation on October 14.

JAPAN BEFORE PERRY

FROM THE MIDDLE
AGES TO MODERN
TIMES

Most of the objects featured in this exhibition and catalogue were made during the years from 1868 to 1912, referred to by the Japanese as the Meiji Era. Since the beginning of written history, Japan has followed the traditional Chinese practice of numbering the years, not as we do from some fixed point in the past, but according to their order within eras of varying length. These eras are always given lucky names ("broad and eternal", "long-lived treasure", and so on), but the two characters making up the word *Meiji*, "enlightened government", were chosen with more than usual care, since the year 1868 marked a revolution in the way the country was to be governed, and heralded a half-century of change so profound that, as one historian has recently written, Japan "was not subjected to a long-term course of medical treatment, but rather underwent a major, and sudden, surgical operation".[1]

This drastic medical intervention came about partly because of unresolved tensions within Japanese society and partly because of the growing commercial and military reach of the nations of the Western world; the relative importance of these two factors, and their respective contribution to the nature of the changes Japan underwent, are the subject of continuing scholarly debate. It remains a matter of historical fact, however, that it was not the older European powers but the youthful and expansionist American nation which made the decisive moves that would force Japan into a new relationship with the rest of the world. Commodore Matthew Calbraith Perry's two visits to Japan in 1853 and 1854, conducted with a masterly combination of firmness and tact, set in motion a chain of events that would lead within fourteen years to the downfall of a system of government more than two and half centuries old, the reestablishment of the emperor as the symbolic, if not actual, center of power, and the intensification of a process of reform that made one British scholar comment at the turn of the century:

> To have lived through the transition stage of modern Japan makes a man
> feel preternaturally old; for here he is in modern times ... and yet he can
> himself distinctly remember the Middle Ages.[2]

THE EARLY PERIOD

We shall return to Perry's visit later on, but in order to understand the Meiji Era it is necessary to sketch in, however briefly, the history of Japan up to the moment of his arrival.

The exact sequence of migrations that contributed to the formation of the modern Japanese race is still a matter of scholarly debate, but it is thought that during the Paleolithic Period, from about 50,000 to 10,000 B.C., part of Japan was occupied by hunter-gatherers using stone tools, with a mostly nomadic lifestyle. The millennia from around 10,000 to 300 B.C. saw the development of a society of more settled hunter-gatherers who made the earliest pottery yet found anywhere in the world. This pottery is often decorated with impressed cord-marks, *jomon*, which have given the period its modern name. Towards the end of Jomon, peoples from South China and North-East Asia, the first of several waves of immigrants until about A.D. 500, entered Japan by way of Korea, and rice was grown for the first time. In the six centuries from 300 B.C. to A.D. 300, called the Yayoi Period after the location of an important archeological site, a fully agricultural society developed, and bronze and iron were introduced from the Asian continent. Later in the period contact was made with China, and from this time the influence of China, whether directly or indirectly, via the Korean Peninsula, was to have a profound effect on the development of Japanese culture. From A.D. 300 to 710 the sequence of historical events gradually becomes clearer thanks to the adoption of the Chinese writing system by the Japanese and the abundance of well-preserved archeological evidence. Political leaders at this time were buried in huge tombs, nowadays called *kofun*, which have given their name to the period. Kofun tombs were filled with sophisticated goods in a range of materials, many of them made by immigrant craftspeople from Korea.

The Kofun Period was particularly important as a time of state formation, first along distinctively Japanese lines, and later in imitation of the organizational structures of Tang-Dynasty China, at that time the largest and most powerful political entity in the world. The emperors of Japan are thought to be descended from the ruling family of the Yamato state, formed in the fifth and sixth centuries in the Yamato region of Japan, near present-day Kyoto and Osaka. These rulers worshipped Amaterasu, Susano-o, and other *kami* [deities] associated with the native religion that later came to be called Shinto. At the end of the sixth century the very different Buddhist religion, of Indian origin, was introduced to Japan from Korea, and the first Buddhist temples were built. Despite efforts in the Meiji Era to reduce the status of Buddhism, the religion's many different sects have flourished to the present day in peaceful coexistence with Shinto, and Buddhism has played a key role, similar to that of Christianity in Europe, in the development of Japanese literature, philosophy and, above all, arts and crafts.

During the Nara Period (710–94) the capital was established at Nara, between Kyoto and Osaka. Contact with Tang-Dynasty China increased, and Buddhism assumed a key political role, for a time becoming virtually a state cult centered around the ruling family. Political and religious reform culminated in the decision to cast a *Daibutsu* [Great Buddha] on the orders of the Emperor Shomu. This enormous image of the Sun Buddha, dedicated in 752, has survived to the present day, although it has been much damaged and restored, and bears little resemblance to the original. The technical challenges involved in its construction laid the foundations for the tradition of bronze-casting, always intimately associated with the manufacture of Buddhist images and religious implements, which enabled Japanese metalworkers to astonish Europe and America with their skills some 1,100 years later. This was also a time of growing interest in other luxury crafts. Inspired by the example of Tang aristocrats, the Nara courtiers imported a wide range of furniture, ceramics, glass, lacquer, silver, carpets, and other items, not just from China but even from as far afield as present-day Vietnam and Iran. These were copied and adapted by court-sponsored craftsmen whose activities, as well as the raw materials they needed for their work, were strictly regulated to ensure both stability and exclusivity of supply.

In 794 the capital was moved to Heian-kyo, the "City of Peace and Tranquility", better known today by its more prosaic name Kyoto, meaning simply the "Capital City". Kyoto remained the official capital until the Meiji Era, although it was often not the true center of power. Traditional histories of Japan have presented the Heian Period (794–1185) as a golden age, akin to Athens in the fifth century B.C. or Florence in the fifteenth century. Although such comparisons have become unfashionable, there is no doubt that the tenth and eleventh centuries witnessed Japan's greatest flowering of court culture, as manifested in romantic literature (especially the very long novel *Tale of Genji* written by Murasaki Shikibu, a female courtier), lyric poetry, and Buddhist architecture and sculpture. The comparatively few surviving masterpieces of lacquer, metalwork, and other applied arts demonstrate that Japanese craftspeople had broken away from their continental, Korean and Chinese origins to forge a distinctive identity. Politically, the period saw a steady decline in the wealth and power of the imperial house. The main beneficiary of this process was the Fujiwara clan, whose members built up huge land holdings, frequently intermarried with the imperial family, and assumed the role of "regents" with more real power than the emperor himself. In time, however, the struggle for political power moved away from the Heian court to regional warrior families who assumed control over much of the country. From 1156 to 1185, two of these families, the Taira and the Minamoto, struggled for supremacy, and the Minamoto ultimately emerged as victors. The Genpei Wars, named after the characters used for writing parts of the names Taira and Minamoto, were the source of a vast body of heroic myth and legend that formed a treasure-trove of subject matter for craftsmen during both the Edo Period and the Meiji Era.

The Minamoto victory, and the move of the government to Kamakura, not far from present-day Yokohama, symbolized the transition from civil to military rule. Although emperors continued to reign and a few unsuccessful attempts were made to restore their authority, real power remained in the hands of the military aristocracy and their samurai retainers until the Meiji Restoration. In 1192, the Minamoto leader Yoritomo

THE AGE OF THE SHOGUNS

assumed the title *Seii-tai-shogun* [barbarian-quelling generalissimo], subsequently abbreviated to *shogun* [general]. This name had been awarded to senior officers on various occasions since the eighth century, but from the end of the twelfth century it became the traditional title for the hereditary military dictators who were to control Japan for most of the next seven hundred years. In the early Kamakura Period (1185–1333), political power passed from the Minamoto to the Hojo family who set themselves up as regents, established a branch of the military government in Kyoto, and intervened in the imperial succession. The prestige of the shogunate was enhanced for a time by its success in beating off two attempted invasions of Japan by the Mongols in 1274 and 1281, but in 1333 the Emperor Go-Daigo was able to overthrow the Hojo with the help of the Ashikaga family. Three years later, Ashikaga Takauji forced the emperor to flee the capital, assumed the title of shogun, and established his government in the Muromachi district of Kyoto, from which the Muromachi Period (1333–1568) takes its name. Despite the ultimate failure of Go-Daigo's efforts to restore his authority, the warriors who supported him in his struggle, especially Kusunoki Masashige (see catalogue number 156) and Nitta Yoshisada (see catalogue number 94), were often celebrated in Meiji-Era art as heroic examples of unswerving loyalty to the imperial cause.

Although they took the title of shogun, the Ashikaga were heavily dependent on the goodwill of provincial military leaders and were never able to exercise effective control. The Muromachi Period is characterized by a gradual dispersion of power to a large number of *daimyo*, regional feudal lords, and a state of almost ceaseless civil war until the end of the sixteenth century. This was accompanied by rapid economic expansion and the development of long-distance communication by land and sea, as well as the emergence of towns around temples, *daimyo* castles, or on the coast as a result of increased maritime trade. Money replaced barter as the main medium of commerce, and craft workers gained improved status, furthering their interests through the establishment of *za*, organizations similar to the medieval European craft guilds. The Kamakura and Muromachi Periods witnessed the development of some of the social and cultural forms that are most closely associated with the Western image of Japan. In 1191, the priest Eisai returned from a visit to China and introduced Japan to both the meditative form of Buddhism called Zen and the practice of drinking an infusion from the leaves of the tea plant, a practice that would develop into the tea ceremony, a kind of formalized social gathering that is still widely popular today. Zen monasteries developed rapidly in both Kyoto and Kamakura, and Zen philosophy combined with martial codes developed during the twelfth-century wars, to form the samurai ethical system later codified as *bushido* (the "way of the warrior"). As well as providing the shogunate with an ideology, the introduction of Zen, together with some other less austere devotional sects of Buddhism, inspired a renaissance in the visual and performing arts: ink painting, stone gardens, flower arrangement, and the *No* theater all developed during this period. Zen brought with it a renewed taste for all things Chinese, including lacquer, bronzes, and ceramics. The influence of Chinese styles is apparent in many craft goods made in succeeding centuries, and was still a powerful factor in the design of some goods manufactured for foreign exhibition during the Meiji Era.

The so-called *sengoku jidai* [age of the country at war] was brought to an end in the second half of the sixteenth century by the successive efforts of three warlords, Oda Nobunaga, Toyotomi Hideyoshi, and Tokugawa Ieyasu. Ieyasu finally defeated his massed enemies at the huge battle of Sekigahara in 1600. Three years later he had himself named shogun, and established his capital at a little fishing village called Edo, in the same part of Japan as the earlier shogunal capital of Kamakura. This city's change of name from Edo to Tokyo (the "Eastern Capital"), would be one of the most symbolic reforms of the early Meiji Era. Despite the violence of the short Momoyama Period (1568–1600), the arts flourished under the patronage of Ieyasu's predecessor, the flamboyant Hideyoshi, setting the scene for the development of sophisticated urban craft workshops that were active through the Edo Period (1600–1868) and into the Meiji Era.

INTERNATIONALISM
AND SECLUSION

The eastward spread of the European "Age of Discoveries" reached Japan in 1543, when three Portuguese sailors were shipwrecked on a remote southern island. For nearly a century afterwards, Japan was an active player on the international scene, greatly extending its overseas shipping and even attempting an invasion of Korea in the 1590s. Portuguese and Spanish missionaries soon arrived in Japan and, at first, Christianity made great headway, but the authorities' attitude towards the foreign religion was always unpredictable. Hideyoshi was alternately friendly and hostile, and there were increasingly severe persecutions under the second and third Tokugawa shoguns, culminating in the 1637 Shimabara Rebellion which ended with the massacre of tens of thousands of believers. At the same time, early enthusiasm for secular, commercial contact with the outside world waned as the government became fearful of the threat of foreign conquest. A series of edicts prohibiting Japanese people from going abroad on pain of death, and confining Chinese traders to the southern port of Nagasaki, was followed in 1641 by the move of the Dutch trading post from Hirado, another southern port, to a small artificial island called Deshima, also in Nagasaki. From 1641 until 1854, China, Korea, the Ryukyu Islands (modern Okinawa), and the Netherlands were the only foreign territories in regular contact with Japan. In the early years of *sakoku* [national seclusion], there was a thriving export trade in Japanese porcelain, manufactured in the southern island of Kyushu, using technical know-how brought back by prisoners-of-war captured during the Korean invasion. Because of political disruption in China, Japan was able to capture a significant percentage of the export market to Europe until the Chinese took over again towards the end of the seventeenth century. The same thing happened, on a smaller scale, in the case of lacquer.

Despite the limited nature of foreign trade, the picture of Edo-Period Japan as a culture almost entirely cut off from outside contact has been rejected by many recent scholars who stress that there was a high degree of awareness of world events, Western technology, and Western objects, not only among the ruling elite but also among the cultivated merchant classes of the great cities. Just as seventeenth- and eighteenth-century Japanese exports of porcelain and lacquer readied the West for a much larger influx of craft goods in the second half of the nineteenth century, so Japanese knowledge of Western medicine, optics, and military technology (mostly gathered from books written in Dutch) facilitated the country's rapid industrialization after the Meiji Restoration. Although graphic art and painting fall outside the scope of this exhibition, it is worth noting that some of the Japanese print designers who were most popular in Europe and America during the early years of the Meiji Era, for example Hokusai and Hiroshige, were among the artists who had been most influenced by Western notions of perspective and shading during the supposed seclusion of the early nineteenth century.

Nevertheless, it would be misleading to suggest that Edo-Period Japan was a truly international country. Aside from the special case of porcelain and lacquer, the crafts mostly followed an autonomous line of development, assisted by Tokugawa Ieyasu's success in establishing a system which maintained peace and security and prevented a return to civil war. The strict rules his successors imposed on foreign contact were mirrored on a much larger scale in the measures they took to keep the *daimyo* in their place. Under a system called *sankin kotai* [attendance by turn], the *daimyo* were obliged to spend one year in every two at Edo and to leave their womenfolk there as hostages, devoting a large part of their wealth to maintaining luxurious establishments in the capital and making expensive ceremonial journeys to and from their domains, often many hundreds of miles away. Not only did this system consolidate Tokugawa control, it also provided a dependable living for a range of craftspeople, including lacquerers, weavers and, above all, metalworkers who created and embellished the swords which were the proudest possessions of the *daimyo* and their samurai vassals.

Although Buddhism and Shinto continued to play a key role in national life, Confucianism, a Chinese philosophy based on the sayings of the sage Confucius who lived in the sixth and fifth centuries B.C., formed the ideology of the Tokugawa shogunate. Confucianism was useful to the shoguns because of the emphasis it placed on decorum and the maintenance of correct hierarchical and family relationships; it also provided the basis for the division of Japanese society into four ranks called *shi*, *no*, *ko*, and *sho*, samurai (of all kinds from shogun to petty retainer), peasants, workmen, and merchants. In the long term, the contradiction between this theoretical scheme and the realities of economic life proved to be a major source of political instability. Prolonged peace, economic growth and the bureaucratization of the samurai class, who were turned from warriors into officials or, in some cases, even lost their stipends altogether, turned the *shi-no-ko- sho* system almost on its head. In terms of actual wealth rather than formal rank, the new urban merchant class came first, dominating much of the economy. As a result of the combination of the *sankin kotai* system with a flourishing market economy, Edo in the eighteenth century was the largest city in the world, with more than a million residents (Japan had a population of about thirty million), half of them members of the samurai class and the other half people who supplied goods and services needed by the whole population, including high-quality craft goods. Both Kyoto and Osaka are thought to have had populations of around 600,000, the former continuing to thrive as a center of the arts, and the latter developing into a great merchant city and the hub of the trade in rice, *sake* [rice wine], soya beans, and other essentials. Thanks to the combined patronage of *daimyo*, merchants, and urban samurai who had adopted merchant ways, metalwork, lacquer, ceramics, textiles, and carving flourished as never before.

Despite the growing prosperity of the cities and a more modest increase in living standards in the countryside, frequent disasters such as earthquakes, tidal waves, fires (an estimated 100,000 lives were lost in the great fire of Edo in 1657) and famines (which killed far more people), made for increasing social instability and tension between rich and poor, and town and country. Periods of inflation in the price of necessities, particularly rice which served as the main measure of wealth in much the same way as the U.S. dollar in today's world economy, made life difficult for everyone except the richest merchants, and were particularly wounding to the esteem of middle-ranking and junior samurai who depended on fixed incomes. The shogunate tried to arrest its declining economic power through a series of bungled reforms, but by the time of the devastating Tenpo famine, which ran from 1833 to 1838, a sense of national decay, coupled with an awareness of the growing threat from the great European powers, led many senior members of the elite to question the regime's ability to cope. The Japanese were well aware of the might of Russia (which had tried to establish contact a generation earlier) and France, and knew that Britain had easily defeated once-powerful China in the First Opium War of 1842. They also had occasional contacts with the United States, thanks to the expansion of the New England whaling industry into the North Pacific. In 1837, for example, the *U.S.S. Morrison* unsuccessfully tried to land Japanese castaways near Edo, and in 1841 a shipwrecked young Japanese whaler, John Manjiro, was rescued by an American ship, eventually reaching New Bedford, Massachusetts and not returning to Japan until 1851.

JAPAN OPENS UP: THE ARRIVAL OF COMMODORE PERRY

From an American point of view, the opening of Japan can be seen as part of the young nation's rapid westward expansion in the decades before the Civil War. The advance to the Oregon Territory, the accession of California and Texas to the Union, and the growth of the whaling industry all drew American attention towards East Asia. From a Japanese standpoint, the United States did not appear to be a predatory Great Power in the same way as Russia or Great Britain; like Japan it was a comparative newcomer to the world of geopolitics. Following unsuccessful diplomatic missions to Japan in 1846 and 1849, on July 8, 1853, the largest United States fleet ever seen in the Pacific arrived off Uraga at the southern end of present-day Tokyo Bay under the command of Commodore Perry, with orders from President Fillmore not to tolerate insults or slights of any kind. Perry's ships waited for several days while the shogunate decided how to respond to this new threat. He was eventually ordered to go to Nagasaki, the only port officially open to trade with Western countries, but this response had been anticipated in Washington, and Perry was under instructions not to agree to it. On July 14, Perry and some of his officers and men were allowed to land long enough to hand over a letter from the President requesting proper treatment of shipwrecked seamen, ports of refuge where ships could obtain coal and stores, and the opening of trade. Perry added a more strongly worded letter of his own stating that if his "very reasonable and pacific overtures" were not at once accepted, he would have to return for a reply the following spring, "with a much larger force".

While Perry's squadron steamed off for a tour of South-East Asian ports, the Japanese struggled to reach a decision on the best way to deal with his proposition. Tokugawa Nariaki, the leader of a powerful branch of the ruling family, suggested a call to arms and limited importation of Western weapons until the country was in a position to respond with military force. Nariaki also suggested that it might be necessary to restore the power of the emperor in order to deal with the situation, a recommendation that heralded the events of the late 1860s. Abe Masahiro, a senior councilor, took the unusual step of consulting with the *daimyo*. Most of them rejected the idea of acceding to the President's request, citing the time-honored nature of the seclusion policy, the dangers of Christianity, and China's recent experience at the hands of the British, but a few of them conceded that Japan was too weak to have much choice in the matter. The sudden death in August of the shogun Ieyoshi heightened the sense of crisis, and a decree of December 1, 1853 eventually suggested that since Japan's defenses were inadequate Perry should be given no clear answer; if he used force, however, Japan must do what it could to defend itself.

Commodore Perry returned on February 13 the following year, and it soon became clear to the Japanese authorities that he would not be satisfied by a vague response. A formal meeting and exchange of papers between Perry and the Japanese side took place on March 8 at Kanagawa, a village near Yokohama at the mouth of Edo Bay, and on the last day of the month the Treaty of Kanagawa was signed. The opening paragraph of the Treaty declared that:

> There shall be a perfect, permanent and universal peace, and a sincere and cordial amity, between the United States of America on the one part, and the Empire of Japan on the other, and between their people, respectively, without exception of persons or places ...[3]

Under its other terms, the ports of Shimoda and Hakodate were opened as ports of refuge, and it was agreed to appoint consuls at a later date. The treaty did not, however, give specific permission for trade. Although the concessions exacted by Perry, as well

Figure 1.
William Heine, *First Landing of Americans in Japan, under Commodore M.C. Perry at Gobe-Hama, July 14th, 1853*. Color lithograph published by Eliphalet Brown Jr., New York. Courtesy of Mystic Seaport Museum, Inc. All rights reserved.

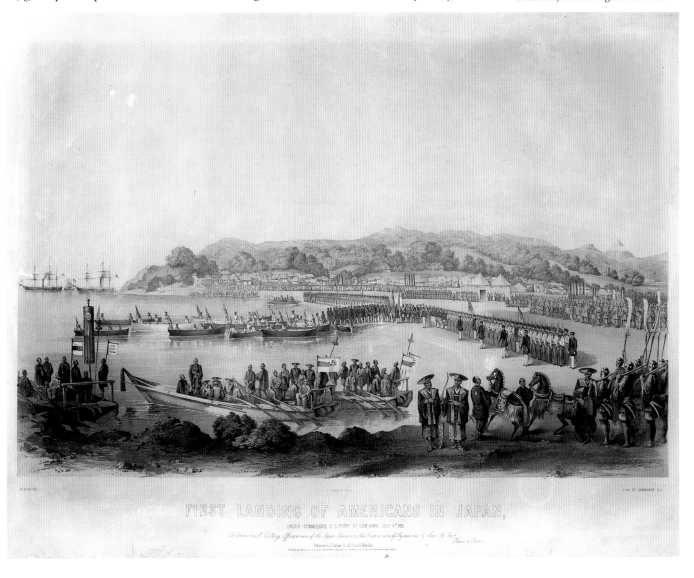

FIRST LANDING OF AMERICANS IN JAPAN,

LANDING OF COMMODORE PERRY, OFFICERS & MEN OF THE SQUADRON,
TO MEET THE IMPERIAL COMMISSIONERS AT YOKU-HAMA, JAPAN, MARCH 8TH 1854.

Figure 2.
William Heine, *Landing of Commodore Perry, Officers & Men of the Squadron, to meet the Imperial Commissioners at Yoku-Hama [Yokohama], Japan, March 8th 1854*. Color lithograph published by Eliphalet Brown Jr., New York. Courtesy of Mystic Seaport Museum, Inc. All rights reserved.

as similar deals concluded soon afterwards by the Russians and the British, failed to satisfy mercantile opinion in Europe and America, they were the first step in a process that would quickly build up an unstoppable momentum.

Just as important as the exact content of the Treaty of Kanagawa was the symbolism and pageantry of the meeting between the two nations. Perry was keenly aware of the importance of ceremony and fully understood the significance of the Japanese rituals of formal entertainment and gift exchange. Authorized to spend the then enormous sum of $20,000 to buy presents for the "emperor" (Perry and his staff were hazy about the respective roles of shogun and emperor), Perry brought with him such treasures as a complete set of John James Audubon's *Birds of America* and *Quadrupeds of North America*; these lavish publications were valued at an astronomical $1,000 each. There was also a case of firearms made by Samuel Colt, a daguerreotype camera, and a telegraph machine from Samuel Morse, the inventor of the code which bears his name, but most impressive of all was a quarter-scale locomotive which ran on a 350-foot circle on a narrow-gauge track. The Japanese delegation lined up for hours to take a ride:

> and as they were unable to reduce themselves to the capacity of the carriage ... they betook themselves to the roof and, clinging to its edge, went whirling round, their robes flapping in the breeze, grinning with intense interest.[4]

The gifts Perry received in return included:

> ... specimens of rich brocades and silks, of their famous lacquered ware, such as chow-chow boxes, tables, trays, and goblets, all skillfully wrought and finished with an exquisite polish; of porcelain cups of wonderful lightness and transparency, adorned with figures and flowers in gold and

variegated colors, and exhibiting a workmanship which surpassed even that of the ware for which the Chinese are remarkable. Fans, pipe cases, and articles of apparel in ordinary use, of no great value but of exceeding interest, were scattered in among the more luxurious and costly objects.[5]

This enthusiastic description was written by Francis L. Hawks, author of a narrative of the expedition, but one of his less open-minded fellow officers, Edward Yorke McCauley, was unimpressed, recording in his diary that the Japanese presents were "nothing very remarkable, or which could not be produced superior in the U.S."[6] The next fifty years were to demonstrate that despite McCauley's scepticism, the skills of Japan's lacquerers, metalworkers, potters and enamelers would find a ready market in the United States.

NOTES
1. Jean-Pierre Lehmann, *The Roots of Modern Japan* (London, 1982), p.165.
2. Basil H. Chamberlain, *Things Japanese*, (fourth edition; London, Yokohama, Shanghai, Hong Kong and Singapore, 1902), p.1.
3. Francis L. Hawks, *Narrative of the Expedition of an American Squadron to the China Seas and Japan Under the Command of Commodore M. C. Perry, United States Navy*, edited by Sidney Wallach, (London, 1954), pp. 204–6.
4. Pat Barr, *The Deer Cry Pavilion, A Story of Westerners in Japan, 1868–1905* (New York, 1969), p.16.
5. Hawks, *Narrative of the Expedition* ..., p.186.
6. Allan B. Cole (ed.), *With Perry in Japan: The Diary of Edward Yorke McCauley* (Princeton and London, 1942), p.99.

"Old Yedo [Edo] has passed away forever. Tokyo, the national capital is a cosmopolis." Utagawa Yoshitora (active about 1850–80), Old and new vehicles on the streets of Tokyo. Color print from woodblocks, signed *Yoshitora ga* [painted by Yoshitora]; 1870. Courtesy of the Metropolitan Museum of Art, Gift of Lincoln Kirstein, 1960; photograph by Otto E. Nelson.

Shosai Ikkei (active about 1870), *Shiodome yori jokisha tsuko no zu* [Passing steam trains seen from Shiodome]. Color print from woodblocks, signed *Shosai Ikkei hitsu* [painted by Shosai Ikkei]; 1872. Courtesy of the Metropolitan Museum of Art, Gift of Lincoln Kirstein, 1959; photograph by Otto E. Nelson.

THE MEIJI ERA (1868–1912): AN OUTLINE

1868–77

The new government of Japan consolidates its power, introduces basic reforms, and promotes the export of raw silk, tea, and craft goods.

1868

The Meiji ["Enlightened Government"] Restoration reestablishes imperial power in the person of the fifteen-year-old Emperor Mutsuhito, usually called the Meiji Emperor. The Emperor moves to the new capital, Tokyo. An edict separates Buddhism and Shinto.

1870

Shinto is declared the national religion.

1871–3

The Iwakura missions travels to the United States and Europe to study Western institutions and technology.

1871

All the feudal domains are replaced by prefectures and the tax system is centralized.

1872

A steam railroad between Shinagawa (Tokyo) and Yokohama is formally opened by the Meiji Emperor. The first government-sponsored exhibition is held in a Tokyo temple. Universal compulsory primary education is introduced.

1873

Japan plays a major part in the Vienna World Exhibition, devoting nearly one percent of national expenditure to the event. Military conscription for men is introduced.

1874

The Kiritsu Kosho Kaisha Trading Company is set up after the Vienna Exhibition to promote Japanese crafts in the United States and Europe.

1876

Japan plays a major part in the Philadelphia Centennial Exhibition. The Kiritsu Kosho Kaisha opens a branch in New York at 865 Broadway. The samurais' annual salaries are ended and they are forbidden to wear swords in public.

1877

The First Domestic Industrial Exposition is held in Tokyo. A rebellion led by the conservative Saigo Takamori is put down by government forces.

1877–89

Its power secured, the new government presses ahead with a program of industrialization and political, legal, social, economic, educational, and military reforms. A more critical attitude develops towards the West and Western art.

1878

Paris Universal Exposition.

1879

The Ryuchikai Society is formed to reawaken Japanese interest in Japanese art forms and resist excessive Westernization.

1879

General Ulysses S. Grant visits Japan.

1881

The Second Domestic Industrial Exposition is held in Tokyo.

1881

Plans begin for creation of a National Diet (Congress).

1884

The Rokumeikan Building opens and becomes a symbol of wholesale Westernization.

1885

Japanese works are widely acclaimed at the Nuremburg International Metalwork Exhibition.

1889–1912

Japan establishes itself as a world power, ending the system of 'unequal treaties' with the West, winning two international wars, and embarking on a period of strong economic growth dominated by powerful industrial conglomerates.

1889

Paris Universal Exposition. The Tokyo Art School opens. The Meiji Constitution is promulgated, declaring the divinity of the Emperor and establishing a two-chamber parliamentary system, but giving most real power to the cabinet.

1890

The Imperial Museum (later the National Museum) opens. The Third Domestic Industrial Exposition is held in Tokyo. The first Artists to the Imperial Household are appointed. The first Diet (Congress) convenes.

1891

The Kiritsu Kosho Kaisha Trading Company is closed down. A nationalist fanatic attempts to assassinate the Tsarevitch (later Tsar Nicholas II) at the beginning of a state visit to Japan.

1893

The Japanese exhibits at the World's Columbian Fair in Chicago attract widespread acclaim.

1894-95

Japan's victory in the Sino-Japanese War symbolizes its rapid modernization and extends its control over Korea.

1895

The Fourth Domestic Industrial Exposition is held in Kyoto.

1899

A treaty with Great Britain ends the practice of "extraterritoriality" and gives Japan equality with the Western powers.

1900

Paris International Exposition.

1902

The Anglo-Japanese alliance is formed and Japan accelerates her military build-up.

1903

The Fifth Domestic Industrial Exposition is held in Osaka.

1904–5

Japan's victory in the Russo-Japanese war establishes Japan as a regional superpower, but at massive human and financial cost.

1904

Louisiana Purchase Exhibition, St. Louis.

1905

Universal and International Exposition, Liège, Belgium.

1907

The Tokyo Industrial Exhibition is held, continuing the tradition of the Domestic Industrial Expositions.

1909

Completion of the Akasaka Detached Palace by Katayama Tokuma symbolizes Japanese mastery of Western architecture.

1910

Japan annexes Korea. The Japan-British Exhibition is held in London.

1912

Death of the Meiji Emperor.

Portrait of the Meiji Emperor as a young man.

REVOLUTIONS AND EXHIBITIONS:
FROM PERRY TO THE CENTENNIAL

THE MEIJI
RESTORATION

The sequence of diplomatic and political developments leading from the Treaty of Kanagawa to the Meiji Restoration of 1868 was extremely complex. The aim of the Western powers, led first by the United States and later, with the outbreak of the American Civil War, by Great Britain and France, was to open Japan to trade. Once the Japanese had realized that Western military might made it impossible to carry on with the policy of seclusion, the leadership was roughly divided into two factions. The conservatives advocated minimal concessions and minimal changes to the existing political system in the hope of an eventual return to the old ways. The reformers, mainly senior samurai from the west of the country, wanted a radical reform of government and society so that Japan could protect herself, compete with her foreign rivals, and change the terms of treaties she had signed under indirect threat of military force.

After the conclusion of the first tentative treaties, the United States, in the person of its first Consul-General, Townsend Harris, pushed ahead with plans for more substantial agreements, and in early 1858 submitted a Treaty of Amity and Commerce under which a further six ports, including Edo and Osaka, would be opened to foreign trade between 1859 and 1863. The Japanese authorities hesitated, but news of Britain and France's victory over China in the "Arrow" War and their plans to send an expedition to Japan at last forced them to sign, although the treaty was described as "a blemish on our Empire and a stain on our divine land".[1] As in 1854, it was followed by similar agreements, with Britain, France, the Netherlands, and Russia. Under the provisions of these "unequal treaties", Westerners in Japan enjoyed extraterritorial rights and were not subject to the laws of Japan, but Japanese residents abroad received no such privileges in return.

In an effort to lessen the effects of the concessions they had already made, the Japanese demanded that facilities for trade should be built in the fishing village of Yokohama instead of nearby Kanagawa as laid down in the treaties. This move would, it was thought, cut the foreign community off from the main Edo-Kyoto-Osaka road and make it easier to control its activities. Western diplomats agreed under protest, but the new town quickly grew and prospered, becoming the focal point of Japan's foreign relations and the center of its trade; many of the works of art reproduced in this catalogue would have left Japan via Yokohama, and quite a few of them were manufactured there as well. Yokohama was a dangerous place in the early years. From 1859 there was a series of attacks by junior samurai on Western officials and traders in both Yokohama and Edo, and their nationalist anger was not directed solely against foreigners: on March 24, 1860, Ii Naosuke, a senior government figure and architect of Japan's response to the second wave of treaties, was cut down outside Edo Castle. For a short time, the United States and Britain offered to tone down the treaties in an effort to shore up the shogunate and pacify its opponents, but further murders in 1862 caused a hardening of British attitudes. Twelve British warships were assembled at Yokohama to support demands for an indemnity of £100,000 and a full apology from Satsuma, a domain in the far south of Japan whose soldiers had killed a British subject. In 1863 the forces of Choshu, a domain in the western part of Honshu Island, fired on American, Dutch and French ships, inflicting casualties and effectively closing the strategic Straits of Shimonoseki to foreign shipping. Shortly afterwards, the British navy sustained heavy damage when it bombarded the town of Kagoshima, capital of Satsuma. These partial successes encouraged some samurai to believe that Japan was already strong enough to repel the foreigner, but in September 1864 a multinational force of seventeen ships bombarded the Choshu batteries and put men ashore to dismantle the military installations.

The shogunate at last agreed to pay an indemnity of three million dollars and, despite desperate efforts by lesser samurai to bring down the regime, the focus of opposition moved from conservative fanatics to moderate realists. As the great statesman Ito Hirobumi put it on his return from a visit to Great Britain in 1865:

... so-called irrational extremists have for the most part had their eyes
opened so that they have come to argue the impossibility of expulsion and
even recommend the opening of the country.[2]

An alliance of three powerful domains, Satsuma, Choshu and Tosa, whose views were
shared by some figures within the administration, culminated, towards the end of 1867,
in a *coup d'état* and a brief civil war that brought down the Tokugawa shogunate and
marked the end of the Edo Period. Much of the opposition to the Tokugawa had been
carried out in the imperial name, and the death in 1867 of the Emperor Komei gave the
leaders of the reform faction the opportunity to enlist the tacit support of his fifteen-year-
old successor, who moved from Kyoto to Tokyo, the new capital, in 1868. However,
although the events of 1867–8 are called the "Meiji Restoration", this does not mean
that the emperor actually wielded executive power. Just as in previous centuries, the
small and powerful oligarchy that would oversee the most sweeping changes in the country's history based its authority on the fact that it ruled with his consent. His role
remained ceremonial, but became more public. As well as performing the ancient court
rituals, he received visiting dignitaries, opened exhibitions and railways, and presided at
solemn state occasions such as the announcement of the new constitution in 1889.

JAPAN REFORMS
AND THE WEST
TAKES NOTICE

During the decade from 1867 to 1877, the new Japanese government's chief priorities
were the consolidation of its power, the introduction of basic reforms, and the rapid
development of Western technology. It is a tribute to the Meiji leaders' determination and
keen commercial sense that, despite these urgent tasks, the same era also marks the
beginning of the Japan craze that would sweep Europe and America in the last quarter
of the nineteenth century. By 1877, when a rebellion led by a conservative samurai, Saigo
Takamori, was successfully put down by the new conscript army, the Meiji government
had found the time and resources to participate successfully in two international expositions and mount a major domestic exposition of its own. Already in the 1850s and 1860s
the pace of technological and institutional innovation had quickened. The *daimyo* of
Satsuma appointed Western experts to help with his industrialization plans and even the
conservative shogunate set up a translation bureau. This willingness to reform meant
that as early as 1858 a British diplomat could note that, compared to backward China,
"the Japanese, if not actually in a state of progressive advancement, are in a condition to
profit by the flood of light that is about to be poured in upon them".[3] The urgent sense
of the need to learn as much as possible from the West was evident in the decision to send
what would now be called fact-finding missions to America and Europe in 1860 and
1861. The Japanese delegation to the U.S. visited several cities and was seen on
Broadway by Walt Whitman, who wrote these verses in the *New York Times*:

> Over the Western sea hither from Niphon come,
> Courteous, the swart-cheeked two-sworded envoys,
> Leaning back in their open barouches, bare-headed, impassive,
> Ride to-day through Manhattan ...
>
> My sail-ships and steam-ships threading the archipelagoes
> My stars and stripes fluttering in the wind
> Commerce opening, the sleep of ages having done its work, races reborn,
> refresh'd,
> Lives, works resumed - the object I know not - but the old, the Asiatic
> renew'd as it must be,
> Commencing from this day surrounded by the world.[4]

By 1872, things were changing so fast that the American teacher William Griffis, back
from only a year in the provinces, enthused:

> Tokyo is so modernized that I scarcely recognize it ... No beggars, no guard-
> houses, no sentinels ... no swords worn ... new decencies and proprieties
> observed; less cuticle visible; more clothes. The age of pantaloon has come.
> Thousands wearing hats, boots, coats; carriages numerous; jin-riki-shas
> countless. Shops full of foreign wares and notions. Soldiers all uniformed,
> armed with ... rifles. New bridges span the canals. Police in uniform.

> Hospitals, schools and colleges ... Railway nearly finished ... Old Yedo
> [Edo] has passed away forever. Tokyo, the national capital is a cosmopolis.[5]

Griffis's words aptly sum up the keynotes of those early years: industrialization, abolition of old institutions and their replacement by Western equivalents, and a craze for the outward aspects of Western fashion and manners. Speed is the most striking aspect of all the reforms. In the four years to the end of 1872, the old feudal domains had been abolished, systems of national primary education and military service had been announced, telegraphs were in widespread use in the capital region, the railway between Tokyo and Yokohama was completed, and the first government-sponsored exhibition was held in a Tokyo temple.

The envoys sent to Europe ten years earlier were probably the first to become aware of the growing importance there both of museums and of international expositions, and even before then, a few Japanese items had made their way into Western public collections. It was not until 1862, however, that the groundwork for what would become the Japan craze was laid by the British diplomat Sir Rutherford Alcock, an assertive and independent-minded figure who is also said to have been the first Westerner to climb Mount Fuji. Alcock's Japanese display for the London International Exhibition in 1862 included nearly a thousand objects, providing an introduction to Japanese art for more than six million visitors. By this date, the great government-sponsored exhibition had become a familiar feature of international commercial and cultural life. The epoch-making 1851 Great Exhibition at the Crystal Palace in London was soon imitated in many countries. Americans erected their own (not very successful) Crystal Palace in New York City in 1853–4, and there were similar events in Dublin (1853), Munich (1854), and Paris (1855). Later, instead of being held in a single large building, fairs spread over many acres and included great halls devoted to such topics as agriculture, education, electricity, gardening, "liberal arts", machinery, transportation, and even crime and punishment. Typically they took place in specially constructed buildings (which sometimes outlasted the exhibitions they held for only a few months), included outdoor as well as indoor displays and were enlivened by a host of extra attractions such as "native villages", "plaisances", bazaars, and fairgrounds. The numbers attending them were huge (fifty million at the 1900 Paris exposition) and they often covered a vast area. In the years after the Civil War, Philadelphia (1876), Chicago (1893), and St. Louis (1904) were to host some of the greatest expositions ever held.

JAPAN AT THE WORLD EXPOSITIONS

The fact that Japan's emergence on the world stage coincided with the development of this new means of truly global communication gave the Meiji leaders a powerful incentive to ensure that their country was fully represented at every major show. Already in the late eighteenth century the scholar and reformer Honda Toshiaki had promoted the virtues of efficient shipping, colonization, and trade, and Japan had participated in two major exhibitions even before the Meiji Era. The first occasion, as we have seen, was in 1862, and in 1867 both the shogunate (which showed more than 1,300 items) and its enemies in Satsuma and Saga (another part of Kyushu Island) organized rival displays at the Paris exhibition, causing the event's director to ask despairingly, "Who are the *real* Japanese?"[6] The Meiji government's first formal participation in a world exhibition took place at Vienna in 1873. Although a number of factors, in particular the international banking crisis of 1872, made the Vienna World Exhibition a financial disaster, it was still an enormous event, and one of the first to follow the example of the 1872 Moscow Polytechnic Exhibition in setting up separate halls for Machinery, Fine Art, and Agriculture. It covered every aspect of contemporary science, art and technology and attempted to outdo anything accomplished in London or Paris over the preceding twenty years. For example, the Paris exhibition of 1867 had featured a large scale model of the Suez Canal (opened in 1869), complete with ships passing through it. Not to be outdone, the Vienna display included a model of the entrance to the Mont Cenis Tunnel between Italy and France, with railroad track, signaling, and a train. As the official British report commented:

> It may well be doubted whether the practical and the picturesque, the modern
> and the medieval, the East and the West, will ever again mingle in one
> harmonious whole... as on the Prater of 1873, in the Buildings on the Park.[7]

All of this presented an unmissable opportunity for research and study. One of the multifarious aims of the Iwakura mission, a high-level Japanese group that traveled in North America and Europe from 1871 to 1873, was to visit the exposition and see what lessons their country could learn from the achievements of the West. Echoing Honda Toshiaki, one member of the mission wrote:

> ... if the country is to be enriched, the army strengthened, and education established, then first production must be encouraged among the people, products of every kind manufactured and exported overseas, goods imported that our country lacks ...[8]

On its return the Iwakura delegation produced a massive report which provided Japan with much of the information it needed in order to become a fully industrialized nation.

For its own display at Vienna, the Japanese government allotted 500,000 yen from its limited national resources (this was 0.8 percent of the entire national expenditure for 1873), and entrusted much of the policy-making to a German, Gottfried Wagener, who was teaching chemistry in Japan as one of many foreign specialists invited by the government. In view of Japan's low level of industrial development, he decided that the Japanese displays should center not on canals or railroads but on technically refined decorative arts, thus appealing to a taste for exotic goods already kindled by the displays of 1862 and 1867. Both at Vienna and at later exhibitions, Japan's success was the result of centralized organization, meticulous preparation, and early recognition of the need to cater to Western interests. Even more important, the very lack of modern industrial products made the government focus on the decorative arts in exhibitions and other forms of trade promotion, so much so that they accounted for about one-tenth of total national exports from the late 1870s until the early 1890s. Considering that the great majority of such goods were made entirely by hand, this is an extraordinarily high figure. As late as 1904, when the country had developed a modern industrial sector as well as vastly increased its production and export of copper, raw silk, and tea, the displays at St. Louis were still dominated by hand-produced craft goods. For about forty years from 1870 to 1910, government sponsorship, coupled on occasion with the patronage of the emperor and his family, provided leading craftspeople with an almost ideal environment in which to refine the skills they had inherited from their Edo-Period forebears, and made it possible for them to produce the works, of a technical excellence not seen before or since, that are the subject of this exhibition and catalogue.

By insisting on the highest standards, the authorities ensured that the Japanese displays were always among the most highly praised, but they were also determined to see that this praise was turned to commercial advantage. Because there was no other organization in the early Meiji Era capable of taking on the role, the central government played an unusually direct part in the promotion of crafts for export after the Vienna exhibition was over, by setting up a semi-public trading company, the Kiritsu Kosho Kaisha. The initiative for this promising move came from Sano Tsunetami, a leading reformer and the vice-president of the Japanese Exhibition Bureau at Vienna, but day-to-day management was entrusted to a tea merchant, Matsuo Gisuke, and an art dealer, Wakai Kenzaburo. These two expanded the business by acting as representatives of the government and complementing the national displays at international exhibitions, a unique position which soon resulted in their opening overseas branches in New York (1876) and Paris (1878). After a good start, Kiritsu Kosho Kaisha later got into financial difficulties, since exhibitions were organized on political as much as commercial grounds, and it was often forced to display products which were so expensive as to be unsalable. Before it was eventually forced to close down in 1891, however, it exerted a strong influence on the overall direction of wares made for export, commissioning more than 2,000 preliminary drawings, employing many of the leading potters, lacquerers, embroiderers, and enamelers of the day, and buying a comprehensive range of ready-made products from other artists. After 1891, the Kiritsu Kosho Kaisha's role was taken over by other, purely commercial companies which had sprung up in the 1870s and 1880s. The government also sought to maintain high standards at the exhibitions by directly commissioning a further 2,500 design sketches in preparation for the 1876 Centennial Exhibition at Philadelphia, the first and second Domestic Expositions in 1877 and 1881, and the 1878 Paris Exhibition.

THE PHILADELPHIA CENTENNIAL: AMERICA SALUTES JAPAN

Japan's preparations for Vienna had been hurried. An official commission was not appointed until June 1872, barely one year before the fair opened, and although some magnificent pieces were eventually displayed, and several prizes were won, this did not allow enough time for the elaborate planning that was necessary if Japan was to make a lasting impact on the international public. Japanese involvement in America's first great exposition, the Centennial Exhibition held at Philadelphia in 1876, was a very different matter, reflecting the superior organization of the entire event. Herman Joseph Schwarzmann, the twenty-seven-year-old engineer who was responsible for the planning and layout of the exhibition grounds, as well as the design of the Art Building, created at Philadelphia the first properly landscaped and planned international exhibition, paying meticulous attention to all the practical details we take for granted at comparable events today. The first concrete proposal for a centennial celebration was made in 1866 and planning for the festival began in March 1871, when Congress passed an act establishing the United States Centennial Commission, followed in 1872 by a Centennial Board of Finance to manage the budget. In 1874 officials were appointed and construction began on a site in Fairmount Park by the Schuylkill River. The exhibition would cover some 236 acres and include around 250 buildings, some of them quite small but others among the largest in the world: the Main Building was 1,880 feet long by 464 feet wide.

The Japanese learned about the centennial celebration as early as June 1873 and decided to participate in 1874, committing $600,000 to the event, the largest sum invested by any of the thirty participating nations. Okubo Toshimichi, a member of the Iwakura mission and, from 1873, Minister for Home Affairs, set up a Centennial Office and made his priorities clear by putting it under the control of a new Board of Commerce, Trade, and Agriculture. Once again, foreign help was enlisted in commissioning and selecting the exhibits, but this time the range of advisors was wider, including an Englishman and an American in addition to Gottfried Wagener. In July 1875 a special envoy, Sekizawa Akeo, arrived in Philadelphia to take charge of the local office and immediately set about achieving his superiors' three main objectives. These were to ensure that they could arrange the exhibits as they wished, get much more space for them, and be allowed to sell them afterwards. Sekizawa was extremely successful in the inevitable battle for space,

Figure 1.
The Main Building of the Centennial Exposition, Philadelphia, 1876. Photograph courtesy of the Print and Picture Collection, The Free Library of Philadelphia.

eventually securing 17,831 square feet, an impressive increase on the 7,290 originally offered. This extra floor area was certainly going to be needed, since up to 30,000 items were gathered from all over Japan. The total freight, brought by sea to San Francisco and then carried free of charge by the Central Pacific Railroad Co., was estimated at 1,300 tons. In addition, the Japanese erected a Japanese Dwelling for their high officials and, in a pattern repeated at many international arts events down to the present, the workmen sent to build the structure, with their dark blue uniforms, unfamiliar tools, deadpan expressions, and manual dexterity, excited widespread comment and served as an excellent curtain-raiser to the main event. Such crowds gathered to watch the strange, "almond-eyed" carpenters at work that a special fence had to be erected to protect them.

Although the presence of the Emperor of Brazil meant that the Japanese delegation was rather overshadowed on the opening day, May 10, the size and splendor of the Japanese exhibit made a deep impression on visitors and press alike. The display, overhung with large Japanese flags and long banners decorated with the imperial chrysanthemum crest, was arranged on two diagonal platforms with a one hundred-foot frontage (see figure 4). The entrance was flanked by two elaborate five-foot high bronzes and, as at Vienna, bronzes were prominent elsewhere in the exhibit, visitors mentioning in particular a vase surmounted by an eagle with flights of birds forming its handles, as well as bronze cranes, tortoises, hens, and rabbits. One of the centerpieces was a formidable display of ceramics arranged on a wedding cake-like stand twelve feet high, with examples from many of the main Japanese kilns, ranging in size from huge porcelain vases to tiny tea cups. Other cases were filled to bursting with lacquer, ivory, and more metalwork. According to one commentator, the Japanese exhibit was:

> ... one of the great surprises of the fair ... We have been accustomed to regard that country as uncivilized, or half-civilized at the best, but we found here abundant evidences that it outshines the most cultivated nations of Europe in arts which are their pride and glory, and which are regarded as among the proudest tokens of their high civilization.[9]

Figure 2.
Japanese workmen setting a foundation post for one of the exhibition buildings, Philadelphia, 1876, from Frank Leslie Norton, *Illustrated Historical Register of the United States Centennial Exhibition* (New York, 1876), p.64.

Figure 3.
The opening day of the Centennial Exposition, Philadelphia, May 10, 1876. Photograph courtesy of the Print and Picture Collection, The Free Library of Philadelphia.

Figure 4.
Part of the Japanese exhibit in the Main Building of the Centennial Exposition, Philadelphia, 1876. Photograph courtesy of the Print and Picture Collection, The Free Library of Philadelphia.

More condescendingly but no less admiringly, another visitor wondered:

> The quaint little people with their shambling gait, their eyes set awry in their head, and their grave and gentle ways, how can it be in them ... to make such wonderful things?[10]

After studying the Japanese display, visitors could shop in the Japanese bazaar just north of the Main Building. Like the Japanese Residence, this had been constructed by Japanese workmen and it included the first Japanese garden in America, complete with pines, camellias, stone lanterns, a stream, and a bamboo fence. The bazaar itself was an open pavilion and the stalls, run by ordinary Japanese merchants and their families, were stacked with ivories, fans, lanterns, screens, bronze figures, lacquers, toys, pottery, and bamboo, mostly of inferior quality to the pieces in the main display, but still extremely popular. Although some commentators criticized the over-commercial attitude of the Japanese, these items – together with the rest of the exhibits that went on sale at much higher prices after the Centennial closed – started a craze for Japanese artifacts that would last for three decades.

Although many nations took part in the Centennial, Japan stood out sharply and unexpectedly from the rest. This was partly because of the Meiji government's commitment in manpower and resources. Only Great Britain shipped more material to the event, few participants secured more space than Japan in the Main Building, and Japan was one of only nine countries to erect a separate national residence for its officials. But perhaps an even more important reason for Japan's success was the fact that this was, for most Americans, their first contact with Japanese culture. The ten million visitors to Philadelphia in 1876 were highly impressed by the novelty of the Japanese displays and fascinated by the contrast between Japanese design and the predominantly High Victorian style of the European stands. Comparing the masterpieces of European medieval art with the Japanese antiquities on show, one writer criticized the former's "clumsiness of design and execution" and praised the latter's "grace and elegance of design and fabulous perfection of workmanship".[11] Japan also appealed to America for the same reason that had made Commodore Perry the right man to open up the country twenty-three years earlier: both nations were new to the international scene and felt that they could deal with each other on equal terms. Another facet of American interest in Japan was shared with European Japanophiles. While they could admire the antiquity, real or apparent, of much that was put on view and envy Japan's imagined freedom from the ravages of the Industrial Revolution, they were also aware that her society and culture were changing at a tremendous rate. The tension between tradition and modernity was a continuing source of fascination. The officials who planned Japan's participation at later exhibitions were aware of this fascination, and did all they could to ensure that their displays both satisfied the Western love of exoticism and showed that their country was abreast of contemporary international taste.

Figure 5.
The Japanese Bazaar at the Centennial Exposition, Philadelphia, 1876. Stereoscopic photograph published by the Centennial Photographic Co., Philadelphia. Courtesy of the Print and Picture Collection, The Free Library of Philadelphia.

NOTES

1. W.G. Beasley, *The Meiji Restoration* (Stanford, Ca., and London, 1973), p.138.
2. Beasley, *The Meiji Restoration*, p.211.
3. Beasley, *The Meiji Restoration*, pp. 121–2.
4. Clay Lancaster, *The Japanese Influence in America* (New York, 1963), p.20.
5. Edward R. Beauchamp, *An American Teacher in Early Meiji Japan* (Honolulu, 1976), p.78.
6. Dallas Finn, "Japan at the Centennial", *Nineteenth Century,* vol. 2, nos. 3 - 4 (Autumn 1976), p.34.
7. John Allwood, *The Great Exhibitions* (London, 1977), p.49.
8. Beasley, *The Meiji Restoration*, p.370.
9. Neil Harris, "All the World a Melting Pot? Japan at American Fairs, 1876–1904", *Mutual Images: Essays in American-Japanese Relations*, edited by Akira Iriye (Cambridge, Mass. and London, 1975), p.29.
10. Robert W. Rydell, *All the World's a Fair: Visions of Empire at American International Expositions, 1876–1916* (Chicago and London, 1984), p.30.
11. Harris, "All the World a Melting Pot?", p.29.

THE EARLY EXHIBITIONS

This section brings together a range of pieces in different materials, including metal, enamel, lacquer and porcelain, of a type and quality that might have been displayed at the international and domestic expositions of the 1870s and 1880s. The principal exhibitions during that period were the first (1877), second (1881) and third (1890) Naikoku Kangyo Hakurankai [National Industrial Expositions] held in Tokyo, and the Vienna (1873), Philadelphia (1876), Paris (1878 and 1889), Amsterdam (1883) and Nuremburg Metalwork (1885) expositions.

1

INCENSE BURNER
1870s
Bronze, with gilding and *shakudo*
280 X 130 cm.
Signed *Dai Nihon Tokyo Kako chu* [cast by
Kako of Tokyo in great Japan]
By Suzuki Chokichi (1848–1919)

When the Japanese government first began, during the 1870s, to participate in international expositions, bronzes like the ones illustrated on these pages made an immediate and profound impression on foreign observers and attracted much favorable comment. We know from a surviving photograph of objects selected for Vienna in 1873, and views of the extensive Japanese section at the Philadelphia Centennial Exhibition in 1876 (reproduced on pages 34 and 40), that large-scale, multi-part bronzes formed an important part of the Japanese displays. Suzuki Chokichi (see pages 64–5), who directed the manufacture of this piece and signed it with his art-name Kako, was largely responsible for the successful redeployment of Japan's time-honored bronze-casting skills and continued to play an important part in both domestic and international exhibitions throughout the Meiji Era.

This bronze is in one of Chokichi's favorite forms, the *koro* [incense burner], a term which, by the 1870s, often referred to the shape of an object rather than its intended function – it is unlikely that this or many of the other incense burners in different materials featured in this catalogue were ever actually used to burn incense. The combination of rich low-relief ornament, mostly of Chinese origin, with highly expressive, almost humorous sculptural forms and symbols of Japanese pride such as the eagle is typical of Chokichi's early period.

Although this incense burner, which has been in Europe since at least as early as 1886, is clearly of the size and quality we would expect of an exhibition piece, it has not proved possible to establish exactly when it was made or first shown.

2

INCENSE BURNER
1870–75
Bronze; with gilt, silver, *shibuichi*, and
shakudo
154.5 x 66.5 cm.
Signed *Kako chu* [cast by Kako]
By Suzuki Chokichi (1848–1919)

The extraordinarily complex decoration of
this multi-part bronze includes a number of
motifs from Chinese and Japanese legends,
combined with intricate low-relief ornament
to produce a rich and exotic effect designed
to appeal to foreign taste. The finial probably
represents Futen, the god of wind (see catalogue number 126), holding an open box
from which he has just released a storm. The
design on the front of the main body has not
been identified, but the reverse shows an old
man holding a staff and a bell, standing on
one side of a stream, being approached by a
general called Satomi Yoshizane on the other
side of the stream. The same motif is seen on
a contemporary bronze by a different artist in
the collection of the Walters Art Gallery,
Baltimore (inv. no. 54.1617), whose reverse
shows a woman with a dog and a boy riding
an ox, suggesting a scene from *Hakkenden*
[The Tale of Eight Dogs], an immensely long
novel by Takiwaza Bakin published in 106
volumes between 1814 and 1841. In the early
part of the novel, Satomi Yoshizane, besieged
in his castle, jokingly promises to present his
daughter Fusehime in marriage to Yatsubusa,
the family dog, if only it will kill his enemy.
The dog duly carries out its master's wishes
and Fusehime gives birth to eight crystal
beads which are eventually incarnated into
eight human sons, each with the word for
"dog" in his name.

Another bronze, similar to this example,
but considerably smaller (only 105 cm. in
height), appears in a photograph of objects
selected for display at the Vienna World
Exhibition in 1873. This style of bronze
continued to be made throughout the 1870s,
and a pair now in the National Museum of
American History was presented to General
Ulysses S. Grant when he visited Japan in
1879.[1] In 1881, the South Kensington
Museum in London (now the Victoria and
Albert Museum) paid the enormous sum of
£1,586. 7s. 2d. for a bronze by Suzuki
Chokichi which had been shown at the great
exhibition in Paris three years earlier.

1. Yokomizo Hiroko, "Meiji shoki no hakurankai
o kazatta kinzoku [On Metalwork Shown at
International Expositions in the Early Meiji
Era]", *Museum* (Journal of Tokyo National
Museum) no. 492 (March 1992), pp. 28–42,
figs. 1, 2 (no. 496) and 34.

3
VASE
1870s
Bronze, with details in silver
123 × 52.0 cm.
Signed *Kako saku* [made by Kako] and *Kako*
By Suzuki Chokichi (1848–1919)

This bronze is in the form called *usubata*
[literally, "thin edge"]. A much simpler
version of the *usubata* first became popular
for flower arrangement in the seventeenth
century and it was later adopted and
developed, like the incense burner or *koro*,
as one of the most popular shapes of
bronze for foreign exhibition. The rim is
cast with a lady holding a *hiogi* [a court
fan made from slats of wood tied with a
silk ribbon] standing on a verandah
looking out over a moonlit landscape,
identified on a plaque as *Ishiyama no
shugetsu* [autumn moon at the Ishiyama
Temple]. This is one of a celebrated set of
views known as *Omi hakkei* [eight views
of Lake Biwa, Japan's largest lake a few
miles east of Kyoto]. One side of the main
body of the vase is cast with an elderly
lady next to a gravepost. This is the great
ninth-century poetess Ono no Komachi. In
her youth she had many lovers whom she
treated cruelly. When she grew old she was
abandoned by her friends, wandering about
"a tattered, crazy beggar-woman".[1] Her
madness was in fact a form of "possession"
by the spirit of a former lover whom she
had tormented, and she was eventually
released from her suffering by a sacred
sotoba [gravepost] on which she sat down
to rest. The story is the subject of a famous
No play.

1. Arthur Waley, *The No Plays of Japan*
   (London, 1921), pp. 148–9.

◄

Bronze vases displayed by the Kiritsu Kosho
Kaisha Company at the Centennial Exposition,
Philadelphia, 1876. Photograph courtesy of the
Print and Picture Collection, The Free Library
of Philadelphia.

4
PAIR OF VASES

1880s
Bronze; with silver, gold, and *shibuichi*
Height 36.8 cm.
Signed *Kiritsu Kosho Kaisha sei* [made by
the First Industrial Manufacturing
Company] under the Company's double
mountain trademark
Attributed to Suzuki Chokichi (1848–1919)
Produced by the Kiritsu Kosho Kaisha
Company

The Kiritsu Kosho Kaisha was founded by
the Meiji government to exploit the success
of the Japanese display at the Vienna World
Exhibition in 1873. The company ordered
work from many famous artists in all areas
of the decorative arts and opened branches
in New York and Paris. In 1891, it was
wound up and the business divided between
Marunaka Magobei (see number 12) and
Hayashi Tadamasa (see number 218). Much
of the metalwork commissioned by the
company features a combination of cast
bronze with chiseled decoration in metals
such as gold, silver, and the special alloys
known as *shibuichi* and *shakudo*. The
original drawing for this pair of vases is
among 1,969 designs, commissioned by
the company and dating mostly from
1881–3, that have been preserved in
Tokyo University of Arts.[1]

1. Hida Toyojiro, *Kiritsu Kosho Kaisha kogei
   shitazushu: Meiji no yushutsu kogei zuan*
   [A Collection of Designs and Preparatory
   Drawings for Decorative Arts for the Kiritsu
   Kosho Kaisha: Designs for Meiji Export
   Wares] (Kyoto, 1987).

5
VASE

About 1877–82
Bronze; with gold foil, copper, and silver
Height 49.7 cm.
Signed on the base *Kako* under the double
mountain trademark of the Kiritsu Kosho
Kaisha [First Industrial Manufacturing
Company], and marked in English:

> *Presented to General Thomas B Van
> Buren by the Foreign Residents of
> Yokohama in recognition of his
> services during eight years as Consul-
> General in Japan 7th October 1882*

By Suzuki Chokichi (1848–1919)
Produced by the Kiritsu Kosho Kaisha
Company

This vase is particularly significant as a
datable example of Chokichi's style during
the first phase of his involvement with the
Kiritsu Kosho Kaisha Company: a similar
piece by Yamagawa Koji of Kanazawa, a
town several hundred miles from Tokyo on
the Sea of Japan, was exhibited at the first
Naikoku Kangyo Hakurankai [National
Industrial Exposition] in 1877, confirming
that, already at this early period, both
metropolitan and provincial workshops
had jointly evolved a kind of syncretic
"export" style combining Japanese, Chinese,
and Western elements.[1] Chokichi continued
to make high-quality trade pieces such as
this at the same time as undertaking massive
commissions for international exhibitions.

In the same year that he was presented
with this vase, Van Buren published an
interesting official report about Japanese
manufactures and customs, illustrated with
hand-colored photographs of the Meiji
Emperor and Empress as well as other
favorite subjects such as samurai, geisha and
the Ainu inhabitants of northern Japan.

1. For an illustration of a similar piece made in
   Kanazawa, together with the original design
   by Marunaka Magobei from the *Onchi zuroku*
   (see number 12), see Tokyo National Museum,

Chosa kenkyu hokokusho Onchi zuroku
[Research Report on the *Onchi zuroku*]
(Tokyo, 1997), pp. 87–8.

6

JAR

Early 1880s
Bronze; with gold, silver, copper, *shakudo*,
and *shibuichi*
Height 38.0 cm.
Signed *Dai Nihon Kako zo* [made by Kako
of great Japan]
By Suzuki Chokichi (1848–1919)
Produced by the Kiritsu Kosho Kaisha
Company

This is one of a group of similarly shaped
vessels made by Suzuki Chokichi (whose
art-name was Kako) in association with the
Kiritsu Kosho Kaisha [First Industrial
Manufacturing Company]. These are nearly
all between 27 and 29 cm. in height; the
extra height of this example is accounted
for by the lid, an extremely rare feature.
Several of the designs, which are usually
composed with an elaborately decorated
"front" and a more restrained "back"
bounded by bands of formal lappets at neck
and base, are based on drawings dating
mostly from 1881–3, and commissioned by
the company from artists such as Yamamoto
Koichi (see number 7). While Chokichi
apparently supervised the casting process,
the elaborate soft-metal decoration was
carried out by other craftsmen who had
earlier trained as sword-fitting makers
(see number 15).

7

JAR

Early 1880s
Bronze, gold, silver, and *shakudo*.
Height 28.6 cm.
Signed *Kiritsu Kosho Kaisha sei* [made by
the First Industrial Manufacturing
Company] under the Company's double
mountain trademark; *Koichi zu* [design by
Koichi]; *Yukinari sen* [engraved by Yukinari]
Designed by Yamamoto Koichi
Engraved by Sugiura Yukinari
Produced by the Kiritsu Kosho Kaisha
Company

The three signatures on this piece, one
(for the commissioning company) on the
base, and two (for the artists) on the side,
underline the collaborative nature of much
early Meiji-Era metalwork. Sugiura Yukinari

and his brother Yukimune (see also number
8) had both originally trained as makers of
decorative sword-fittings, but following the
abolition of the samurai privilege of wearing two swords in 1876, they put their skills
to new use.

Yukinari is recorded as working for the
Kiritsu Kosho Kaisha in 1881, and both
artists exhibited at the great Paris Universal
Exposition in 1900. The designer Yamamoto
Koichi was also responsible for one of
Suzuki Chokichi's most famous works, a
great bronze lantern (1880) for the Yasukuni
Shrine in Tokyo, the central focus of state
Shinto.

8
VASE
Early 1880s
Bronze; with gold, silver, copper, *shibuichi*, and *shakudo*
Height 48.0 cm.
Signed *Kiritsu Kosho Kaisha sei* [made by the First Industrial Manufacturing Company] under the Company's double mountain trademark; *Koichi zu* [design by Koichi]; *Yukimune sen* [engraved by Yukimune]
Designed by Yamamoto Koichi
Engraved by Sugiura Yukimune
Produced by the Kiritsu Kosho Kaisha Company

For information about these artists, see number 7.

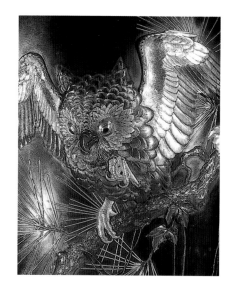

9
VASE
Early 1880s
Bronze, with silver and *shakudo*
Height 60.5 cm.
Signed *Dai Nihon Kako chu* [cast by Kako of great Japan] under the double mountain trademark of the Kiritsu Kosho Kaisha [First Industrial Manufacturing Company]; *Koichi zu* [design by Koichi]; *Yukinari sen* [engraved by Yukinari]
Bronze work by Suzuki Chokichi (1848–1919)
Engraving by Sugiura Yukinari
Produced by the Kiritsu Kosho Kaisha Company

The Japanese metalworker's traditional skill in patinating bronze to a range of colors using solutions derived from minerals and plants is particularly well suited to depicting autumnal hues. The motif of the *aki no nanakusa* [seven grasses of autumn], featured on this vase, has been celebrated in both literature and art since very early times.

10
CHARGER
1880s
Iron; with gold, silver, copper, and *shibuichi*
Diameter 91.5 cm.

Although made from iron rather than bronze,
this outsize dish with its soft-metal design
of a male and female pheasant on a branch
of magnolia can be confidently associated
with the group of metal artists who
regularly received commissions from the
Kiritsu Kosho Kaisha [First Industrial
Manufacturing Company] (see page 31).

11
PAIR OF VASES
1880s
Bronze; with copper, silver, *shakudo*,
gilding, and *shibuichi*
Height 97.4 cm.
Signed *Gyokutosai koku* [carved by
Gyokutosai] and sealed *Mitsukiyo*

This unrecorded artist is possibly
connected with, or even the same
individual as, Hasegawa Issei who
also used the name Gyokutosai. If
this is so, the very different style
of number 51, dating from around
1900, bears testimony to the artistic
flexibility of Meiji-Era metalworkers.

12

BASIN
About 1878
Bronze; with gold, silver, copper, and
shibuichi
Height 35.2 cm.
Signed *Suhodo Hakuzen* and *Dai Nihon
Marunaka sei* [made by Marunaka of great
Japan]
Commissioned by Marunaka Magobei
(1830–1910)

The design for this basin, in the form of a
giant abalone shell encrusted with seaweed
and shellfish, is found in the *Onchi zuroku*,
a collection of over 2,500 sketches commissioned by the Japanese government between
1875 and 1885. This particular design,
including both the exterior and the interior
with the inlaid reflection of the moon,
appears in a volume of drawings prepared
for the Paris Exposition of 1878.[1] Originally
a hat-dealer from the provincial city of
Kanazawa, famous as a metalworking center,
Marunaka Magobei was already known
by the time of the First National Industrial
Exposition in 1877 as a commissioner
and exhibitor of silver- and gold-inlaid
bronzes; he later took over the business of
the Kiritsu Kosho Kaisha [First Industrial
Manufacturing Company] (see page 31).[2]

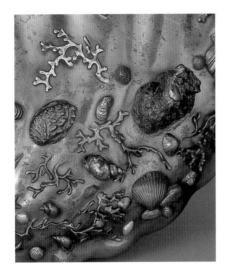

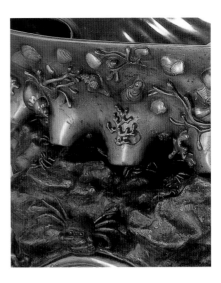

1. Tokyo National Museum, *Chosa kenkyu
   hokokusho Onchi zuroku* [Research Report
   on the *Onchi zuroku*] (Tokyo, 1997), p.69;
   accompanying CD-ROM, 29.17.
2. Hida Toyojiro, "Exporters of Meiji Decorative
   Arts", in *The Nasser D. Khalili Collection of
   Japanese Art*, edited by Oliver Impey and
   Malcolm Fairley, vol. I (London, 1995),
   pp. 70–95, 80–82.

13
VASE
About 1880
Bronze, with silvering and gilding; the perch
inlaid with pearl-shell studs
Height 60.5 cm.
Signed *Ozeki sei* [made by Ozeki]
Produced by the Ozeki Company

For the Ozeki Company, see page 94.
Both in subject matter and in patination,
this vase is untypical of Ozeki work and is
closer to products of the Kiritsu Kosho
Kaisha [First Industrial Manufacturing
Company] (see page 31), though without
the extensive inlay often seen in that
company's metalwork.

14
PAIR OF VASES
1880s
Bronze; with gold, silver, and copper
Height 31.0 cm.

Although unsigned, these vases can be firmly
attributed to a workshop in Takaoka or
Kanazawa. The form is a characteristic early
Meiji combination of an international
baluster shape with the wide flat rim
popular in Japanese flower bronzes from
the seventeenth century.[1]

1. Joe Earle, *Flower Bronzes of Japan* (London,
   1995), pp. 94–9; Yokomizo Hiroko, "Meiji
   shoki no hakurankai o kazatta kinzoku [On
   Metalwork Shown at International Expositions
   in the Early Meiji Era]", *Museum* (Journal of
   Tokyo National Museum) no. 492 (March
   1992), pp. 41–42.

15
VASE
About 1885
Shibuichi; with gold, silver, *shakudo,* and
copper
Height 30.9 cm.
Signed *Ryounsai Moritoshi*, with a seal
Moritoshi; marked on the base *Ozeki sei*
[made by Ozeki]
By Unno Moritoshi (1834–96)
Produced by the Ozeki Company

Unno Moritoshi, the maker of this vase,
was born in Mito, a domain to the northeast
of present-day Tokyo that was controlled
during the Edo Period by a branch of the
ruling Tokugawa family of shoguns. As
such, it was an important center for the
manufacturing of sword-fittings and, during
the early Meiji Era, many specialist metalworkers from Mito made their way to
nearby Tokyo where they transferred their
skills to the manufacture of pieces for
export. This vase is an outstanding example
of such work, utilizing both the techniques
and the subject matter (in this case a party
of travelers on a ferryboat) of traditional
sword-fittings in an entirely novel way.

The Ozeki family, father and son, were
perhaps the most successful of the dealers
in high-quality decorative art throughout
the Meiji Era. Originally a dealer in pipes,
Ozeki Yahei set up the Yokohama branch,
probably under the management of his son
Ozeki Sadajiro, soon after the port was
opened in 1859. In 1877, both father and
son exhibited commissioned pieces under
their separate names in the first Naikoku
Kangyo Hakurankai [National Industrial
Exposition]. By 1880, the company is
recorded as employing twenty-four people
and dealing in enamels, bronzes, ivory,
crystal, carvings, pins, fans, hardstones,
tortoiseshell, lacquer, and a variety of
ceramics.

16
VASE
About 1880–90
Silver; with *shibuichi*, *shakudo*, gold, and
copper; the base with a band of cloisonné
enamel
Height 27.9 cm.
Signed *Kogyokusai* with a seal *Kazuhisa*

For Kogyokusai Kazuhisa, see also number 17.

17
VASE
About 1880–90
Silver; with *shibuichi*, *shakudo*, gold, and
copper
Height 31.5 cm.
Signed *Kogyokusai* with a seal; marked on
the base *Ozeki sei* [made by Ozeki]
Produced by the Ozeki Company

Although we know little about Kogyokusai
Kazuhisa's life, it appears that, like the more
famous Unno Moritoshi (see number 15),
he was originally a maker of sword-fittings
but later turned his hand to other forms of
metalwork.

18
JAR
About 1880
Cloisonné enamels worked in silver and gilt
copper wire; gilt brass rims and foot
Height 16.9 cm.
Attributed to the Namikawa Yasuyuki
Workshop

Although unsigned, this jar and cover can
be firmly attributed to Namikawa Yasuyuki
(1845–1927) by reason of its design and
palette, and also from the method of its
construction. Elements of the scattered
designs can be found in the *Kyo shippo
mon'yo shu* [A Collection of Designs for
Kyoto Enamels], an undated selection of
Namikawa designs,[1] while the colors,
particularly that of the yellow ground, can
be found on other unsigned works that are
more unambiguously in the early Namikawa
Yasuyuki style. This vase marks a considerable breakthrough in the technique of
cloisonné, as one can see by comparison
with number 246. The change from the
work of the late 1870s is astonishing and it
is likely that Namikawa has been helped by
his association with the German scientist
Gottfried Wagener who had been invited
by the Japanese government to advise on
the modernization of Japanese industries
and the organization of Japanese displays
at foreign exhibitions (see page 254). There
is no published illustration of the "copper
vase of elegant shape with opaque and
transparent colors and complicated wirework, with no trace of cracks" for which
Namikawa Yasuyuki won a second prize at
the second Naikoku Kangyo Hakuranaki
[National Industrial Exposition] in 1881,[2]
but it seems reasonable to guess that it may
have resembled this fine piece.

1. Yoshida Mitsukuni and Nakahara Kenji, *Kyo
   shippo mon'yo shu* [A Collection of Designs
   for Kyoto Enamels] (Kyoto, 1981).
2. Suzuki Norio and Sakakibara Satoru, *Nihon
   no shippo* [Japanese Cloisonné Enamels]
   (Kyoto, 1979), p.233.

19

VASE
About 1880
Cloisonné enamels worked in silver wire;
gilt metal rim and foot
Height 18.3 cm.
Attributed to the Namikawa Yasuyuki
Workshop

Although unsigned, this vase is demonstrably
the work of Namikawa Yasuyuki, as the
designs for three of the panels and of a
single sparrow in the fourth are taken
almost directly from the *Kyo shippo
mon'yo shu* (see number 216), nos. 130
and 131. Even though the vase is slightly
later than number 18, the yellow ground,
meant to be even and not mottled, is still
not quite perfectly so. This suggests a date
close to 1879–80, when Namikawa is said
to have perfected the even black ground,
present here on the shoulders between the
panels. A vase of the same shape, with
some identical panels but with differently
shaped cartouches, was exhibited in the
Nuremberg Metalwork Exhibition in 1885
and bought from that exhibition by the
Österreichisches Museum für Angewandte
Kunst [Austrian Museum of Applied Art]
in Vienna.[1]

1. Gunhild Gabbert Avitabile, *Die Ware aus dem
Teufelsland* (Hanover, 1981), no. 168.

20

PAIR OF JARS
About 1885–90
Cloisonné enamels worked in silver and
gilt copper wire; gilt brass rims and foot
Height 15.5 cm.
Each signed *Kyoto Namikawa*
[Namikawa of Kyoto]
Made by the Namikawa Yasuyuki
Workshop

These are the earliest signed pieces by
Namikawa Yasuyuki in the Khalili
Collection.

21
PAIR OF VASES
About 1883
Cloisonné enamels worked in gilt and silver
wire; gilt metal mounts
Height 55.2 cm.
With a paper trade label in English *H. W.
Lea & Co., 166A, Fenchurch Street,
London, E.C.*
Attributed to the Namikawa Sosuke
Workshop

This pair of vases is decorated with designs
in the style of Onishi Chinnen (1792–1851),
an artist who specialized in bird and flower
painting. The flowers depicted include
peonies, Chinese bell-flowers and *susuki*
[pampas grass]. Throughout his career,
Namikawa Sosuke (1847–1910), who was
not related to Namikawa Yasuyuki (see
pages 254–5), constantly developed his
enameling technique so that he could
emulate the work of painters and book
illustrators; even at this early date he had
succeeded in making the wire invisible in
certain places.

The vases were exhibited at the
Amsterdam Exhibition of 1883, where
Sosuke and the Nagoya Cloisonné Company
were awarded the first-class gold medal
and the president of the company, Mr.
Muramatsu, was decorated by the King
of Holland. They are the earliest known
enamels attributable to Sosuke, having
been exhibited only three years after the
Tokyo branch of the Nagoya Cloisonné
Company was established.

22

FIGURE OF A GOOSE
About 1880–1885
Cloisonné enamels worked in silver wire;
shakudo beak and gilt bronze legs
Height 41.3 cm.
Attributed to the Namikawa Sosuke
Workshop

Although unsigned, this extraordinary
study can be tentatively attributed to
Namikawa Sosuke by comparison with the
enamel cock and hen made especially to
decorate a hall in the Imperial Palace, and
illustrated in Namikawa Sosuke's 1896
booklet.[1] The only other recorded cloisonné
model in the round by Namikawa Sosuke
appears to be the "five-colored macaw"
exhibited by him in the fourth Naikoku
Hakurankai [National Industrial Exposition]
in 1895.

1. Anon., *S. Namikawa, Inventor of Cloisonné
   Without Wires, Member of Board of Imperial
   Artists, Decorated with Medal of Green Ribbon*
   (Undated pamphlet, latest dated quotation
   Feb. 9, 1896).

24

SCREEN
1880s
Shosen and cloisonné enamels; lacquered
frame and wood stand
99.3 × 75.8 cm.
Signed *Shoka Itsujin e* [designed by Shoka
Itsujin] with an unread seal
Signed on the reverse *Shippo Kaisha*
Made by the Shippo Kaisha Company after
a design by an unknown artist

In 1880 Namikawa Sosuke took over
the Shippo Kaisha Company and moved
it from Nagoya to Tokyo; this panel is an
early example of his workshop's pictorial
style.

23

TRAY
Late 1880s
Musen and cloisonné enamels
27.6 × 24.4 cm.
Signed *Seitei* with a seal
Attributed to the Namikawa Sosuke
Workshop, from a design by Watanabe
Seitei (1851–1918)

The design is taken almost directly from
a detail of a hanging scroll by Seitei in ink
and color on paper, now in the collection
of the British Museum. Two of the ducks
have been copied, the others omitted
altogether; the ducks have been placed
differently in space, and some reeds have
been added to balance the composition.

25

JAR

About 1880
Stoneware, painted and gilded
Height 24.6 cm.
Sealed *Makuzu Kozan zo* [made by Makuzu Kozan]
Made by the Miyagawa Kozan Workshop

A jar with similar decoration of lotus flowers in low relief was exhibited in the second Naikoku Kangyo Hakurankai [National Industrial Exposition] of 1881.[1]

1. Tokyo Teishitsu Hakubutsukan [Tokyo Imperial Museum], *Dai Nikai Naikoku Kangyo Hakurankai shuppin shashincho* [Photographic Catalogue of the Second National Industrial Exposition] (Tokyo, 1882), cat. no. 41.

26

VASE

About 1885
Silver, with *shakudo* and gold; the body and cover both embellished with cloisonné enamel worked in gold wire
Height 44.0 cm.
Marked *Ozeki sei* [made by Ozeki]
Produced by the Ozeki Company (see number 56)

The luxurious combination of techniques seen on this vase, including silver filigree work, engraving in soft metals, and translucent cloisonné enamels, is typical of the best works by the leading art dealers in the mid-Meiji Era. The figure on the lid is Shoki the demon-queller (see number 137) who looks down threateningly at the three demons, each made from a different metal, supporting the vase. The enamel work may be by Hiratsuka Mohei (see numbers 45, 56, and 188).

SEE OVERLEAF

27
CHARGER
1875–80
Iron; with gold, silver, copper, *shakudo*, and
shibuichi
Diameter 48.2 cm.
Signed *Kyoto no ju Komai sei* [made by
Komai of Kyoto]
Produced by the Komai Company (see
page 67)

The Komai family archives contain a
drawing of an almost identical charger; it is
thought that the design, with a boy to one
side attempting to catch a dragonfly and a
man in a richly patterned kimono, smoking
a pipe, hunched, on the other side, may
refer to the fairy tale *Tonbo Choja* [The
Rich Man and the Dragonfly]. This story
relates that a poor farmer was resting one
day when his wife saw a dragonfly come
flying several times from a mountain
opposite their house and circle around him.
When he woke up, he told her that he had
just been dreaming that he was drinking
delicious wine. Sure enough, they soon
found a spring of wine and endless amounts
of gold, and lived happily ever after.[1] In
typical Komai style, the scenes in the
twelve smaller roundels bear no narrative
relationship to the central design.

1. Fanny H. Mayer, *Ancient Tales in Modern
   Japan* (Bloomington, Indiana, 1984), no. 71
   (pp. 82–3).

28
PAIR OF VASES
Iron, with gold and silver
About 1875–80
Height 30.5 cm.
Each signed *Nihonkoku Saikyo no ju*
Komai sei [made by Komai of the Western
Capital (Kyoto) in Japan]
Produced by the Komai Company

For the Komai Company, which was reput-
edly founded in 1841 and started to become
involved in the export trade around 1873,
see page 67. These vases demonstrate the
finest quality work of the company and are
clearly of a particularly early date. All the
details are worked in *nunome zogan* inlay
(see number 30), the only additional
engraving being on the vine-leaf borders.
The name of Komai seldom appears in the
lists of artists for international or national
exhibitions until 1903, presumably because
a Kyoto dealer, Ikeda Seisuke, marketed
most of their work. It was Ikeda, for
example, who won a gold medal at the
Paris Universal Exposition of 1900 for a
plate of gold and silver which may well
have come from the Komai workshop.

29
PAIR OF VASES
About 1880
Iron, with gold and silver
Height 30.3 cm.
Each signed *Kyoto no ju Komai sei* [made
by Komai of Kyoto]
Produced by the Komai Company

The silver-outlined panels around each vase
depict the *Omi hakkei* [eight views of Lake
Biwa, Japan's largest lake a few miles east
of Kyoto].

30
PAIR OF VASES
About 1875–80
Iron; with *shibuichi*, silver, *shakudo*, gold,
and silver
Height 46.0 cm.
Signed *Saikyo Inoue sei* [made by Inoue of
the Western Capital (Kyoto)]
Possibly by Inoue Kichibei

These vases are decorated in the so-called
nunome-zogan [literally, "cloth inlay"]
technique in which the softer gold, silver
and other metals are hammered onto a key
previously scratched into the harder metal
of the body. The technique, akin to Western
damascening, is mainly associated with the
work of the Komai Company (see number
27) of Kyoto, but this pair of vases seems
to have been made by a different Kyoto
family, about whom little is known, although
the signature may refer to a certain Inoue
Kichibei who is recorded in the Paris
Universal Exposition of 1900. An almost
identical pair of vases is illustrated in *The
Ornamental Arts of Japan* (sect. 6, pl. 8),
a work by the British connoisseur George
Audsley published in London in 1882–4.
The word "Saikyo" in the signature means
literally "Western Capital" and is an archaic
term for Kyoto, Japan's capital until 1868.
It was much used by Kyoto artists in the
early Meiji Era. The pictorial decoration
shows the various stages of rice preparation, including cultivation, threshing, and
final delivery into store.

31

CABINET
About 1873
Bronze; with gold, silver, copper, *shibuichi*,
and *shakudo*
35.8 × 35.4 × 17.3 cm.
Signed *Otake Norikuni* with a gold seal
Nori; the base signed *Shinsai*
By Otake Norikuni (*b.* 1852)

This is a particularly fine and early
example of the application of traditional
metalworking techniques, originally used in

sword-decoration, to pieces made for overseas exhibitions. A very similar miniature
cabinet, decorated with a battle scene
instead of the more peaceful motifs seen
here and said to be the work of a certain
Otake Kiyonaga (which may perhaps be
another name used by Otake Norikuni),
appears in a photograph of objects selected
for display at the Vienna World Exhibition
in 1873 (see also number 2).[1] For Otake
Norikuni, see number 231.

1. Yokomizo Hiroko, "Meiji shoki no hakurankai
o kazatta kinzoku [On Metalwork Shown at
International Expositions in the Early Meiji
Era]", *Museum* (Journal of Tokyo National
Museum) no. 492 (March 1992), pp. 28–42,
figs. 1 and 2 (no. 463).

32

BOX FOR WRITING UTENSILS AND BOX FOR WRITING PAPER

Second half of the nineteenth century
Wood lacquered in *hiramaki-e*, *takamaki-e*, and other techniques; gilt metal water-dropper; silver fittings to the writing utensils
4.9 x 23.0 x 26.0 cm. (box for writing utensils); 15.1 x 34.5 x 43.1 cm. (box for writing paper)

Throughout the Edo Period, matching sets of writing- and paper-boxes offered lacquerers an opportunity to show off the full range of their technical and artistic skill. The box for writing utensils contains an ink-stone for grinding solid sticks of ink, a gilt metal water-dropper in the form of chrysanthemums floating in water, an inkstick holder, a knife, and a skewer.

33
BOX FOR WRITING UTENSILS AND BOX
FOR WRITING PAPER
About 1860–70
Wood lacquered in *hiramaki-e*, *takamaki-e*,
and other techniques on grounds of *nashiji*
and *hirame*; *shakudo* water-dropper and
fittings to the writing utensils
4.8 × 24.3 × 27.4 cm. (box for writing
utensils); 15.7 × 34.2 × 43.2 cm. (box for
writing paper)
Signed in gold lacquer under the ink-stone
Hokkyo Komin kore o saku [Hokkyo
Komin made this], with a seal *Komin*
By Nakayama Komin (1808–70)

Nakayama Komin is highly regarded for
his success in reviving the classical style of
lacquer decoration, with lavish use of gold
and silver ground, at the end of the Edo
Period. Late in life he was awarded the
honorary Buddhist title of *Hokkyo*. The
landscape design seen on these boxes occurs
on a number of other unsigned lacquers of
about the same date, suggesting that they
were based on the same, as yet unidentified,
pattern book.

34
PANEL
1881
Wood, lacquered in a variety of techniques
including *hiramaki-e*, *takamaki-e* and
togidashi-e
49.0 × 77.0 cm.
Signed in seal form *Koma* and *Zeshin*
By Shibata Zeshin (1807–91)

One of the most famous of all Japanese
lacquerers, Shibata Zeshin originally studied
his craft in the prestigious Koma family
and continued to make occasional use of
their surname, as on this piece, throughout
his very long working life. He also, unusually
for a lacquerer, received formal instruction
from two great masters of painting and
was famous as a painter as well as a
lacquerer. Unlike Nakayama Komin (see
number 33), Zeshin constantly experi-
mented with new lacquering techniques

and was open to outside influences. Both
the composition and the overall format of
this framed panel reflect his awareness of
Western oil painting.

The panel is believed to be the same
piece as the "black *roiro* and *takamaki-e*
panel with a rice-boat and sparrows" which
is recorded as having won a bronze medal
at the second Naikoku Kangyo Hakurankai
[National Industrial Exposition] held in
Tokyo in 1881. For another work by Zeshin,
see number 391.

METALWORK

NEW MARKETS AND NEW CHALLENGES: BRONZE-CASTING

All of Japan's traditional industries had to adapt to the social and economic upheavals that were set in motion by the Meiji Restoration, but metalworking was dealt an especially heavy blow. This was because the arts of casting bronze, forging steel, and chiseling gold and silver were closely connected with some of the most distinctive and traditional aspects of everyday life and belief in Edo-Period Japan (1615–1868). Bronze, for example, had been associated with Buddhism ever since the Indian religion was introduced into Japan from Korea in the sixth and seventh centuries. Although there had been times when much religious sculpture was carved in wood, during the Edo Period most of the larger images, as well as other major features of Buddhist temples such as bells, cauldrons for incense, and architectural decorations, were cast from bronze. One of the earliest actions of the new government, in the very first year of the Meiji Era, 1868, was the formal separation of Buddhism from Shinto, Japan's indigenous faith, which was declared the state religion two years later. This downgrading of the imported religion meant that Buddhist temples and the artifacts they housed often suffered neglect. Prominent citizens no longer banded together to pay for Buddhist images, and the introduction of Western clocks removed the need for the bronze temple bells that had sounded in nearly every street of old Japan.

As well as losing their traditional customers, Japan's metalworkers were faced with an additional problem. Lacquer and porcelain, two of Japan's other national crafts, had been "market-tested" in the seventeenth century when, for a brief period, Japan rivaled China as a source of exotic trade goods for Western consumers. Not only were some of the shapes and patterns of the Japanese wares later copied by the Chinese for the enormous export trade they carried on in the eighteenth century, Japanese goods were still exported to the Netherlands in limited numbers during the early part of the nineteenth century. Thus, there was already some idea in Europe and America as to what Japanese lacquer and porcelain could or should look like. Japan's metalwork, by contrast, was virtually unknown. Nevertheless, Japanese bronzes were often singled out for praise by commentators on the early exhibitions. American writers were astonished that simple workshops with no machinery could have produced such complex and ostentatious objects, "so abounding in the drollest conceits, and the most grotesque shapes of birds, beasts, and human beings ... that no description of them is possible without ... engravings or photographs."[1] Another critic considered the Japanese cast bronzes at the 1876 Centennial Exhibition as "the most marvelous objects here"[2] before describing in some detail the stages of their production by the traditional "lost wax" process. In this method, the desired shape, worked up in a mixture of beeswax and pine resin, is coated with many layers of a sand and glue mixture, after which the original model is melted away leaving a hollow mould for casting. The whole process, as visitors were informed by the Japanese at the exhibition, could take 2,250 days of work, from creating the moulds to final decoration and polishing. At the 1893 World's Columbian Exposition, where the Japanese mounted a much more varied display and even put up a modified recreation of one of the country's most famous religious buildings, metalwork continued to attract special mention. *The Timesaver*, an unofficial handy guide claiming that it "... names and locates 5,000 things at the World's Fair that visitors should not fail to see", rated every significant exhibit or attraction with "1 (Interesting)", "2 (Very Interesting)" or "3 (Remarkably Interesting)". A Japanese iron eagle, "two feet high, with 3,000 individually handcrafted feathers" was awarded a "3", the same status as the guns that fired the first and last shots of the Civil War.[3] Commenting on the bronze-caster Suzuki Chokichi's most important contribution to the exhibition, now in the Japanese Imperial Collection, *The Graphic History of the Fair* considered that:

> Some of the bronze works were so beautiful that the most careless of the uninitiated could not pass them by. The twelve bronze falcons in the upper gallery were the result of years of labor, and they repaid the most careful study.[4]

Suzuki Chokichi, one of the heroic figures of Meiji craft, was at the heart of the great national project to redirect Japanese traditional industries towards the export market, and his career is typical of the era. Born in a Tokyo suburb at a time when the city was still called Edo, he was apprenticed to a traditional workshop where he underwent five years of rigorous training before setting up on his own at the age of seventeen. Although there is no evidence to confirm that he exhibited at the Vienna World Exhibition (1873), the elaborate incense burner reproduced on page 38 bears his signature and is very close in design to an example seen in a photograph of the Vienna display.[5] The even more impressive and much larger incense burner on pages 36 and 37, also signed by Chokichi and also unrecorded, was discovered recently in Germany and must have been intended for foreign exhibition, so it seems probable that documents relating to his early work are far from complete. What is certain is that Chokichi played a leading role at subsequent exhibitions, contributing some of the most impressive Japanese entries to the Philadelphia (1876) and Paris (1878) Expositions, as well as casting a great bronze lantern for the Yasukuni Shrine in Tokyo, the central focus of state Shinto (1880), a fountain for the Second National Industrial Exposition (1881), and an eagle which won first prize at the specialist Nuremburg Metalwork Exhibition (1885), where 492 Japanese pieces were shown. In 1874, Suzuki became director of the metalworking department of the government-sponsored Kiritsu Kosho Kaisha Company (page 31), setting up his own business after it folded in 1891. He was appointed *Teishitsu Gigeiin* [Artist to the Imperial Household] in 1896; this honor, which Chokichi used to the full in his advertising, is discussed on pages 347–9. The obscurity of his last fifteen years reflects wider changes in the Japanese economy, when conventional manufacturing industry assumed a more central role, not only in daily life, but also in Japan's contribution to many of the later exhibitions such as the one held in San Francisco in 1915. Chokichi abandoned bronze-casting and became a dealer in polishing-stones, no doubt of the kind his workers had used in producing the superb finish of his bronzes, until his death in 1919.

Some writers have suggested that the bronzes shown by Chokichi and his contemporaries owed nothing at all to traditional design and can only be considered as export wares, opportunistically created for an impressionable foreign audience. This is far from the truth. Just as many scholars have recently come round to the view that many of the economic achievements of the early Meiji Era built on the distinctive form of capitalism developed independently in Japan during the Edo Period, so it is now widely accepted that the design of these great bronzes is an adaptation of elements within the indigenous metalworking tradition. The large, multi-sectioned vases, encrusted with complex scenes from myth and legend, shown at Vienna and Philadelphia, are the result of superimposing the dramatic style of 1840s and 1850s warrior prints and illustrated books with a particular bronze form, the *usubata* that had been used for centuries in large, formal flower arrangements. Similarly, the three *oni* [demons] supporting Chokichi's great incense burner (page 37) are outsize versions of a popular mythical being frequently depicted in Edo-Period carvings and prints. Even the highly naturalistic eagles and falcons trace their origins to eighteenth- and nineteenth-century painting styles – themselves reflecting earlier European influence – which continued to flourish in the Meiji Era. The response to Western taste did not lead to the direct import of Western styles and motifs; rather it encouraged the selection and sometimes the exaggeration of disparate Japanese elements. The success of Suzuki's design policy was confirmed in 1881 when the South Kensington Museum in London (now the Victoria and Albert Museum) paid the enormous sum of £1,586. 7s. 2d. for an incense burner of his which has much in common with the giant piece reproduced on pages 36 and 37.

While Buddhism had sustained the Japanese bronze-casting tradition, the patronage of the samurai class had led to the creation of some of the finest arms and armor ever seen. The forged steel blades of the two swords, one long and one short, worn by every member of the samurai class are without a parallel anywhere in the world for their combination of rigidity, elegance of form, and deadly sharpness. Japanese mastery in wrought-iron work is demonstrated in samurai armor, made up of numerous metal plates joined by silk bands, and with carefully patinated helmets, masks, arm-guards, and other details. But it was, above all, the skills of the decorative metal craftsman, working in copper, silver, gold and their alloys, which was most easily adaptable to changing times. As early as 1873, the first steps were taken to form a conscript army equipped with modern weapons, and in

NEW MARKETS AND NEW CHALLENGES: DECORATIVE METALWORK

1876, the very same year as the Philadelphia Centennial Exhibition, a law was enacted which brought to a permanent end the right of Japan's two million samurai to bear their traditional weapons. This meant that makers of sword-fittings now had to adapt their work to new customers, both by adding decoration to bronzes cast by other craftsmen (see catalogue numbers 6–9) and, more often, by manufacturing a huge variety of smaller pieces in other metals (see catalogue numbers 45–55).

Over the centuries, Japan had developed a number of special alloys which could be patinated using naturally-derived acids and pickling solutions to produce an extraordinary range of beautiful finishes. Copper itself could vary from red to pale brown, but the most frequently used of the Japanese alloys are *shakudo* and *shibuichi*. *Shakudo*, a mixture of copper with a tiny percentage of gold, is patinated to a lustrous blue-black hue, while *shibuichi*, literally "one-quarter", although the actual proportions vary, is made from copper and silver and can be patinated to a range of colors from dark grey to pale green. Combined with silver and gold (itself appearing in several different shades) against a copper background, these alloys could create the illusion of full-color decoration, as noted by the British designer Christopher Dresser, who visited Japan in 1876–7:

> No people but the Japanese have understood the value of color in metal ...
> In many of their works we see gold, silver, copper, zinc, black-metal, tea-urn bronze, green bronze, and other metals ... To them [these metals] are only so many materials with which things of beauty may be produced.[6]

Perhaps Dresser was thinking of items like the miniature bookcase, see catalogue number 31, again very similar to one shown at Vienna just three years before the samurai sword was banned. Every inch an exhibition piece, it is a perfect example of the smooth transition from a traditional to a modern use for these time-honored techniques and it shows how well the pictorial style of late Edo-Period sword decoration could be adapted to a quite different shape.

Like Suzuki Chokichi in bronze, several leading workers in soft metal were to receive the title *Teishitsu Gigeiin* [Artist to the Imperial Household] later in the Meiji Era. The most famous of them, Kano Natsuo (1828–98) was among those first honored in this way in 1890. This was in recognition not only of his great skill and artistry in decorative metalwork but also of his practical contribution to Japan's economic transformation, since Natsuo had earlier worked for several years as designer and die-maker for his country's first modern coinage. Another great name is that of Natsuo's pupil Unno Shomin (1844–1915), who received the honor in 1896. Shomin included a subtle boast about his skill in the characters of his name, since *Sho* can mean "to be superior to" and *min* forms part of the name of a much earlier metalworker, Somin, who is considered the inventor of a new chiseling technique that allowed for variation in the width of the engraved line. This was also Shomin's speciality, and his copper plaques (numbers 395 and 396) are really paintings in metal, with every natural, flowing detail of Shoki the Demon-Queller's beard and whiskers or Kanzan's and Jittoku's hair painstakingly delineated with countless strokes of the hammer on the chisel in place of the delicate, and a hundred times more rapid, touch of a Japanese brush on paper.

After he had seen the exhibits for the Paris Exposition of 1889, Kano Natsuo wrote a list of the metalworkers he most admired. This list naturally included his pupil Shomin, but another artist he placed in the first division was Namekawa Sadakatsu (1848–after 1900), one of several Meiji-Era masters whose families had originally worked in the Edo Period for a branch of the ruling Tokugawa family in the Mito district to the north-east of Tokyo. His pair of silver vases (see catalogue number 228), dating from around 1895, shows just how far these former servants of the samurai had developed. Not only was silver hardly ever used before the Meiji Era as the material for whole vessels, the subtle color scheme is worlds away from the slightly ostentatious little bookcase made twenty years earlier. The decoration on Namekawa Sadakatsu's vase was intended to mimic the muted appearance of traditional painting on paper or silk. This effort to out-paint the painters is seen again in a vase by Jomi Eisuke II (1839–99, number 38), a craftsman and dealer from Kyoto. The vase is decorated mainly in *shakudo* and *shibuichi* inlay so as to emulate the soft, atmospheric effect of a landscape painted using a brush heavily loaded with black ink. An even more striking adaptation of traditional techniques, this time to emulate Chinese rather than Japanese painting, appears on a cigarette box by Kajima Ikkoku II (1846–1925, see catalogue number 62), decorated in so-called *sumie zogan* [ink-painting inlay]. In this case, a very thin sheet of silver was hammered onto the *shibuichi* lid of the box, which had previously been carefully scored in order to provide a key, a technique known in the West as damascening. The silver sheet was then either cut back to the *shibuichi* ground or carefully polished to different depths with a stone, enabling the artist to achieve some extremely subtle effects.

This box was made around 1910, at the very end of the Meiji Era, but damascening had been put to spectacular use some forty years earlier by the Komai family of Kyoto. Around 1873 Komai Otojiro started selling his distinctive wares in the nearby port of Kobe, a center of foreign trade like Yokohama, and within a few years his chargers, plaques, cabinets, model pagodas, and vases (numbers 27–29, 40, 44, 137, 154, 156–7), made from iron overlaid with minute decoration in gold and silver, were in such demand that he was prosperous enough to buy a large house. In 1901, despite earlier business problems, he was able to expand into new premises and started manufacturing a wide range of smaller objects such as cigarette cases and jewel boxes, making his wares among the best-known products of Japan in the early years of this century.

The Komai Company in some ways resembled a modern manufacturing concern, nurturing and developing its brand at the same time as employing most of the tradespeople involved in making its products. Another type of of organization that was very active in the second half of the Meiji Era was the commissioning company, which might directly employ a few people but sourced most of its merchandise from independent workers. The Ozeki Company is the most famous of these companies, putting its distinctive trademark on work in both enamel and metal. Although it was not as big as the semi-nationalized Kiritsu Kosho Kaisha, it survived for much longer and played a very active part in the five National Industrial Expositions (page 212), where it would usually be awarded the lion's share of the more important official prizes and medals, the artists themselves receiving lesser honors. The incense burner and cover on page 152 is an outstanding example of a collaboration between the Ozeki Company and a leading craftsman, in this case Yamada Motonobu (1847–97). Yamada worked for the Imperial Household and enjoyed the patronage of the Kuki family, whose leader, Kuki Ryuichi, was one of the most influential cultural administrators of the day. The incense burner's unusual spherical form and innovative fusion of traditional techniques, including both chiseling in iron (originally used on armor) and details of gold and *shakudo* derived from sword-decoration, is an excellent example of the late Meiji-Era artist's success in achieving a style that is unmistakably Japanese and yet also highly marketable to foreign buyers.

NOTES

1. William Hosley, *The Japan Idea* (Hartford, Conn., 1990), p.55.
2. Hosley, *The Japan Idea*, p.55.
3. John E. Findling, *Chicago's Great World's Fairs* (Manchester and New York, 1994), p.29.
4. [Anon.], *The Graphic History of the Fair, Containing a Sketch of International Expositions, a Review of Events Leading to the Discovery of America, and a History of the World's Columbian Exposition, Held in the City of Chicago, State of Illinois, May 1 to October 31, 1893* (Chicago, 1894), p.201.
5. Yokomizo Hiroko, "Meiji shoki no hakurankai o kazatta kinzoku [On Metalwork Shown at International Expositions in the Early Meiji Era]", *Museum* (Journal of Tokyo National Museum) no. 492 (March 1992), pp. 28–42, figs. 1 and 2.
6. Hosley, *The Japan Idea*, p.52.

METALWORK

This section features examples of the many different traditional styles and techniques of metalwork that were adapted during the Meiji Period and applied to new types of products designed for both the domestic and the international markets. These have mostly been arranged according to the main metal from which they are made, including bronze, iron, silver, and the copper-gold and copper-silver alloys known respectively as *shakudo* and *shibuichi*.

35

ORNAMENT
About 1880–1900
Bronze; with copper, *shakudo*, gold, and silver
14.3 × 36.2 cm.
Signed *Shoami Katsuyoshi*, with a silvered seal *Katsuyoshi*
By Shoami Katsuyoshi (1832–1908)

Shoami Katsuyoshi is one of several Meiji-Era craftsmen who originally trained as a maker of sword-fittings (starting at the age of thirteen), but had to change to new styles and products in the 1870s. He exhibited extensively in both domestic and international exhibitions, winning many prizes. This *okimono* [literally "thing to place", a word used in this period for any high quality decorative item with no direct practical purpose] is made from bronze and copper which have been carefully patinated to a variety of autumnal colors and embellished with gold, silver, and *shakudo*, an alloy of copper and a very small percentage of gold, patinated to a lustrous blue-black.

43
PAIR OF VASES
About 1880
Iron, with gold and silver; the panels
worked in a variety of copper alloys
Height 62.5 cm.
Signed and sealed *Yoshimori*; signed inside
the covers *Dai Nihon Tokyo Tekkodo zo*
[made by Tekkodo of Tokyo in great Japan]
By Unno Yoshimori II (Bisei, 1864–1919)
Produced by the Tekkodo Company

Unno Yoshimori II, also known as Unno
Bisei, was one of the most important

metalwork artists of his period. Born in
Tokyo, he started to learn chasing and
engraving in 1875, as well as studying
drawing, painting, and Western-style
sculpture. He became a professor at the
Tokyo School of Art in 1898.

The panel depicting the two sages closely
resembles, both in technique and in the faces,
the panel on the incense burner, number 42.

44
DISH
About 1885
Iron; with copper, *shibuichi*, silver, and gold
Diameter 48.6 cm.
Signed *Nihonkoku Kyoto no ju Komai sei*
[made by Komai of Kyoto in Japan]
Produced by the Komai Company

The central panel is decorated with two
rakan [disciples of the Buddha, see
number 170].

45
VASE
About 1890
Shakudo; with *shibuichi*, copper, silver, and enamels
Height 29.0 cm.
Signed *Bokusui no ju Motonobu koku* [carved by Inshi Motonobu of Bokusui]; sealed *Ozeki sei* [made by Ozeki]
By Yamada Motonobu (1847–97)
Produced by the Ozeki Company

Yamada Motonobu was one of the finest Meiji-Era metalwork artists. His family had worked for the Tokugawa family in the Mito area to the north-east of Tokyo. He first started metal-carving in 1864, at the age of thirteen, and is recorded as working for the Imperial Household in

1877. "Bokusui", given as his place of residence in the signature on this piece, is another name for the Sumida River and district in the east of Tokyo, where many craftsmen lived and worked during the Meiji Era. It is possible that the enamel work was carried out by Goto Shozaburo or Hiratsuka Mohei (see numbers 26, 56 and 188), as both are recorded as having won prizes at the first Naikoku Kangyo Hakurankai [National Industrial Exposition] of 1877 for work exhibited by Ozeki Sadajiro.

46
VASE
About 1900
Shibuichi; with silver, gold, copper, and enamel
Height 34.5 cm.
Signed *Takasaki* and *Horyusai Koichi*
By Takasaki Koichi (dates unknown)

Takasaki Koichi exhibited a pair of silver vases, decorated in cloisonné enamels with peony and poppies, at the Paris Universal Exposition of 1900.[1]

1. *Bijutsu gaho, Daini rinji zokan bijutsu gaho; Pari hakurankai shuppin kumiai seisakuhin* [Extra Issue no. 2 of Fine Arts Magazine Containing Illustrations and Descriptions of Products of the Paris World Exposition Exhibitor's Union] (Tokyo, 1900), unpaginated.

47
INCENSE BURNER
About 1880
Shibuichi; with *shakudo*, gilding, silver,
and copper
Height 37.0 cm.
Signed *Ichiryu Tomotoshi* with a *kao*
[cursive monogram]
By Ichiryu (Hitotsuyanagi) Tomotoshi
(1831–89)

Ichiryu Tomotoshi was one of several sword-
fitting makers from the domain of Mito,
north-east of Tokyo, who first worked for
a branch of the Tokugawa family, and later
moved to Tokyo and Yokohama. On this
piece, in theory an incense burner but in
reality an *okimono* [ornament], the body of
the drum is made from *shibuichi* [literally,
"one part in four"], an alloy primarily of
gold and silver patinated to a dull gray-green
color. The *kankodori* [cock on a drum]
motif symbolizes good government. Drums
were supposedly placed outside the palaces
of early Chinese kings so that their subjects
could beat on them if they had a complaint;
this drum has been so little used that it has
become a perch for the farmyard bird.

48
ORNAMENT
About 1900–10
Shibuichi in two different colors; with
shakudo, *sentoku* [a form of brass], and
copper
Length 22.1 cm.
Signed *Joun saku* [made by Joun]
By Oshima Joun (1858–1940)

For Oshima Joun, see number 245.

49
PAIR OF VASES
About 1880–90
Shibuichi, with a variety of other metals
and alloys
Height 13.9 cm.
The panels variously signed *Inshi
Motonobu koku* [carved by Inshi
Motonobu], *Motonobu*, *Inshi*, *Bokusuihen
Motonobu koku* [carved by Bokusuihen
Motonobu], *Ittosai Masatoshi*, and
Ukishima hen; sealed on the base *Ozeki sei*
[made by Ozeki]
By Kaneyasu Masatoshi (1845–1908 or
later) and Yamada Motonobu (1847–97)
Produced by the Ozeki Company

Most of the panels depict various stages
in the cultivation of silkworms and the
manufacture of silk. For Yamada
Motonobu, see number 45.

50
VASE
About 1900
Silver; with cloisonné enamels, *shakudo*,
and gilding
Height 26.2 cm.
Signed *Takasaki seizo* [made by Takasaki]
By Takasaki Koichi (dates unknown)

For Takasaki Koichi, see numbers 46
and 288.

51
VASE
About 1900
Shibuichi, with gold and silver
Height 19.6 cm.
Signed *Issei zo* [made by Issei]
By Hasegawa Issei (dates unknown)

Hasegawa Issei, who worked in Tokyo in
the Meiji and Taisho Eras, was known for
his metal *okimono* [ornaments], and was
presumably responsible for the dragon on
this piece (see also number 288). He is
recorded as exhibiting at the Liège Exposition
of 1905 and the Paris Universal Exposition
of 1900, where he showed silver vases,
incense burners, and groups of birds.[1]

1. Ch. Desoer (ed.), *Catalogue Officiel de la
   Section Japonaise, Exposition Universelle et
   Internationale de Liège* (Brussels, 1905), p.88,
   no. 179; *Catalogue spécial officiel du Japon:
   Exposition Internationale de 1900* (Paris,
   1900), p.86.

52
INCENSE BURNER
About 1895
Shibuichi; with silver, *shakudo*, gold, and bronze
Height 14.9 cm.
Signed *Kaneyasu Masatoshi zo* [made by Kaneyasu Masatoshi]
By Kaneyasu Masatoshi (1845–1908 or later)
Probably produced by the Ozeki Company

The panels depict Shoki, the demon-queller, being teased by two demons: one performs a New Year dance on his hand, while the other runs away with his sword.

53
TRAY
About 1890
Shibuichi; with silver, gilding, *shakudo*, and copper
26.9 × 20.9 cm.
Signed *Higashiyama*, sealed *Motonobu*
By Higashiyama Motonobu (dates unknown)

54
BOX
About 1885
Shibuichi; with *shakudo*, silver, gold, and
copper
9.2 × 13.9 cm.
Signed *Tokasai Shomin*, sealed *Sho*
Probably by a follower of Unno Shomin
(1844–1915)

The top shows the warrior Raiko (944–1021),
famed for his success in clearing the Kyoto
region of demons and brigands, being
haunted by a large spider-demon which
appears above him, its hands holding
cobwebs with which to bind him. A similar
box is in the collection of the Walters Art
Gallery, Baltimore (inv. no. 52.1177).

55
VASE
About 1895
Shibuichi, with a silver neck and relief
decoration in various metals
Height 27.2 cm.
Signed *Ryounsai Moritoshi* and sealed
Ryoun; the base sealed *Ozeki sei* [made
by Ozeki]
By Unno Moritoshi (1834–1896)
Produced by the Ozeki Company

For Unno Moritoshi, see number 15. This
vase shows Urashima Taro, the hero of a
popular legend, being approached by a
minogame [hairy-tailed tortoise]. During
a fishing trip, he was transported by sea
turtles to the palace of the sea goddess,
where he was detained for several centuries.
At last, he was allowed to return home
with a chest containing the years of his life
that had slipped away, but the goddess
gave him strict instructions not to open it.
At first he was able to resume his normal
life at the age he had been before his
disappearance, but he was eventually
overcome by curiosity. He opened the box
and immediately became an old man.

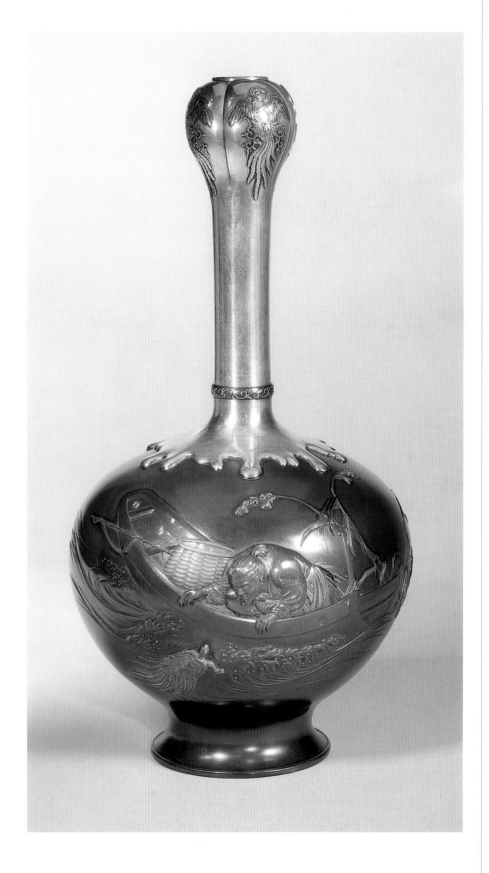

56

TEA AND COFFEE SERVICE
About 1900
Silver; with gold, silver, and enamels
The tray 72.6 × 44.5 cm.
Signed in English *Musashiya Yokohama*
and in Japanese *Musashiya sei* [made by
Musashiya]
The enamels attributed to Hiratsuka Mohei
(dates unknown)
Produced by the Ozeki Company

The service comprises a coffee pot and cover;
teapot and cover; hot-water jug, cover, and
stand with spirit burner; milk jug; sugar
bowl and tongs. The enameling is possibly
the work of Hiratsuka Mohei (see numbers
26, 45 and 188), who worked for the Ozeki
family at the first Naikoku Kangyo
Hakurankai [National Industrial
Exposition] in 1877.

57
BOX
About 1900
Shibuichi; with silver, *shakudo*, gold,
and copper
4.0 × 9.4 × 7.7 cm.
Signed *Michihiro koku* [carved by
Michihiro]

The artist is possibly Suzuki Michihiro,
who showed an iron incense burner at the
third Naikoku Kangyo Hakurankai
[National Industrial Exposition] in 1890.

58
BOX
About 1910
Silver, with *shibuichi* and gold
5.3 × 11.4 × 15.3 cm.
Signed *Bunkei sen*, sealed *Bunkei no in*
[seal of Bunkei] and *Shomin no in* [seal of
Shomin]; the base marked *Tokyo Hattori
tokei-ten kinsei* [respectfully made by the
Hattori Clock Store, Tokyo]
By Unno Shomin (1844–1915) and Bunkei
(dates unknown)
Produced by the Hattori Clock Store

The two figures reading a scroll, depicted
on the *shibuichi* panel, are Kanzan and
Jittoku, two legendary monks of Tang-
Dynasty China (618–907). They lived in
the kitchen of a monastery and spoke a
private language. Because of this, they were
considered mentally unbalanced. For Unno
Shomin, see numbers 395 and 396, another
work by him depicting Kanzan and Jittoku.
Nothing is known of Bunkei, who worked
with Shomin on this piece.

59
INCENSE BOX
About 1890
Silver; with *shakudo*, copper, and gold
Height 8.0 cm.
Signed *Seppo Hidetomo koku* [carved by
Seppo Hidetomo]

The upper part of the monkey detaches at
waist level to reveal the silver interior.

60
INCENSE BURNER
About 1900
Silver; with *shakudo*, gilt, and copper
13.5 × 14.0 cm.
Signed *?mi zo* [made by ?mi], sealed *Ozeki
sei* [made by Ozeki]
Produced by the Ozeki Company

This incense burner takes the form of a
lion-like creature of Chinese origin, known
as a *shishi*, playing with a ball made from
silver and *shakudo*.

61
INCENSE BURNER
About 1890
Silver, with copper and gilding
12.9 × 11.2 cm.
Signed *Takachika*
By Sano Takachika (dates unknown)

For Sano Takachika, see number 235 and
328–9.

62

BOX

About 1910
Silver and *shibuichi*
5.2 × 15.9 × 12.3 cm.
Signed *Ikkokusai* and *Mitsutaka*
By Kajima Ikkoku II (1846–1925)

Kajima Ikkoku II was the eldest son of Ikkoku I, taking over the name on his father's death in 1882. He started exhibiting in 1881, under the name Eijiro, and showed a large group of objects at the third Naikoku Kangyo Hakurankai [National Industrial Exposition] in 1890; his works were also on view in Liège (1905) and London (1910), where he showed a vase with horses.[1] This was apparently decorated in *sumie zogan*, a style of inlay also seen on this box, in which a thin sheet of silver is applied to the scored *shibuichi* body and then either cut back to the *shibuichi* or carefully polished to different depths with a stone, enabling Ikkoku to produce delicate effects that are uncannily reminiscent of ink-painting.

The Chinese sage depicted on the cover, who may be Jurojin, a god of longevity, is surrounded by auspicious motifs, including pine, plum, a deer, a crane, and a bat.

1. Office of the Imperial Japanese Government Commission to the Japan-British Exhibition, *An Illustrated Catalogue of Japanese Modern Fine Arts Displayed at the Japan-British Exhibition, London, 1910* (Tokyo, 1910), no. 199.

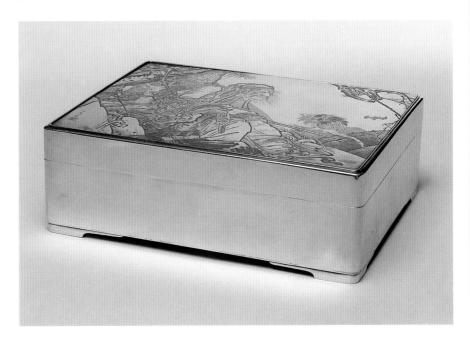

63
SCREEN
About 1890
Silver; with *shakudo*, gold, copper, and
shibuichi
23.9 × 18.1 cm.
Signed *Inshi Motonobu sen* and *Inshi*,
sealed *Motonobu*; the base sealed *Ozeki sei*
[made by Ozeki]
By Yamada Motonobu (1847–1897)
Produced by the Ozeki Company

The panel humorously depicts Emma-O, one
of the Buddhist judges of hell, dreaming of
a beautiful courtesan in an unguarded
moment.

64
DISH
About 1875–1900
Silver, with a panel of *kinji* lacquer decorated
in Shibayama style (see pages 93–4)
6.4 × 16.5 × 21.7 cm.
Signed *Katsumitsu*

Nothing is known of the artist Katsumitsu,
who probably worked for one of the silver
companies based in Yokohama.

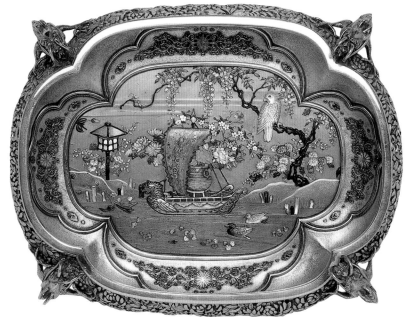

67
VASE
About 1875–1900
Wood, lacquered in *kinji* and *hirame*,
with encrustation of shell, ivory, and other
materials; silver edgings
Height 20.2 cm.

Most early examples of Shibayama work
were probably made in Tokyo, but
Shibayama artifacts were so popular that
later in the Meiji Era craftsmen in other
workshops centered around Yokohama
began to manufacture similar pieces.
The fact that a large number of different
workshops produced Shibayama-style
wares accounts for the enormous variety
in the selection illustrated here.

68

PAIR OF VASES

About 1875–1900

Wood, lacquered in gold, silver, black, and red *hiramaki-e* and *takamaki-e* and with encrustation of ivory and other materials; silver rims. Each vase on a copper stand inlaid in high relief with copper, silver, gold, and *shakudo*

Height 16.2 cm.

Many examples of Shibayama work feature not only organic materials, such as ivory, shell, and coral, but also metalwork derived from the earlier tradition of sword decoration in gold, silver, copper, and the special Japanese alloys *shakudo* and *shibuichi*. The decoration of these vases refers to the regular embassies from Korea and Ryukyu (Okinawa) which had taken place during the Edo Period. These foreign delegations occasionally included exotic animals such as elephants and were sometimes reenacted by the Japanese at annual festivals.

69

PAIR OF VASES

About 1875–1900

Wood, lacquered in *kinji* and *hirame*, and with encrustation of shell, ivory and other materials; silver edgings

Height 25.5 cm.

Signed *Shibayama* on one vase and *Ekisei* on the other

By Shibayama Ekisei (see below)

Shibayama Ekisei is said by one Japanese writer to have worked in the middle of the nineteenth century and is described as the ancestor of the Shibayama inlay workers. The Ekisei who made this piece is a later individual, possibly the same as the artist called Ekisei who won prizes at the second (1881) and third (1890) Naikoku Kangyo Hakurankai [National Industrial Expositions].

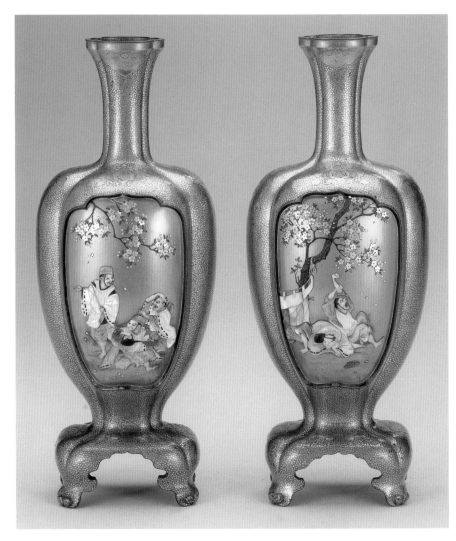

70

BOX IN THE FORM OF A DRUM

About 1890–1900
Wood, lacquered in *kinji* and *hiramaki-e*, with encrustation of ivory and shell; fitted with ivory carvings
Height 33.8 cm.

Although no reliable chronology has been established for the development of Shibayama ware, the style of the ivory carvings attached to this piece, in particular the figure of a woman holding a hibiscus, suggests a date towards the end of the nineteenth century. The figure on the face of the drum is Gama Sennin [the toad deity], whose story is explained in the caption to number 141.

71

TWO-FOLD SCREEN
About 1875–1900
Wood, lacquered in *maki-e*, *kirikane*, and *kinji*, with encrustation of shell, ivory, and other materials; silver hinges
20.5 × 23.5 cm.

This screen depicts a *hanami* [cherry blossom viewing] party, a leisure pursuit which was frequently depicted by wood-block print artists during the Edo Period and remains popular today.

72

TWO-FOLD SCREEN
About 1875–1900
Wood, lacquered in *maki-e* and *kinji*, and with encrustation of shell, ivory, and other materials, and translucent enamel inlays; silver hinges and fittings
30.5 × 32.2 cm.

73
PAIR OF VASES
About 1890–1900
Wood, lacquered in *hiramaki-e*, *togidashi-e*,
and *kinji*, and with encrustation of shell,
ivory, and other materials; silver stands and
rims with decoration in gold, silver, and
other metals
Height 17.5 cm.

74
TWO-FOLD SCREEN
About 1875–1900
Wood panels lacquered in *hiramaki-e*,
togidashi-e, and *kirikane* on a *fundame*
ground, and with encrustation of shell,
ivory and other materials; set in silver frames
38.3 × 36.9 cm.

The repoussé frames are probably the work
of one of the Yokohama firms specializing
in silverware for export, of which the best
known was Y. Konoike. The Konoike
Company, whose curio store was located at
17 Honcho-dori [Main Street] in Yokohama,
also sold items made entirely from silver,
such as teaspoons, teapots, and napkin rings.

75

PAIR OF VASES
About 1890–1900
Wood, lacquered in *hiramaki-e, kirikane,*
and *kinji,* and with encrustation of shell,
ivory and other materials; silver stands and
stoppers; *shakudo* collars
Height 17.2 cm.

76

PAIR OF VASES
About 1890–1900
Wood, lacquered in *hiramaki-e, kirikane*
and *kinji,* and with encrustation of shell,
ivory, and other materials; silver fittings
Height 21.0 cm.

77
PAIR OF VASES
About 1875–1900
Wood panels lacquered in *hiramaki-e*,
togidashi-e, and *kirikane* on a *kinji* ground,
and with encrustation of shell, ivory, and
other materials; set in silver frames with
cloisonné enamel decoration
Height 15.9 cm.
Signed *Soya*

Nothing is known about the artist whose
name is impressed on the base of these vases.

78

CABINET

About 1875–1900

Silver filigree inset with panels of silver, ivory, and *kinji* lacquer; decorated in *hiramaki-e* lacquer; with encrustation of shell, ivory, and other materials

14.1 × 11.2 × 16.0 cm.

The use of differently shaped overlapping panels of decoration is very common in smaller objects made for export; for other examples see numbers 188 and 194.

79

CABINET

About 1875–1900

Wood, lacquered in *takamaki-e*, *togidashi-e*, and *kinji*, and with encrustation of shell, ivory, and other materials; silver fittings

12.9 × 11.6 × 15.1 cm.

The figure riding on a carp, shown on the inside of the door, is the Chinese magician Kinko (see also number 230), who is supposed to have lived in the state of Zhao at the end of the Zhou Dynasty (traditional dates: 1122–255 B.C.) or, perhaps, in the Han Dynasty (206 B.C.–A.D. 221). Sent into exile by the king of Zhao, he wandered with his many followers to the bank of a river, dived in, and eventually emerged at an appointed hour riding on the back of a carp. Later, he dived in a second time and was never seen again.

80

VASE
About 1875–1900
Wood, lacquered in *takamaki-e*, *hiramaki-e*,
hirame, and *kinji*, and with encrustation
of shell, ivory, and other materials; silver
fittings and liner
Height 30.5 cm.
Signed *Gekko*

The signature, incised on a shell tablet
inlaid into the base of the vase, may be
that of a metalworker with the same
name which appears on a *shibuichi*
and copper netsuke in a British private
collection.[1]

1. E. A. Wrangham, *The Index of Inro Artists*
   (Harehope, Northumberland, 1995), pp. 57–8.

81
VASE
About 1875–1900
Metal body of *shakudo*-colored alloy
decorated in cloisonné enamels; panels
lacquered in *maki-e* and *kinji*, and with
encrustation of shell, ivory and other
materials; silver fittings
Height 37.5 cm.
Signed *Masamitsu*

Towards the end of the nineteenth century,
Japanese metalworkers developed new
pickling solutions in an effort to impart
the characteristic blue-black color of
shakudo to copper without adding the
gold. The color of the metal on this vase
is slightly different from that of true
shakudo, suggesting that this is an
example of such work.

82
VASE
1880s
Porcelain, painted in underglaze blue and
enamels
Height 23.1 cm.
Signed *Kozan sei* [made by Kozan]
Made by the Miyagawa Kozan Workshop

The revival of Japanese porcelain in the
mid-Meiji Era was spearheaded by
Miyagawa "Makuzu" Kozan. Originally
from a long line of potters based in Kyoto,
he took over the family business in 1860 at
the age of nineteen, and in 1870 opened a
workshop in Yokohama. This was a bold
move for, despite the obvious advantages
of being close to the new capital, Tokyo,
and the tourist shops and trading houses of
Yokohama, there was no tradition of
porcelain manufacturing there. Before long,
however, Kozan was producing a wide
range of ceramics for both domestic and
export markets. The early products of
Kozan's Yokohama workshop are sometimes rather heavily potted and awkwardly
shaped, but they are already an advance on
the overly ornate earthenware he produced
in the 1870s.

83
VASE
1880s
Porcelain; painted in underglaze blue,
mauve, and olive green
Height 26.8 cm.
Signed *Kozan sei* [made by Kozan]
Made by the Miyagawa Kozan Workshop

84
TEAPOT
1880s
Porcelain, painted in underglaze blue and
olive green
Height 24.0 cm.
Signed *Kozan sei* [made by Kozan]
Made by the Miyagawa Kozan Workshop

85
VASE
1880s
Porcelain with a pale green glaze, painted in
underglaze brown
Height 19.5 cm.
Signed *Kozan sei* [made by Kozan]
Made by the Miyagawa Kozan Workshop

86
VASE
1880s
Porcelain, with a flambé glaze running
down the side of the vessel, the base
painted in underglaze blue
Height 21.6 cm.
Signed *Kozan sei* [made by Kozan]
Made by the Miyagawa Kozan Workshop

Kozan's so-called *yohen* [transmutation] or
flambé glazes were very popular in the West,
first gaining international recognition at the
Paris International Exposition of 1889,
where he won a gold medal.

87
VASE
About 1890
Porcelain with a celadon (pale green) glaze,
painted in underglaze red and blue
Height 25.2 cm.
Signed *Kozan sei* [made by Kozan]
Made by the Miyagawa Kozan Workshop

The lotus scroll decoration of this vase
reflects the influence of Chinese porcelain
of the early Ming Dynasty (1368–1644).

88
BOWL
1890s
Porcelain, with decoration in underglaze
green and pink, and white enamel on a
coral ground
Height 21.0 cm.
Signed *Makuzu-gama Kozan sei* [made by
Kozan at the Makuzu kiln]
Made by the Miyagawa Kozan Workshop

89
INCENSE BURNER
About 1890
Porcelain, painted in pale yellow enamel on
a coral ground, the details finely delineated
in coral, the enamel lightly incised
Height 13.2 cm.
Signed *Kozan sei* [made by Kozan]
Made by the Miyagawa Kozan Workshop

90
VASE
1890s
Porcelain, painted in underglaze copper-red,
black and green
Height 17.6 cm.
Signed *Makuzu-gama Kozan sei* [made by
Kozan at the Makuzu kiln]
Made by the Miyagawa Kozan Workshop

This is an example of the freer style of
porcelain decoration, with several different
underglaze colors, developed at the Makuzu
kilns during the 1890s.

91

PAIR OF SAMURAI FIGURES
About 1890
Bronze, with gilding, silver, and *shakudo*;
wood stands
Overall heights 223 and 226 cm.
Signed *Nihonkoku bijutsusho Miyao sei*
[made by the Miyao Art Workshop in Japan]
Produced by the Miyao Company

This pair of figures reproduces in loving
detail the complex structure of Japanese
armor, with its multiple iron plates joined
by silk ribbons, and rich silk brocade sleeves
and leggings. The Miyao Company of
Yokohama was one of the more prolific
workshops of the Meiji Era, producing
generally good-quality bronzes bearing rich
brown patinas with details picked out in
gilding. The subject of warriors was a
favorite theme which presumably appealed
to the company's Western clientele. Although
the overall appearance is very ornate and
apparently detailed, the company used
virtually no inlay, relying on the gilt details
to give the general effect. The main part of
the Miyao business was concerned with
bronzes, but the company is also recorded
in the second Naikoku Kangyo Hakurankai
[National Industrial Exposition] of 1881
exhibiting pieces in wood.

92
FIGURE OF A DRAGON
About 1880
Bronze, with gilt, *shakudo*, and silver;
wood stand
Height 227 cm.
Signed *Dai Nihon Tokyo Miyao zo*
[made by Miyao of Tokyo in great Japan]
Produced by the Miyao Company

For the Miyao Company, see page 95.

93
SAMURAI FIGURE
About 1890
Bronze with gilt details; wood stand
decorated with black and gold lacquer
Height 191 cm.
Signed *Gyoko saku* [made by Gyoko]
Produced by Akasofu Gyoko

Akasofu Gyoko lived in Tokyo, his
workshop, like that of Miyao Eisuke
(see numbers 91 and 92), producing cast
metalwork for export. His given name was
Sotojiro and he is recorded as a member of
the Tokyo Chukinkai [Tokyo Cast
Metalworkers Association] in the second
half of the Meiji Era. For another example
of his work, see number 234.

94
CABINET
1880s
Lacquer, mounted with enameled and gilded porcelain panels; *shakudo* and gilt fittings
208 × 120 × 46.0 cm.

This cabinet is a good example of the sumptuous combination of techniques that was sought after by many Japanese-art enthusiasts at the height of the Japan craze in the 1870s and 1880s. Also characteristic of this period is the optimistic use on the metal fittings of the hollyhock *mon* [crest] of the Tokugawa family who had ruled Japan as shoguns for more than two centuries until 1867. The Tokugawa *mon* is particularly inappropriate on this piece, since the large porcelain panel at the top right shows the warrior Nitta Yoshisada (1301–38), a loyalist hero who struggled to depose the Hojo, an earlier family of military rulers, and restore Imperial rule (see page 146). On his way to capture the city of Kamakura, Nitta threw his sword into the waves as an offering to Ryujin, the Dragon King of the Sea. The tide immediately drew back, opening up a route by which Nitta was able to make a successful surprise attack. After the restoration of Imperial rule in 1868, tales like this were promoted by the new government and this particular episode was illustrated in an official history book published in 1888.[1]

1. Osumi Kazuo *et. al.* [ed.], *Nihon kaku densho jinmei jiten* [Dictionary of Imaginary and Traditional Personalities] (Tokyo, 1986), p.369.

"SATSUMA" WARE

THE MYTH OF
ANTIQUITY

An elaborately enameled and gilded Japanese ware called "Satsuma" captured the imagination of both European and American writers at the very start of the Meiji Era, and was perhaps the most extravagantly praised of all Japan's newly-discovered arts and crafts. In 1875, for example, the British connoisseurs George Audsley and James Bowes wrote enthusiastically of:

> those beautiful works in soft-toned faience, decorated with flowers, birds, and other objects, in a style more delicate and artistic than can be found throughout the entire range of Keramic Art outside the islands of Japan.[1]

This was praise indeed, since Europeans had already been buying East Asian porcelain for nearly three hundred years, but no one was prepared for the exuberance of Satsuma. In an early demonstration of Japanese skill in adapting product to market, it combined dazzling decoration with mysterious subject matter, both responding to prevailing Western taste and appearing to offer a privileged window onto the myths, legends, and customs of "old Japan". It was thus perhaps the most successful of all Meiji Japan's many efforts to produce goods that, while seemingly traditional, were deliberately designed to appeal to a Western taste for the exotic. Better still, its origins were soon shrouded in mystery.

As we saw earlier (page 30), the Paris Exhibition of 1867 included not only an official Japanese section organized by the Tokugawa government, but also contributions from the two southern domains of Saga and Satsuma. The Satsuma exhibit included a few examples of what would later be called Satsuma ware, and one of these was purchased by the South Kensington Museum in London, forerunner of the Victoria and Albert Museum. Compared to later pieces, the decoration of this vase was quite restrained, and the examples illustrated in 1875 by Audsley and Bowes were already much more elaborate. This elaboration of design went hand-in-hand with the concoction of fanciful stories about the history of Satsuma: in 1877, for example, there was a public sale in London of "old Satsuma" which had supposedly been made for the Popes just after Christian missionaries first visited Japan in the sixteenth century! It soon became essential for anyone with the slightest pretension to a knowledge of Japanese art to possess the ability to distinguish between "old" and "new" Satsuma, even though nobody could be quite certain just how old "old" might be. Often the products of two different factories, working in different parts of Japan at the same time, were given widely varying dates.

Audsley and Bowes were aware that the antiquity of Satsuma was already being exaggerated and thought that they were striking a blow for historical accuracy when they stated "the most ancient examples which have come under our observation do not date further back than two hundred and fifty years".[2] We know now that wares in the style were probably made no earlier than the middle years of the nineteenth century, about twenty-five years before the two British writers published their lavish volumes on *Keramic Art of Japan*, but a lack of documentary evidence has meant that even today the precise early history of Satsuma is hard to trace. This shortage of hard information encouraged exaggerated opinions on both sides of the argument about the true age of Satsuma. In 1888, the American ceramic expert Edward Sylvester Morse used the columns of *Harper's New Monthly Magazine* to deride the extravagance of Audsley and Bowes's publication, their acceptance of the very idea that there was really a single body of ceramics that could be called Satsuma and their belief that this had been made over a very long period of time:

> What was called Satsuma enriched the collections of the amateur; museums of art paraded colossal Satsuma vases in pairs, gorgeous with glitter and gold; costly books, with triumphs of the chromo-lithographer's skill, depicted what was supposed to be different periods of this Satsuma ware .[3]

In 1893 the learned but highly opinionated writer Frank Brinkley, of Irish origin but resident in Japan for over forty years (see also page 93), offered this cutting comment on the delusions that accompanied the Satsuma craze in his remarks on the Japanese exhibits sent to the Chicago World's Fair:

> These things are eagerly acquired ... as Japanese specimens, and in one
> sense they certainly merit the term, for it is emphatically curious that there
> should have sprung into prosperous existence within the past twenty years
> a large class of objects which are absolutely without prototypes in Japanese
> art, do open violence to the canons of that art, have their origin solely
> in the Japanese keramist's [potter's] deluded conception of foreign taste,
> and nevertheless pass among foreigners for genuine representations of
> Japanese taste.[4]

Although Brinkley was exaggerating when he claimed that the history of the ware went back no more than twenty years and that it had no prototype in Japanese art, it is interesting that this supposedly most Japanese of products in fact incorporated a number of recently-invented European techniques and was later influenced by Western styles. Imported pigments were soon being applied alongside Japanese ones for overglaze decoration, and from 1884 most of the distinctive gilt color in the versions of Satsuma made at Awata in Kyoto and Kutani in Kanazawa was made from "liquid gold", a material developed at the Meissen Factory in Germany and imported by traders in Yokohama. The imported paint became increasingly popular with ceramic decorators because it did not change color during firing and did not require thick application, allowing the painter to produce more delicate designs. Foreign travel exposed the manufacturers of Satsuma to further outside influences. Yabu Meizan of Osaka (see below) would be especially inspired in his later career by new examples of porcelain from Sèvres in France, which he brought home from the 1900 Paris Exposition.

YABU MEIZAN AND THE DEVELOPMENT OF SATSUMA WARE

The general term "Satsuma" could, if used correctly, cover all the pottery made in the Satsuma area at the southern tip of Kyushu, the southernmost of Japan's main islands. Kyushu has been a center of the ceramics industry since the 1590s, when Korean potters were brought back to Japan after two attempted invasions of Korea (see page 18). Kyushu kilns had produced many different types of ware over the centuries, most of them looking nothing like Satsuma as we know it today. The immediate precursor of the first wares to be called "Satsuma" in the West was a kind of white-bodied earthenware with a crackled glaze and decoration in polychrome enamels which may have been made in Kagoshima, since examples of this type are often marked with the word "Satsuma" or the crest of the Shimazu family, hereditary lords of the Satsuma domain. It was apparently not until the Paris 1867 Exposition that the term "Satsuma" was first used by Westerners to describe the gilded and enameled earthenware discussed and illustrated on these pages. As a result of the success of Satsuma ware, orders began to come in from both Europe and America and very soon potters from other parts of Kyushu were helping to meet the demand. Already "Satsuma" referred not simply to a geographical place, but to a style, or rather, a romantic vision of the exotic Orient.

Satsuma pottery was widely admired and bought at the 1873 Vienna World Exhibition, and many potters, not just in Kyushu but also in other parts of Japan, began to cash in on the new fashion. Satsuma-style wares were made in Awata (a district of the old capital Kyoto), in the new capital Tokyo, in the great trading center of Osaka, in the burgeoning international port of Yokohama, and at the Kutani kilns in the old ceramic center of Kanazawa on the coast of the Sea of Japan. Sometimes the entire process of manufacture was carried out in one place, but more often ceramic bodies made and glazed in Satsuma itself were sent to Osaka and Tokyo to be decorated with minute painting of figures in imaginary landscapes between dense floral borders. Such pieces were shown at the first National Industrial Exposition held in 1877.

Yabu Meizan of Osaka (1853–1934) was the most prolific of all the manufacturers of Satsuma ware. In 1880, after a time in Tokyo learning the art of pottery-painting, he opened the Yabu Meizan workshop in Osaka, buying his undecorated blanks from a kiln in Satsuma operated by Chin Jukan, a potter who had revived Satsuma ware, then in decline as a result of the short-lived "Satsuma Rebellion" of 1877. During the economic depression of 1881–4 Yabu Meizan struggled to stay in business. Eventually, he gained recognition and won a bronze medal at the Fourteenth Kyoto Exhibition in 1885. Throughout his career he continued to make full use of the marketing opportunities offered by both domestic and international expositions. His family still own many of the medals that he won at events from 1885 until 1916, in cities as diverse as Kyoto, Paris, Chicago, Hanoi, St Louis, Portland, London, Osaka, and Semarang in Dutch Indonesia. Although he had a habit of storing his workshop's products for a long time before displaying them, thus making it hard to identify pieces that can be precisely dated, a study of his career throws some light on the development of Satsuma from the 1880s until the end of the Meiji Era. Like many other businesses, the Meizan workshop benefited from an economic upturn in the late 1880s; from 1888 he concentrated on exporting, particularly to the United States, and was inundated with direct orders. During this early period, Yabu Meizan wares were often decorated with Chinese or Buddhist subjects: *rakan* [disciples of the Buddha] with large gold halos (see catalogue number 105), or groups of *karako* [Chinese children] taking part in festivals and games or acting out adult roles (see catalogue number 145). The *karako* theme, also called the "hundred boys", had its origins in China's Ming Dynasty (1368–1644), and it might have been difficult for foreign buyers to understand why Chinese subjects were shown on Japanese wares. This may explain a change during the 1890s in favor of native subjects such as samurai combat (see catalogue number 98) or fishermen (see catalogue number 99), sometimes directly copied from popular Japanese prints, such as Hiroshige's series of views depicting the Tokaido Road from Edo to Kyoto (see catalogue number 152).

From the late 1890s until 1910, Yabu Meizan concentrated most of his energy on three of the great exhibitions: Paris (1900), St Louis (1904), and London (1910). For the Paris Exhibition he traveled to France as a member of the consultative committee as well as visiting the Hague and Berlin. Although he achieved high sales, second only to the porcelain workshop of Miyagawa (Makuzu) Kozan, he was not granted the official status of "artist" and still showed in the Chemical Industry section of the Domestic Industrial Exhibitions. Despite their slightly condescending attitude towards his work, the Japanese authorities clearly regarded him as a reliable and energetic administrator, and in August 1903 he was named secretary of the Louisiana Purchase Exposition Japan Exhibits Association, responsible for arranging the exhibits, decorating the hall, and organizing sales at the craft gallery on the exhibition site. Even though Japan was engaged in a desperate and costly war with Russia, the Japanese pavilions were the only ones to be completed by the official opening date of the Exposition. Thanks to his direct involvement in the project, Yabu Meizan was able to achieve his highest-ever exhibition sales, and for the first time his works were ranked by the Exhibition Bureau in Japan as works of art, allowing him to exhibit in the Art Palace at the Exposition. He also played a prominent, although less central, role in the 1910 Japan-British Exhibition, once again exhibiting a few of his best-quality works in the Art Palace as well as thirty-one pieces in the Chemical Industry section.

Nearly all of the work he showed during this, the most productive and successful period of his long career, was decorated in a minute style requiring extremely precise painting, which was achieved by using copper-plates for the designs; many of these remain, like the exhibition medals, in the possession of the Yabu family. They were not used for painting directly to vases or plates, but they allowed the same outline design to be traced on paper an unlimited number of times and transferred to many different pieces. First the engraved copper-plate was used to print the design on a sheet of paper, then the design was cut out from the printed paper and placed on the pottery, and the outline was impressed on the white background. Towards the end of the Meiji Era, when the output of the Yabu Meizan Workshop reached its peak, thanks to the use of this technique of semi-mass production, there was an even greater emphasis on intricate decoration including grounds made of literally thousands of flowers or butterflies (see catalogue number 97) or Japanese scenes, especially processions, sometimes with hundreds of figures (see catalogue number 102). A conservative in matters of design, Yabu Meizan was unmoved by the negative comment, both domestic and foreign, heaped on Japanese work before and during the 1900 Paris Exposition by opinion-formers such as Maeda Kosetsu who, in 1897, had given a speech criticizing the tendency to paint figures, landscapes, flowers, and birds inside a frame. Yabu Meizan continued for several years to apply his decoration within intricately painted borders in a way which virtually ignored the shape of the vessel. It was not until the very close of the Meiji Era that some, but not all, of his production showed a radical change, eliminating border decoration and concentrating instead on a single motif making dramatic use of the entire surface (see catalogue number 125). This experiment was not commercially successful. At the Japan-British Exhibition in 1910, a vase in his new style won a prize but sold for less than one-tenth of the price fetched by a bowl with an out-of-date, crowded design (see catalogue number 120 for a virtually identical example). Miraculous workmanship and exotic subject matter, rather than dramatic design, gave Satsuma ware its enduring popularity with overseas buyers. But by the time that Yabu Meizan returned to Japan from London in January 1911, his export business was already in decline. The outbreak of the first World War in 1914 and the economic crisis in 1919, coupled with a gradual but profound shift of taste in favor of Chinese rather than Japanese art, made it difficult to export his exotic earthenware to Europe and America. The Panama Pacific International Exposition, held in San Francisco in 1915, marked the end of his serious export business to Europe and America.

Figure 1.
Detail of catalogue number 108.

Although Yabu Meizan is by far the most famous of the manufacturers of Satsuma, there were several other workshops, some of them producing equally impressive examples of fine decoration. One workshop actually used Yabu Meizan's name and style to sell its output, inferior to the genuine article but by no means bad, to less discerning customers who could not afford or did not appreciate the subtle coloring and attention to detail seen in true Meizan work. The best known of the other high-quality Satsuma wares was Kinkozan, made by a workshop at Awata in Kyoto operated by Kobayashi Sobei (1867–1927). His father, of the same name, is supposed to have been the first potter in the old capital to imitate the newly fashionable Satsuma style, and it may have been this type of work that he showed at Philadelphia in 1876 and Paris in 1878, but the true Kyoto Satsuma was made by his son who, like Yabu Meizan, participated in all the major exhibitions until the end of the Meiji Era and may have visited London in 1910. Sobei employed a range of painters of whom we know nothing except their names which appear as seals on the base of Kinkozan vases alongside the name of the workshop (see catalogue number 114). Although the style tends towards the extremely fine detail demanded by European and American buyers, it is strikingly different from the work of the Osaka decorators and, especially in the later pieces, there is a much stronger sense of the relationship between the design and the vase to which it is applied. Another highly skilled and distinctive decorator working in a similar manner was Takebe Shoko (see catalogue number 126), an enigmatic character of whom we know very little except that he seems to have worked with Thomas Bates Blow, an English dealer living in Japan who also supplied the great Swiss collector Alfred Baur.

The vast quantities of cheap, sketchily painted plates and vases that flooded the curio shops of the Western world from the 1870s until well into the twentieth century have given Satsuma ware a bad name among today's connoisseurs of Japanese art. It is only when we view a selection of the very finest examples from the leading workshops of the Meiji Era that we can understand just how it was that the combination of absorbing subject matter with infinitely painstaking craftsmanship exercised such a fascination among those Europeans and Americans who could afford the best work.

NOTES
1. George Ashdown Audsley and James Lord Bowes, *Keramic Art of Japan*, 3 vols., (Liverpool and London, 1875), vol. 1. p.35.
2. Audsley and Bowes, *Keramic Art of Japan*, vol. 1. p.34.
3. Edward Sylvester Morse, "Old Satsuma", *Harper's New Monthly Magazine* (Sept. 1888), pp. 512–29.
4. Frank Brinkley, *Artistic Japan at Chicago: A Description of Japanese Works of Art Sent to the World's Fair* (Yokohama, 1893), p.27.

"SATSUMA" WARE

This section features a selection of "Satsuma", an extravagantly enameled and gilded ware that captured the imagination of European and American buyers at the very start of the Meiji Era. Most of the examples illustrated here were decorated in the workshop in Osaka operated by Yabu Meizan (1853–1934), but a few pieces from other centers are also included.

95
PLATE
About 1890
Earthenware, painted and gilded
Diameter 21.0 cm.
Signed *Yabu Meizan*
Made by the Yabu Meizan Workshop

96
VASE
About 1890
Earthenware, painted and gilded; wood stand
Height 37.0 cm.
Signed *Yabu Meizan*
Made by the Yabu Meizan Workshop

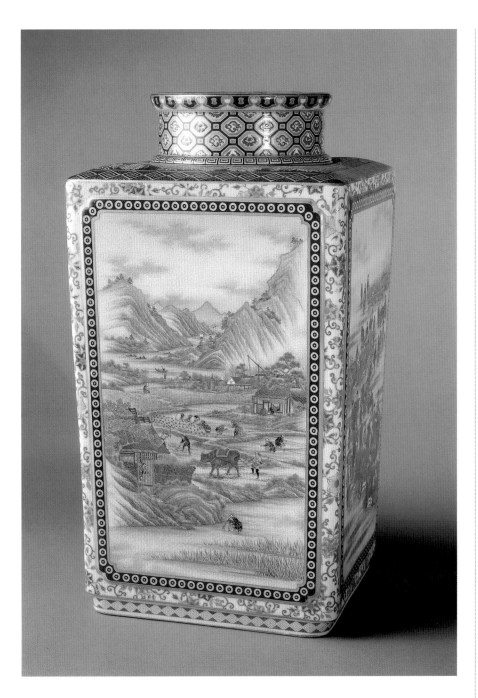

97
BOWL
About 1890–1905
Earthenware, painted and gilded
Diameter 12.5 cm.
Signed *Yabu Meizan*
Made by the Yabu Meizan Workshop

The interior of this bowl, with its dense
decoration of chrysanthemums and other
flowers, is a good example of the minute
painting style favored by Yabu Meizan in
his later period. To achieve the required
level of precision under conditions of
semi-mass production, copper plates
were used to transfer the outline design
onto the surface of the pottery.

98
VASE
About 1890–1905
Earthenware, painted and gilded
Height 17.9 cm.
Signed *Yabu Meizan*
Made by the Yabu Meizan Workshop

99
BOTTLE
About 1890–1905
Earthenware, painted and gilded
Height 20.7 cm.
Erased signature: *Yabu Meizan*
Made by the Yabu Meizan Workshop

100
PLATE
About 1890–1905
Earthenware, painted and gilded
Diameter 21.7 cm.
Signed *Yabu Meizan*
Made by the Yabu Meizan Workshop

101
BOWL
About 1890–1905
Earthenware, painted and gilded
Diameter 17.0 cm.
Signed *Yabu Meizan*
Made by the Yabu Meizan Workshop

102

PLATE

1894 or earlier
Earthenware, painted and gilded
Height 21.3 cm.
Signed *Yabu Meizan*
Made by the Yabu Meizan Workshop

This plate was purchased by H. J. Allcroft
from Yabu Meizan's workshop on October
27, 1894 for 55 yen.

103

PLATE

About 1890–1905
Earthenware, painted and gilded
Diameter 15.9 cm.
Signed *Yabu Meizan*
Made by the Yabu Meizan Workshop

104
JAR
About 1890–1905
Earthenware, painted and gilded
Height 19.6 cm.
Signed *Yabu Meizan*
Made by the Yabu Meizan Workshop

105
VASE
About 1900
Earthenware, painted and gilded
Height 86.0 cm.
Signed *Genroku gonen Toen ga, Ishuin
Kanzan saku* [painted in the fifth year of
Genroku (1692) by Toen, made by Ishuin
Kanzan]

Several large pieces of Satsuma are known
which bear spurious dates relating to the
Genroku (1688–1704) and other eras of
the Edo Period. The decoration on this
example depicts the *bodhisattva* Kannon,
venerated in Japan as a goddess of mercy
(see number 163), surrounded by *rakan*,
disciples of the Buddha, who were said to
be sixteen or five hundred in number.

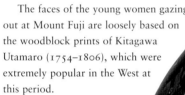

106
JAR
About 1900
Earthenware, painted and gilded
Height 29.2 cm.
Signed *Kyoto Ryozan dai Nihon no sho*
[designed by Ryozan of Kyoto in great
Japan] and with the trademark of the
Yasuda Company and the *mon* [crest] of
the Shimazu family

This is an example of a piece in Satsuma
style by one of several workshops in Kyoto
that specialized in this type of ware. The
crest of the Shimazu family, lords of the
Satsuma domain in the south of Japan, many
hundreds of miles from Kyoto, is added to
the signature to stress the supposed ancestry
of the ware, which many Western buyers
continued to believe was actually made
in Satsuma.

The faces of the young women gazing
out at Mount Fuji are loosely based on
the woodblock prints of Kitagawa
Utamaro (1754–1806), which were
extremely popular in the West at
this period.

107
VASE
About 1900
Earthenware, painted and gilded
Height 46.0 cm.
Signed *Dai Nihon Suizan zo* [made by
Suizan of great Japan]

Towards 1900, a number of decorators, of
whom Suizan was one, began to change the
style of Satsuma ware by reducing the size
and number of the decorative borders, and
increasing the area available for pictorial
composition.

108
BOWL
About 1900–1910
Earthenware, painted and gilded; wood stand
Diameter 15.3 cm.
Signed *Yabu Meizan*; the foot-rim impressed
Meizan
Made by the Yabu Meizan Workshop

109
TRUMPET VASE
About 1900–10
Earthenware, painted and gilded
Height 29.6 cm.
Sealed *Yabu Meizan*
Made by the Yabu Meizan Workshop

This is another excellent example of the very
detailed and delicate decoration achieved by
Yabu Meizan's workshop towards the end of
the Meiji Era. The interior is painted with a
minute design of tiny flowers.

110
BOWL
About 1900–10
Earthenware, painted and gilded
Diameter 18.0 cm.
Sealed *Yabu Meizan*
Made by the Yabu Meizan Workshop

111
BOWL
About 1910
Earthenware, painted and gilded
Height 14.8 cm.
Sealed *Yabu Meizan*
Made by the Yabu Meizan Workshop

At the end of the Meiji Era, Yabu Meizan's workshop began to make a number of vases and bowls that were decorated with a single motif, carefully placed so as to complement the overall shape of the piece, instead of treating the pottery merely as a vehicle for virtuoso miniaturist painting. This return to a more traditional approach to ceramic decoration was highly praised, but it was not commercially successful and the workshop continued to produce work in the conventional Meizan style.

112
JAR
About 1900–10
Earthenware, painted and gilded
Height 17.8 cm.
Sealed *Yabu Meizan*
Made by the Yabu Meizan Workshop

113
VASE
About 1910
Earthenware, painted and gilded
Height 18.0 cm.
Sealed *Yabu Meizan*
Made by the Yabu Meizan Workshop

The original copper-plate design for this
vase is in the possession of the Osaka City
Museum, donated by the Yabu family. Such
copper plates were used to print the design
on a sheet of paper, after which the design
was cut out from the printed paper and
placed on the pottery, and the outline
impressed on the white background.

114
VASE
About 1905–10
Earthenware, painted and gilded
Height 30.2 cm.
Signed *Kinkozan zo* [made by Kinkozan];
red seal *Chokusai*
Painted by Chokusai (dates unknown)
Made by the Kinkozan Workshop

Kinkozan Sobei VI (1868–1928) of Kyoto started to make earthenware in the Satsuma style in the 1870s and exhibited in Philadelphia in 1876, but it was the seventh bearer of the Kinkozan name who supervised the production of all the pieces signed *Kinkozan* in the Khalili Collection. Kinkozan Sobei VII seems first to have exhibited abroad at the International Exhibition of Barcelona in 1888; he also exhibited in Chicago at the World's Columbian Exposition of 1893 and showed three vases at the fourth Naikoku Kangyo Hakurankai [National Industrial Exposition] in 1895. He won a silver medal in Paris in 1889, gold and silver medals at the Paris Universal Exposition of 1900, a *meiyo ginpai* [honorable silver prize] at the fifth National Industrial Exposition of 1903, a Grand Prize at St. Louis in 1904, and a Grand Prize in Liège in 1905. Kinkozan employed a number of specialist decorators whose signatures or seals sometimes appear on the base alongside the workshop mark.

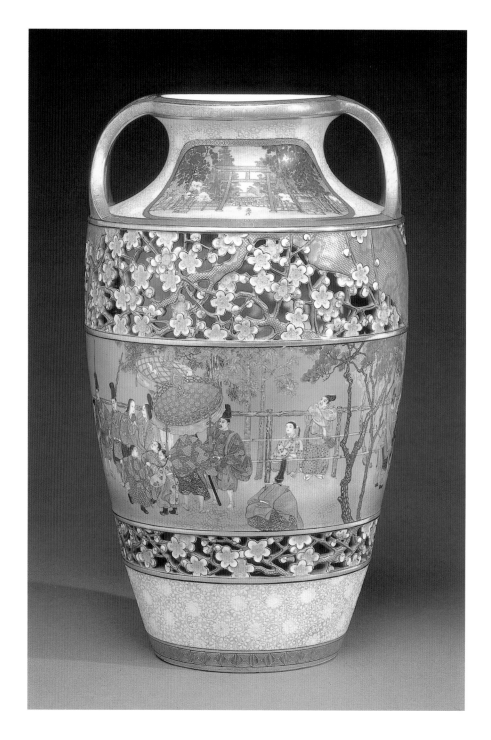

115
VASE
1908
Earthenware, painted and gilded
Height 55.0 cm.
Signed *Kyoto Kinkozan zo* [made by
Kinkozan of Kyoto]; the panels signed
Sozan; the based inscribed *James Robinson
Esq., with Mr. G. Kobayashi's Compliments*
Made by the Kinkozan Workshop

An accompanying letter from Mr Kobayashi,
dated 1908, advises Mr Robinson of the
dispatch of the vase, stating:

> having had the desire to send you
> something which you may keep merely
> as commemoration of the bond of our
> eternal friendship, I have had rather
> difficulty in selection because there in
> Japan is nothing superior to match
> with those excellent article produced in
> England, except only few of such as
> China-ware or silk-goods. But the lat-
> ter is not at all fit to the purpose, so I
> have chosen the former, besides Kyoto
> is most prominent district of its manu-
> facturing. The reminiciences [*sic*], of
> that when you paid a visit to this coun-
> try you were deeply impressed by the
> beauty of Nikko, still being lodged in
> my mind, I have ordered a flower vase
> to the best maker in the district to be
> painted, by the eminent artist, the
> scene of the Shogun's proccession [*sic*]
> marching out of the gate, Yomei-mon,
> the pride of our old architecture after
> celebrating the anniversary of his
> ancestors. Though it took nearly five
> months, considerablly [*sic*] long time
> to finish only one vase it has made
> splendidly and the maker himself was
> very proud of it. The vase has been sent
> to the shipper to forwarded to you by
> the Suez route, and I hope it would
> reach you in perfect condition.

116
BOWL
About 1910–15
Earthenware, painted and gilded
Height 17.8 cm.
Sealed *Yabu Meizan*
Made by the Yabu Meizan Workshop

117
BOX
About 1905–10
Earthenware, painted and gilded
5.7 × 12.5 × 9.2 cm.
Signed *Kinkozan zo* [made by Kinkozan],
red seal *Fuzan*
Made by the Kinkozan Workshop

In the late Meiji Era, craftsmen in several different media began to manufacture cigarette boxes in response to the growing fashion for cigarette smoking in Europe and America. Such boxes are often decorated with scenes from popular tourist spots that would have been familiar to foreign buyers (see also numbers 147–152). The lid of this box depicts the arch of the Itsukushima Shrine, near Hiroshima in the west of Honshu, Japan's main island.

118
VASE
About 1910
Earthenware, painted and gilded
Height 10.7 cm.
Sealed *Yabu Meizan*
Made by the Yabu Meizan Workshop

119
VASE
About 1910
Earthenware, painted and gilded
Height 11.7 cm.
Sealed *Yabu Meizan*
Made by the Yabu Meizan Workshop

The tradition of caricaturing human
activities by substituting insects, amphibia,
and other animals has a very long history
in Japan, the most famous example being
the *Choju giga* [humorous pictures of birds
and beasts], a set of thirteenth-century
picture scrolls.

120

BOWL
About 1910
Earthenware, painted and gilded
15.0 x 15.8 cm.
Sealed *Yabu Meizan*
Made by the Yabu Meizan Workshop

In a discreet effort at self-advertisement, one of the banners carried in the procession shown on this vase has been inscribed *Dai Meizan* [Great Meizan]. An almost identical bowl was exhibited at the Japan-British Exhibition, London, 1910.[1]

1. Office of the Imperial Japanese Government Commission to the Japan-British Exhibition, *An Illustrated Catalogue of Japanese Modern Fine Arts Displayed at the Japan-British Exhibition, London, 1910* (Tokyo, 1910), no. 146.

121
VASE
About 1910–15
Earthenware, painted and gilded
Height 21.7 cm.
Sealed *Yabu Meizan*
Made by the Yabu Meizan Workshop

122
VASE
About 1910
Earthenware, painted and gilded
Height 29.5 cm.
Sealed *Yabu Meizan*
Made by the Yabu Meizan Workshop

123
VASE
About 1910
Earthenware, painted and gilded
Height 21.7 cm.
Sealed *Yabu Meizan*
Made by the Yabu Meizan Workshop

This is an example of the manner of
decoration sometimes adopted by the Yabu
Meizan workshop and other producers of
Satsuma ware at the end of the Meiji Era,
whereby the number of panels is reduced,
enabling the decorator to achieve a more
pictorial effect.

124
VASE
About 1910
Earthenware, painted and gilded
Height 18.3 cm.
Signed *Yabu Meizan*
Made by the Yabu Meizan Workshop

125
VASE
About 1910
Earthenware, painted and gilded
Height 24.2 cm.
Sealed *Yabu Meizan*
Made by the Yabu Meizan Workshop

HISTORY, MYTH, RELIGION, AND TOPOGRAPHY

TALES OF OLD JAPAN

Throughout the Meiji Era, American and European connoisseurs were fascinated not only by the forms and techniques of Japanese art, but also by the stories told in the elaborate decoration of their treasured bronzes, lacquers, ceramics, and carvings. As one British writer put it, "the subjects, the method of working, all speak of old Japan, its history, its art, its civilisation, its religion and its domestic life."[1] The Japanese, for their part, realized the importance of presenting their country as a place where traditional beliefs and quaint old customs still held their own despite profound changes that were affecting every aspect of national life. This applied both to the scenes depicted on Japanese artifacts and to the conditions under which they were supposed to be made. As early as 1876, the official Japanese government guide to the Philadelphia Centennial Exhibition claimed that "the Japanese artisan is still very much like those of medieval Europe working in his own peculiar way, assisted only by a very few assistants, and being himself both artist and artisan".[2] Statements like this made Japanese art all the more popular as people in the West became increasingly concerned about the dehumanizing effects of industrialized mass production in their own countries.

Interest in Japan's rich stores of myths and legends was stimulated by the publication in 1871 of *Tales of Old Japan*, a collection written by Algernon Bertram Mitford (Lord Redesdale), a British diplomat. Mitford's book included historical accounts of the heroic deeds of the samurai as well as children's fairy stories and the first detailed Western description of *harakiri* or *seppuku* [ritual suicide].[3] Another source of images and information was provided by the *musha-e* [warrior prints] of woodblock print artists such as Utagawa Kuniyoshi (1797–1861) and his contemporaries, which were exported in enormous numbers. More fanciful responses to Japanese history and legend included the British comic operetta *The Mikado* (1885) by Gilbert and Sullivan, and the French novelist Pierre Loti's *Madame Chrysanthème* (1887). This formed the basis for Giacomo Puccini's opera *Madame Butterfly* (1904), set in Nagasaki. From 1890 onwards, the American image of Japan was strongly influenced by the extensive writings of Lafcadio Hearn, a half-Greek, half-Irish writer and adventurer who became so infatuated with the country that he took Japanese nationality, a Japanese wife, and a Japanese name, Koizumi Yakumo.[4] Even though Japan was, by 1910, a major industrial and military power which had won two international wars, a romantic and nostalgic vision of the country still permeated the Western popular imagination. Japanese artists continued to respond to that vision right up to the end of the Meiji Era and beyond.

SHINTO, BUDDHISM, AND CONFUCIANISM

According to ancient legend, the islands of Japan were created from the union of two gods, a brother and sister called Izanagi and Izanami. When Izanami later died giving birth to the God of Fire, her body became a rotting mass and Izanagi purified himself by bathing in a stream. New deities were born from his discarded clothing and from parts of his body. The most important of these were Susano-o (see catalogue number 172), the Impetuous Male God, and Amaterasu, the Sun Goddess (see catalogue number 174), who sent her grandson Ninigi to rule over Japan. Ninigi was the great-grandfather of Jinmu, Japan's first *Tenno* or emperor, who is supposed to have ruled from the year 660 B.C. It is thought that the early *Tenno* were the ruling family of the Yamato state, formed in the fifth and sixth centuries in the Yamato region of Japan, near present-day Kyoto and Osaka. Susano-o, Amaterasu, and the other *kami* or deities worshipped by the early Japanese belong to the native religion that later came to be called Shinto, literally "the way of the gods". Most other *kami*, however, are immaterial spirits residing in natural objects such as trees and stones or offering protection to particular families or occupations.

At the end of the sixth century the very different Buddhist religion, of Indian origin, was introduced to Japan from Korea. Founded by Gautama Buddha (6th–5th century B.C.), Buddhism teaches that the world is an illusion, and that worldly desires are the cause of suffering. While many philosophical forms of the Buddhist faith stress the need to rid oneself of such desires, the most popular Japanese sects offered both practical benefits and spiritual consolations, including freedom from sickness and want, as well as release from the cycle of birth and rebirth. Such favors are often bestowed by *bodhisattvas*, saintly beings who renounce their own enlightenment, remaining on earth to relieve the sufferings of mankind. Buddhism has played a key role, somewhat similar to that of Christianity in Europe, in the development of Japanese literature, philosophy, and art (see catalogue numbers 164–71).

Throughout most of Japanese history, Shinto and Buddhism enjoyed a peaceful coexistence. This is due in part to doctrinal changes made in the eighth and ninth centuries, which are reflected in a story concerning the Emperor Shomu. In 743 he decided to mark the country's conversion to Buddhism by casting a huge bronze image of Dainichi Buddha, the Great Sun Buddha (see page 17). But before work could begin, he had to ask permission of the Sun Goddess. After seven days and nights of prayer she gave her welcome to the project, and her wishes were later confirmed when the emperor had a dream in which the Sun and Buddha were declared to be one and the same. In a similar way, other *kami* were reclassified as manifestations of Buddhas and *bodhisattvas*.

Although the Chinese system of moral and political philosophy that we call Confucianism had been known in Japan since the fifth century, it was not until the seventeenth century that it was widely disseminated among the Japanese elite. First expounded by Kong Fuzi (a name that was later Latinized to Confucius by Jesuit missionaries) in the fifth century B.C., Confucianism emphasizes the importance of harmonious social relationships and loyalty to righteous rulers as well as to fathers, husbands, and elder brothers. As such, it was a valuable ideological tool and was used both by the shoguns and, after a brief interval, by the Meiji government to underpin their authority. During the Edo Period, Confucianism became the dominant political ideology of the ruling class (although it was often no more than an elegant veneer disguising the essentially military nature of the Tokugawa regime), and Chinese studies were pursued at the expense of knowledge of early Japanese history and traditions. From the middle of the Edo Period, however, nativist thinkers such as Motoori Norinaga started to remind their countrymen of the distinctiveness of Japanese culture. This resulted in renewed emphasis on the divinity of the emperor through his direct descent from Amaterasu. Independent-minded members of the samurai class grew increasingly concerned about their government's failure to take action against the threat of Western invasion, and their opposition found expression in emperor-centered nationalism.

After the emperor's status was restored in 1867–8, the Meiji leaders took steps to reduce the importance of Buddhism and increase that of Shinto. The two faiths were formally separated in 1868, and in 1870 Shinto was declared the official national religion, while Buddhism lost much of its financial support. State Shinto gave Amaterasu and her family a prominence they had never enjoyed before, but Buddhist subjects and popular groupings like the Seven Gods of Good Fortune are depicted in Meiji decorative art much more frequently than State Shinto subjects. This reflects the fact that so many Meiji-Era artifacts were made by artists and craftsmen who had received their training, including their vocabulary of motifs, during the late Edo Period before the promulgation of the artificial, government-inspired cult. During the Meiji Era, Shinto subjects were mostly reserved for officially sponsored works designed to promote awareness of Japan's national myths. It is interesting, however, that a handful of very ambitious pieces in the Khalili Collection depict episodes from such legends even though they seem to be in styles that we associate with work made for export; it is unlikely that foreign buyers would have understood their significance. The fact that two of these works (see catalogue numbers 173 and 174) give equal prominence to leading Shinto deities and figures from Chinese mythology suggests that they were probably made before the Sino-Japanese War of 1894–5, which, at both an official and a popular level, fundamentally altered the traditional reverence for Chinese culture.[5]

During the 1870s, as the new Meiji government established its authority over the whole of Japan, foreigners started to move around the interior of the country in comparative safety. For many centuries the Japanese themselves had been enthusiastic long-distance travelers, not just for business but also for sightseeing and pilgrimages to Buddhist temples and Shinto shrines. As a result, the first intrepid Western explorers were able to take

PEOPLE, PLACES, AND CUSTOMS

advantage of a network of roads and simple wayside inns that led them, often in great discomfort, to such established beauty-spots as the great mausoleum at Nikko in the mountains north of Tokyo (see catalogue number 150), the bridge at Uji (see catalogue number 151), the architectural splendors of Kyoto (the former capital and the cultural center of the country), and of course the volcanic cone of Mount Fuji (see catalogue number 147), the "peerless mountain".

CHINESE SUBJECTS

Depictions of Chinese subjects in Meiji decorative art mostly follow a pattern established in the Edo Period. Particularly in lacquer and metalwork, many of the favored motifs are drawn from a vast vocabulary of subject matter based on Chinese Ming Dynasty (1368–1644) artifacts and printed books, including the "hundred boys", *sennin* [semi-divine "immortals"], or the Seven Sages of the Bamboo Grove (see catalogue numbers 140–4). Although Confucianism was neglected in the early years of the Meiji Era, it was soon revived for political reasons since its emphasis on loyalty and obedience, as well as the need for kings and emperors to rule virtuously, was suited as much to the imperial as the shogunal system (see catalogue numbers 325–6). Chinese mythical creatures – above all, the dragon, a symbol of imperial power – were also a favorite subject, particularly on porcelain, but here the motivation was often commercial rather than political. By imbuing his vases with a Chinese feeling, the porcelain decorator Makuzu Kozan, for example, was able to appeal to the existing Western taste for Chinese porcelain, which had already been exported to Europe and America in enormous quantities for over two centuries (see catalogue numbers 132 and 136).

THE SAMURAI

Literally meaning "one who serves", the word *samurai* describes a class of warriors, each owing unswerving allegiance to his feudal lord, who first came to prominence in the civil wars of the twelfth century. Throughout the period during which the country was run by shoguns – generals – ruling in the name of the emperor, the samurai played a prominent part in Japanese life. During the largely peaceful Edo Period (1615–1868) their role was sometimes bureaucratic rather than military, but as late as the 1850s and 1860s, a number of foreign traders and diplomats were attacked and killed by dissident, anti-reform samurai who objected to their presence in Japan. Despite this brutal reality, European and American writers quickly came under the influence of late Edo-Period Japanese views of the traditional warrior class. The popular literature, drama, and art of that time had often depicted the samurai as heroic figures whose conduct was guided by an idealistic moral code, an image which coincided with renewed Western interest in medieval European chivalry. Especially after their traditional annual salaries were abolished in 1876 and they were forbidden to wear their two deadly sharp swords, the samurai, with their elaborate armor and picturesque customs, became a favorite subject for the decoration of items intended for export to Europe and America (see catalogue numbers 153–160). Many of these scenes were apparently chosen more or less at random but in a few instances the subject matter was influenced by prevailing government ideology. In such cases the stories shown usually date from the early fourteenth century, when loyalist heroes like Kusunoki Masashige (1294–1336) and Nitta Yoshisada (1301–38) struggled unsuccessfully to depose the Hojo, a family of military rulers, and restore imperial rule (see catalogue numbers 94 and 156). The obvious parallels with recent Japanese history ensured that tales like this were actively promoted by the new government.

A lacquer cabinet in the Khalili Collection, originally purchased in Yokohama in 1909, is decorated with fourteen scenes from Japanese history, each identified by a short inscription. These offer such a comprehensive overview of some of the most popular military tales that they are presented in detail here. Reading from left to right and top to bottom, the scenes are as follows:

> TOP ROW, LEFT
> In the course of his fight with Yokogawa Kakuhan, Sato Tadanobu (1161–86) climbs up the pagoda of a temple in the Yoshino district. Sato Tadanobu was one of the leading retainers of Minamoto no Yoshitsune, the great twelfth-century warrior who played a leading part in the overthrow of the Taira clan. Following the decisive battles of Ichinotani (1184) and Dannoura (1185), Yoshitsune's half-brother Minamoto no Yoritomo turned against him and pursued him into the Yoshino district. To help his master

escape, Sato donned Yoshitsune's distinctive armor and fought a desperate rearguard action against a band of warrior monks who had sided with Yoritomo. After a fight in which all Sato Tadanobu's men were slain, he entered the monks' temple, revealed himself as Tadanobu (and not Yoshitsune), set fire to the buildings, pretended to commit *seppuku* [ritual suicide], climbed to the top of the pagoda, leapt through the air to a nearby hill, and made his getaway. In the best-known version of the tale, Sato kills the leader of the monks, Yokogawa Kakuhan, before he enters their temple, but according to the inscription on this cabinet he is still in pursuit of Yokogawa as he climbs the pagoda.[6] Tadanobu died soon afterwards and his master Yoshitsune was pursued to the north of Japan where he was eventually overcome in battle, killing his wife and children before committing suicide at the age of thirty-one (1189). Yoshitsune's heroic failure has made him one of the most admired figures in the whole of Japanese history and a host of legends has gathered around his name – according to one of these he escaped to Mongolia and became the famous Genghis Khan.

TOP ROW, MIDDLE
Minamoto no Yoritomo (1147–99) meets Minamoto no Yoshitsune (1159–89) at the Kisegawa River. In 1180 Yoshitsune, learning of his half-brother's revolt against Kiyomori, leader of the Taira clan, hurried to join him with 2,000 horsemen.[7] Here we see the two warriors in court dress, each with attendants. This peaceful scene belies the bloody struggle with the Taira that would follow for the next five years and culminate in Yoritomo hunting down his former comrade-in-arms.

TOP ROW, RIGHT
Minamoto no Yorimasa (1104–99) makes his report after slaying the *nue*. In 1153 the young emperor was taken ill, troubled by the scratching and howling of a monster which visited the palace at night. Yorimasa shot the creature with an arrow and his servant Ino Hayata finished it off with his sword. The *nue*, as it was called, turned out to have the head of a tiger, the body of a monkey, and the tail of snake.

SECOND ROW, LEFT

Tokugawa Ieyasu (1542–1616), Oda Nobunaga (1534–82), and Toyotomi Hideyoshi (1536–98) compose the *Song of the Cuckoo* at the Kitano Tenmangu Shrine in Kyoto. In this imaginary scene, the three late sixteenth-century unifiers of Japan (see page 18) gather to compose poetry; one of them holds a brush in his hand. The Kitano Tenmangu was an appropriate location for this activity since it was sacred to the memory of Sugawara no Michizane, god of literature (see below). The *Song of the Cuckoo* is referred to in one of the closing lines of the sentimental patriotic song mentioned under catalogue number 156. The song, composed in the late nineteenth century, celebrates the parting of Kusunoki Masashige from his son Masatsura

(see also below), so that even this scene, supposedly set in the late sixteenth century, refers to the heroic failures and imperial loyalists of the fourteenth century.[8]

SECOND ROW, MIDDLE

Minamoto no Tsunemasa plays the *biwa*, a lute-like instrument of Chinese origin, while praying at the shrine to the goddess Benzaiten on Chikubushima Island in Lake Biwa, Omi Province (for Benzaiten, also called Benten, see catalogue numbers 148 and 173). The inscription on this panel reads in columns from left to right, instead of the usual arrangement in columns from right to left. This reflects the fact that the cabinet was intended for export so that its maker could take liberties which would not have been acceptable to a Japanese buyer.

SECOND ROW, RIGHT

The young Sugawara no Michizane (845–903) composing a poem on a moonlit night. A leading courtier of Emperor Uda, Sugawara no Michizane was an imperial loyalist who attempted to diminish the power of the Fujiwara family (see page 17). Eventually he was falsely accused of trying to dethrone the emperor and sent into exile. After his death, he became the first Japanese subject to be officially recognized as a deity, under the name Kitano Tenjin. Sugawara no Michizane is famed for his scholarship and his skill as a calligrapher and poet.

Like Nitta Yoshisada and Kusunoki Masashige (see below), he is also renowned as one of the great failed heroes of Japan.[9]

THIRD ROW, LEFT
Honda Tadakatsu (1548–1610) at the Battle of Nagashino. Honda, one of the leading generals of Tokugawa Ieyasu (see above and page 18), is always depicted wearing a helmet decorated with stag antlers.

THIRD ROW, MIDDLE
The female warrior Tomoe Gozen setting off for battle. This so-called "Japanese Amazon", also shown in catalogue number 157, was active in the late twelfth-century civil wars. Here she is seen going off to fight, armed with a *naginata* [spear]. The seated figure may be her husband Kiso Yoshinaka.

THIRD ROW, RIGHT
Kusunoki Masashige (1294–1336) reading a scroll predicting the future history of Japan. The career of this great imperial loyalist is discussed under catalogue number 156. In this episode, he visits the Tennoji Temple and consults a scroll supposedly written by Shotoku Taishi, which predicts that in the reign of the ninety-fifth emperor "Violence shall rise up in the land; distress shall afflict the sovereign ..." but "370 days after the sun has sunk ... thereafter for three years the state will be one".[10] This was taken to refer to the exile of the Emperor Go-Daigo, who three years after being banished to Chiburi Island succeeded in returning to the mainland and briefly resuming the throne. Eventually, however, both Kusunoki Masashige and Nitta Yoshisada (see below) were defeated by Ashikaga Takauji and the emperor was forced to abandon the capital forever.

FOURTH ROW, LEFT

Nitta Yoshisada (1301–38) fighting at the battle of Yahagi River. Nitta Yoshisada (see above and catalogue number 94) was originally a retainer of the Kamakura shogunate but later switched sides and supported the Emperor Go-Daigo in his struggle with Ashikaga Takauji (see page 18). He defeated Takauji at the battle of the Yahagi River (1335), but was killed in battle three years later.

FOURTH ROW, MIDDLE

Taira no Kagekiyo performing a sword-dance before the battle of Dannoura (1185). This is another example of doomed defiance: at the battle (see above) the Taira were crushed by the Minamoto, and Kagekiyo was taken prisoner. He was led off to the Minamoto headquarters at Kamakura but starved himself to death. Legend has it that he plucked out his own eyes so as not to see his enemies' triumph.

FOURTH ROW, RIGHT

Minamoto no Tametomo (1139–70) about to sink a ship with a single arrow. It is said that the mighty archer Tametomo was seven feet tall and his left arm grew much longer than his right so that he could fire arrows further. He was banished to the island of Oshima by Taira no Kiyomori, and his tendons were cut so he could no longer use his bow, but in time they grew back miraculously, enabling him to establish control over Oshima and the neighboring islands. In 1170 a fleet of ships was sent to arrest him. He sank the first ship with a single arrow before committing *seppuku*, knowing that he would be overwhelmed by superior forces.

BOTTOM ROW, LEFT

Kusunoki Masatsura (1326–48) rescuing the court lady Ben no Naiji. The story of Masatsura's parting from his father Masashige is told under catalogue number 156. In a later incident, Ben no Naiji was tricked by a counterfeit letter (purporting to be from her mother) into returning to Kyoto after she had fled the city with the Emperor Go-Murakami. Masatsura heard her crying inside her *kago* (palanquin) and rescued her. The emperor offered Masatsura her hand in marriage but he refused, knowing that he was destined for a short life. Two years later he was killed in battle; once again the villainous Ashikaga Takauji was responsible.

BOTTOM ROW, RIGHT

Tamamo no Mae dancing in the mountains of Yoshino. A twelfth-century emperor fell dangerously and mysteriously ill. The court astrologer was consulted and reported that the cause was someone in the emperor's immediate entourage. Shortly afterwards it was noticed that a court dancer, Tamamo no Mae, had a halo around her head when it was dark. To settle the matter an exorcism ceremony was arranged: Tamamo no Mae was reluctant to attend but was forced to dance and when he did so she started to turn into a magic fox with nine tails. She fled to Nasu Moor and became the spirit of a stone.

NOTES

1. Ernest Hart, *Lectures in Japanese Art Work* (London, 1887), p.7.
2. Quoted in William, *The Japan Idea: Art and Life in Victorian America* (Hartford, Conn., 1990), p.39.
3. A.B. Mitford (Lord Redesdale), *Tales of Old Japan* (London, 1871; reprinted Rutland, Vt., and Tokyo, 1966).
4. For a collection of Hearn's essays, see Lafcadio Hearn, *Writings from Japan*, edited by Francis King (New York, 1984).
5. The changing attitude to China is examined in Donald Keene, "The Sino-Japanese War of 1894–95 and its Cultural Effects on Japan", in *Meiji Japan: Political, Economic and Social History 1868–1912*, edited by Peter Kornicki (London and New York, 1998), vol. 3, pp. 247–83.
6. Helen Craig McCullough, *Yoshitsune: A Fifteenth-Century Japanese Chronicle* (Stanford, 1966), pp. 175–189.
7. McCullough, *Yoshitsune ...* , p.14.
8. Ivan Morris, *The Nobility of Failure* (London, 1975), pp. 131–2 and 385.
9. Morris, *The Nobility of Failure*, pp. 41–66.
10. Quoted in Helen Craig McCullough, *Taiheiki: A Chronicle of Medieval Japan* (New York, 1959), pp. 161, 142–2.

HISTORY, MYTH, RELIGION, AND TOPOGRAPHY

The pieces catalogued in this section have been selected for their subject matter. Throughout the Meiji Era, American and European connoisseurs were fascinated, not only by the forms and techniques of Japanese art, but also by the stories told in the elaborate decoration of their treasured bronzes, lacquers, ceramics, and carvings. The Japanese, for their part, realized the importance of presenting their country as a place where quaint old beliefs and customs still held their own, despite profound changes that were affecting every aspect of national life. The traditional Japanese love of nature and travel is reflected in pieces depicting some of the tourist destinations favored by late nineteenth-century Western travelers.

126

PLATE

About 1900–10
Earthenware, painted and gilded
Diameter 21.4 cm.
Signed *Shoko Takebe*; inscribed in *katakana*
(one of the Japanese phonetic scripts) with
the name of Thomas B. Blow
Painted by Shoko Takebe (dates unknown)
for Thomas B. Blow

This plate is decorated in Shoko Takebe's characteristic style with Futen, the god of wind, releasing a storm against a procession of children pulling a *takarabune* [treasure ship] on wheels containing the Seven Gods of Good Fortune. The use of large groups of children in ceramic decoration is first seen in China in the late Ming Dynasty (1368–1644). Here they are combined with a group of deities who had become extremely popular in Japan during the Edo Period. The Seven Gods of Good Fortune are, from left to right: Hotei, a god of prosperity and well-being, who is almost being crushed by his treasure sack; Ebisu with his long fishing rod; Fukuro-kuju [literally, "good fortune, high rank and longevity"] with his enormously tall forehead; Benten, a goddess of Indian origin and the only female member of the group; Jurojin, with a long beard and staff; Daikoku, another god of wealth who wears a distinctive headcloth; and the ferocious-looking Bishamon (standing outside the boat) who is a god of war as well as of good fortune. Thomas B. Blow, an English dealer, lived in Japan from at least 1906 until 1914, supplying many leading European collectors with Japanese ceramics, metalwork, and other applied arts.

127
VASE
About 1890
Shibuichi; with *shakudo*, gold, copper,
and silver
Height 33.9 cm.
Signed *Katsuo koku* [carved by Katsuo];
sealed *Katsuo*

Each of the Seven Gods of Good Fortune
(see number 126) is depicted with the
respective attribute. Jurojin holds a *nyoi*
scepter, a deer at his side; Benten holds an
ewer; Ebisu holds a dish, his carp on the
low table; Fukurokuju holds a scroll;
Daikoku leans on his mallet; Hotei sits
beside his large sack; and Bishamon holds
a small shrine.

128

INCENSE BURNER

Dated 1896 and 1897
Shibuichi; with gold, *shakudo*, and silver
Height 16.3 cm.
Signed on the Jurojin panel *Seiryoku sanroku nite Essai kinkoku* [carefully carved by Essai at the foot of Mount Seiryoku] and sealed *Masayoshi no in* [seal of Masayoshi]; signed on the Benten panel *Hinoto-tori shoshun Masayoshi teppitsu* [the iron brush of Masayoshi in early spring of the *hinoto-tori* year (1897)] and sealed *Nihonbi* [Japanese art]; the Hotei panel signed *Hinoe-saru chushu Tesshi sen* [engraved by Tesshi in mid-autumn of the *hinoe-saru* year (1896)] and sealed *Essai*
Sealed *Ozeki sei* [made by Ozeki]
By Oyano Masayoshi (*b.* 1865)
Produced by the Ozeki Company

This incense burner depicts three of the Seven Gods of Good Fortune (see number 126): Jurojin asleep, resting on a deer; Benten beneath a dragon emerging from the clouds; and Hotei and a *karako* [Chinese boy] looking up at the tail of the dragon.

129
VASE
About 1900–10
Earthenware, painted and gilded
Height 23.5 cm.
Indistinctly signed
In the style of Shoko Takebe

For Shoko Takabe, see number 126. This
vase shows Raijin, the thunder god, encir-
cled by drums, above figures fleeing from a
storm of thunder and lightning. Raijin was
originally a snake-shaped Shinto deity, but
was also sometimes imagined as a small
boy, accompanied by a Shinto priestess. It
was not until the Edo Period that he took
the form of an *oni* [demon] with drums,
under the influence of Buddhist iconography.

130
ORNAMENT
About 1880
Copper; with gold, *shakudo*, bronze,
shibuichi, *sentoku*, wood, and horn
10.0 × 17.4 cm.
Signed *Ryounsai*
By Unno Moritoshi (1834–96)

This group shows Raijin and Futen, the
gods of thunder and wind (see numbers
126 and 129) with a *nio*. Nio are guardian
deities who usually, except in non-traditional
artifacts such as this, stand guard outside
Buddhist temples in pairs, one with his
mouth open and one with his mouth
closed. The modeling of this *nio* is based on
the style established for such figures by the
sculptors Unkei and Kaikei in the twelfth
and thirteenth centuries.

131

INCENSE BURNER

About 1895

Iron, cast and engraved, with gold and *shakudo*

Height 24.5 cm.

Signed *Inshi Motonobu koku* [carved by Inshi Motonobu] and sealed *Motonobu*; sealed *Ozeki sei* [made by Ozeki]

By Yamada Motonobu (1847–97)

Produced by the Ozeki Company

The sides are chased and engraved with eleven of the twelve animals of the East Asian zodiac, who are still used in both China and Japan to count the years, and were traditionally used to count the hours and days as well. The twelfth animal, the monkey, forms the handle on the cover.

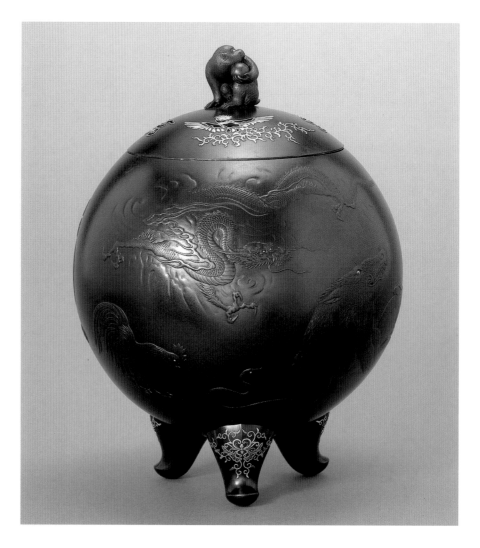

132

INCENSE BURNER

1890s

Porcelain; painted in underglaze green, red, and blue

Height 21.2 cm.

Signed *Makuzu-gama Kozan sei* [made by Kozan at the Makuzu kiln]

Made by the Miyagawa Kozan Workshop

Ever since the development of decorated porcelain in fourteenth-century China, the dragon – zodiac animal, bringer of rain and symbol of imperial power – has been an immensely popular motif for ceramic decoration in the countries of East Asia. Dragons appear frequently in the work of Miyagawa Kozan, many of whose porcelains were inspired by Chinese originals.

133
PAIR OF VASES
1875–1900
Hardwood lacquered in *hiramaki-e*,
with shell
20.1 × 9.9 cm.
Signed *Dai Nihon Tokyo ni oite
Choshisai kore o tsukuru* [this was made
by Choshisai in Tokyo, great Japan]

134
INCENSE BURNER
About 1900–05
Cloisonné enamels worked in gold wire
Height 14.3 cm.
Signed *Kyoto Namikawa* [Namikawa
of Kyoto]
Made by the Namikawa Yasuyuki Workshop

135
ORNAMENT
About 1900
Silver, with gilding, *shakudo*, and copper;
crystal ball
Height 11.7 cm.
Signed *Kuninori*
Possibly by Murasawa Kuninori

The only recorded artist with this name
active in the Meiji Era appears to be the
third Murasawa Kuninori, a member of
a family specializing in inlay who lived in
the important metalworking center of
Kanazawa in the Ishikawa Prefecture.[1]

1. Wakayama Homatsu (Takeshi) (ed.), *Kinko
jiten* [A Dictionary of Metalworkers] (Tokyo,
1972), p.110.

136
VASE
About 1900–10
Porcelain, painted in underglaze blue
and yellow
Height 54.0 cm.
Signed *Makuzu-gama Kozan sei*
[made by Kozan at the Makuzu kiln]
Made by the Miyagawa Kozan Workshop

The *shishi*, a lion-like creature of Chinese
origin, and the peony have been depicted
together in Japanese art since the medieval
period, the *shishi* being seen as the king of
the beasts and the peony as the king of
flowers. On a late Meiji-Era vase such
as this, they should probably be viewed simply as design motifs without any special
significance, but in earlier times they could
symbolize strength and as such were often
used in the decoration of armor.

137
CHARGER
About 1885–90
Iron; with *shibuichi*, *shakudo*, gold,
and silver
Diameter 48.6 cm.
Signed *Nihonkoku Kyoto no ju Komai sei*
[made by Komai of Kyoto in Japan]
Produced by the Komai Company

This charger shows Shoki, the demon-
queller, standing on the back of a dragon,
sword unsheathed. According to Chinese
legend, Shoki was first depicted in the Tang
Dynasty, when the celebrated artist Wu
Daozi (active 720–60) presented a painting
of the demon-queller to the Emperor
Minghuang (Xuanzong). The image of
Shoki reached Japan as early as the

Kamakura Period (1185–1392), when a
pictorial scroll shows him as a hell-judge,
clutching a demon about the neck and
blinding it. By the Edo Period, Shoki had
become associated with the Boys' Festival
held on the fifth day of the fifth month. He
remains a popular figure to this day, especially in the Tokyo area.

138

FIGURE OF CHOHI
About 1880
Hardwood and ivory lacquered in
hiramaki-e and *takamaki-e*, with shell
Height 50.2 cm.
Signed *Hokkyo Hara Shugetsu saku* [made
by Hokkyo Hara Shugetsu]
By Hara Shugetsu (1828–*c*.1880)

139

FIGURE OF KAN'U
About 1880
Hardwood and ivory lacquered in
hiramaki-e and *takamaki-e*, with shell
and bone
Height 36.2 cm.
Signed *Hokkyo Hara Shugetsu saku* [made
by Hokkyo Hara Shugetsu]
By Hara Shugetsu (1828–*c*.1880)

These figures probably represent Chohi (the
standing figure, in Chinese Zhang Fei,
166–221) and Kan'u (the seated figure
with a sword, in Chinese Guan Yu, *d*. 219),
two semi-legendary heroes of China's
Three Kingdoms Period who devoted their
lives to supporting Liu Bei, one of several
contenders for the Chinese throne. Their
exploits have been celebrated in drama
and literature for over a thousand years,
and Kan'u eventually became canonized in
popular Chinese religion as Guan Di, the
god of war. Appropriately for legendary
Chinese heroes, the garments are embellished
with fabulous Chinese beasts: the *kirin* (see
number 42) and *ho-o* birds.

140

VASE

About 1880

Bamboo; encrusted with gold, silver, copper, *shakudo*, brass, and *shibuichi*

Height 54.0 cm.

Signed *Kocho Seki Eisuke, jinbutsu chokoku Serizawa Ryumin, Watanabe Nobuyoshi, shoju Yamaguchi Sadanori, hoshoku Ikeda Yoshitaka, chogan Shibayama Nagahisa* [Supervised by Seki Eisuke, figures carved by Serizawa Ryumin and Watanabe Nobuyoshi, pine tree carved by Yamaguchi Sadanori, decoration by Ikeda Yoshitaka, inlay by Shibayama Nagahisa]

This impressive collaborative work depicts three of the most popular *sennin*: Chokaro with his gourd, Gama with his toad and Tekkai blowing out his spirit (see numbers 142-2).

141

PAIR OF TWO-FOLD SCREENS
About 1890
Hardwood, lacquered in *hiramaki-e* and
takamaki-e, with ivory; gilt metal fittings
Height 171 cm.
Signed *Shigeno Hoen*, *Yasuhara Kiyoshi*,
and *Morikawa Kazuaki*; sealed *Ho*,
Kiyoshi, and *Kazuaki*

All four of the figures depicted on this pair
of screens are *sennin*, semi-legendary figures
of Chinese origin who became popular in
the Edo Period, largely thanks to imported

Chinese illustrated books. Gama Sennin
[the toad immortal], seen on the right-hand
screen, caught a three-legged, white-skinned
toad. He tied it up with a cord and it became
his constant companion and assistant in
various magical arts. He is often seen in the
company of Ri Tekkai, whose name means
"Li with the iron crutch", Li being a common Chinese surname. Tekkai used to leave
his body and take his soul on heavenly journeys, on one occasion entrusting his physical self to the care of a servant. Called away

to his mother's sickbed, the servant burned
Tekkai's body, thinking that his master's
soul had been away for so long that it
would never return. When Tekkai eventually came back to earth, he had to take up
residence in the body of a recently deceased
crippled beggar and is therefore always
shown holding a staff. The *mon* [crests] of
the Tokugawa and Maeda, two of the most
powerful families of Edo-Period Japan, at
the base of the screens have been added
purely for decorative effect.

142

SET OF MOUNTINGS FOR A SHORT SWORD

About 1885–1900

Wood, lacquered in *kinji*, with encrustation of shell, ivory, and other materials; metal fittings in various alloys

Length 45.5 cm.

This ornamental mounting for a *tanto* [dagger], most likely made some time after the 1876 edict rescinding the right of the samurai to bear arms in public, is decorated with two *sennin*: Tekkai (shown blowing out his spirit, see number 141) and Chokaro. Chokaro, like Tekkai, became popular in the Edo Period thanks to imported Chinese picture books. His presence is implied here by the horse on the hilt, reclining by a double gourd, and he is also shown on the *fuchi*, or collar, at the point where the hilt meets the scabbard. Chokaro is first mentioned in an early eighth-century Chinese historical work, when he was already several hundred years old. He used to ride a white mule which covered thousands of miles in a single day, but could be folded up and stored in his gourd when it was not needed.

143

VASE

About 1875–1900
Wood, lacquered in *kinji*, *hiramaki-e*,
takamaki-e, and other techniques, with
encrustation of shell, ivory and other
materials; details in silver and cloisonné
enamels
Height 36.3 cm.
Signed *Sadatoshi saku* [made by Sadatoshi]

The sides of this vase portray the Chinese
sage Shoshi ("the master of the pan-pipes")
mounted on a dragon and playing a mouth-
organ, with his wife on a *ho-o* bird playing
a different type of mouth-organ. According
to mythology, Shoshi taught his wife to play
his favorite instrument, the *sho* (in Chinese,
sheng). One day, while she was playing a
melody about a *ho-o* bird, the bird descended from the sky and came to rest near her.
Shortly afterwards, both husband and wife
entered the Land of the Immortals, he on a
dragon and she on a *ho-o* bird. The figure
on the lid is Jurojin, one of the Seven Gods
of Good Fortune, holding a *sake* cup
engraved with the character *kotobuki*
[longevity] and accompanied by a crane.

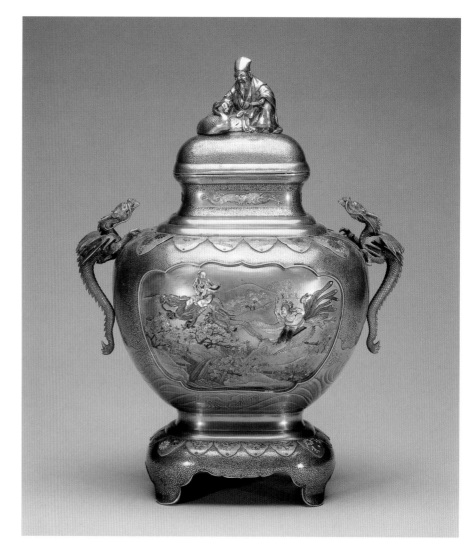

144

PAIR OF TUSKS

1890–1900
Ivory, with encrustation of shell, ivory,
and other materials; metal fittings in
various alloys
Height 51.3 cm.
Each signed *Musashiya* and sealed *Ozeki*
Produced by the Ozeki Company

For this subject, see above.

152
VASE
About 1900
Earthenware, painted and gilded
Height 36.5 cm.
Sealed *Kyoto Tojiki Goshi Gaisha* [Kyoto
Ceramic Joint Stock Company]; signed
Ryozan kore o tsukuru [Ryozan made this],
and with the trademark of the Yasuda
Company and the *mon* [heraldic crest] of
the Shimazu family

This vase is decorated with reproductions
of the *Tokaido Gojusan Tsugi* [Fifty-Three
Stopping-Places on the Tokaido Road],
a series of woodblock prints designed
by Ando Hiroshige (1797–1858) and
published during the late 1830s. Depicting
views along the old road from Edo (Tokyo)
to Kyoto, the prints became very popular in
Europe and America during the early Meiji
Era not only for their artistic quality, but
also for the window they offered into the
interior of a country that was still largely
inaccessible to foreign visitors.

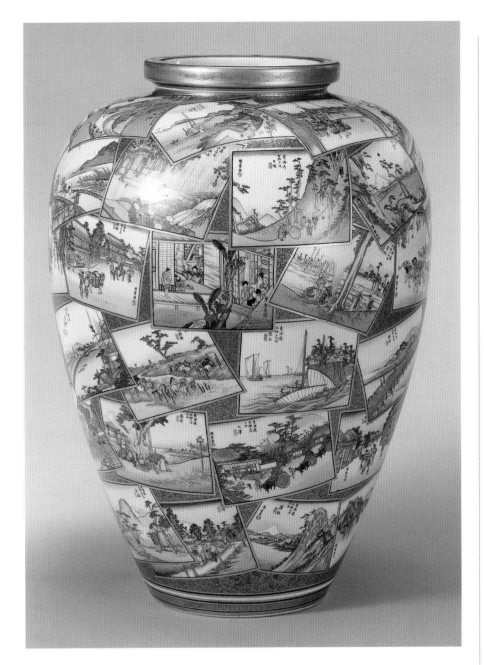

153
INCENSE BURNER
1890s
Earthenware, painted and gilded
Height 17.2 cm.
Signed *Nakamura Baikei kinsei* [respectfully
made by Nakamura Baikei], and with a
long inscription (see below)

Like the landscape prints of Ando Hiroshige
(see above), the warrior prints of Utagawa
Kuniyoshi (1797–1861) and his followers
were very popular in the West during the
Meiji Era. The prints reproduced on this
piece, each with a number and title, depict
the story of the revenge of the Soga brothers
(1172–93 and 1174–93) who vowed, while
still young, to kill their father's murderer.
They eventually succeeded, but both perished
in the attempt.

    The base is inscribed with a long
self-congratulatory inscription:

> This is an extremely fine, detailed, and
> beautiful piece. One of the pictures
> used here looks as if it were fired gold.
> Only the best-quality materials were
> selected, and repeated firings were
> made. It is priceless. It took three hun-
> dred and ten days to make this.
> Specially made by Nakamura Baikei.

154
PLAQUE
About 1895–1900
Iron; with silver, gold, *shakudo*, and
shibuichi
37.8 × 30.3 cm.
Signed *Nihonkoku Kyoto no ju Komai sei*
[made by Komai of Kyoto in Japan]
Produced by the Komai Company

The winged creature shown on this plaque
is Seijobo, king of the *tengu*; on his back
rides the youthful Minamoto no Yoshitsune
(1159–89), the most famous warrior in the
whole of Japanese history. At the very
beginning of his career, Yoshitsune was
trained in swordsmanship on Mount
Kurama outside Kyoto by the *tengu*. It is
thought that they were originally Shinto
divinities, but they were later identified with
the *yamabushi*, Buddhist warrior-monks
who lived in the mountains, practicing
religious austerities and playing an active
part in the ceaseless civil wars of the
medieval period. The famous *Tengu soshi*
scroll of 1296 depicts *tengu* with crow-like
beaks; by the Edo Period, *tengu* were always
represented as either *karasu-tengu* [crow-
tengu] or *hananaga-tengu* [long-nosed
tengu]. In this depiction, the *tengu* king
also carries the young hero's *kendo* [fenc-
ing] equipment, two bamboo staves and a
mask, as well as his tall lacquered *geta*
[clogs].

155
INCENSE BURNER
About 1885
Copper, *shibuichi*, *shakudo*, bronze, silver,
and gold, with enameling
11.9 × 12.0 cm.
Signed *Kyoto Kobayashi Shunko*
[Kobayashi Shunko of Kyoto]
By Kobayashi Shunko (*d. c.* 1890)

During the Edo Period, *tengu* (see above)
were often depicted as *karasu-tengu* [crow-
tengu], and the moment of its emergence
from the egg became a favorite subject for
netsuke carvers. Little is known of the metalworker who modeled this extraordinarily
fine piece; the enameling is probably from
the atelier of Namikawa Sosuke (see pages
254–5).

156
CHARGER
About 1880
Iron, with gold, silver, and *shakudo*
Diameter 49.3 cm.
Signed *Nihonkoku Kyoto no ju Komai sei*
[made by Komai of Kyoto in Japan]
Produced by the Komai Company

This charger shows Kusunoki Masashige
(1294–1336), one of the great loyalist
heroes of Japan. Kusunoki devoted his life
to restoring the authority of the Emperor
Godaigo, who had been expelled from the
capital, Kyoto, by the ill-fated regent Hojo
Takatoki (see number 173). After initial
successes, both Kusunoki Masashige and
his comrade-in-arms, Nitta Yoshisada (see
number 94), were eventually defeated by
the villainous shogun Ashikaga Takauji. The
scene depicted here, among the most
famous in Japanese military folklore, is the
final parting of Masashige from his son,
Masatsura, to whom he presented a scroll
on military strategy and a sword he had
received from the Emperor. This episode
had an obvious appeal in the early Meiji
Era, when the new rulers of Japan liked to
present their "restoration" of Imperial rule
(see page 29) as the completion of the task
begun by the fourteenth-century loyalist
heroes. It was the subject of a patriotic
song before World War II which, although
prohibited by the Occupation authorities in
1945, is still well-known.[1] The original
drawing for this piece is kept in the Komai
family archives.

1. Ivan Morris, *The Nobility of Failure* (London,
   1975), pp. 131–2.

157
PLAQUE
About 1890
Iron; with silver, gold, *shakudo*, and
shibuichi
24.2 × 18.9 cm.
Signed *Nihonkoku Kyoto no ju Komai sei*
[made by Komai of Kyoto in Japan]

The female warrior depicted on the plaque
is Tomoe Gozen, the wife of Kiso Yoshinaka
(1154–84). When her husband met his death
in battle, she was attacked by a warrior
named Uchida Ieyoshi but defeated him
in single combat and sliced off his head.
According to one account of her later life,
although she was subsequently captured by
the victorious Minamoto clan, her life was
spared thanks to the intervention of Wada
Yoshimori, whom she married. Their son
Asahina Saburo, in turn, became a
celebrated warrior.

158
SWORD
About 1880–90
Cloisonné enamels worked in silver wire,
with gilding, *shibuichi*, and *shakudo*; silk
and leather cords
Length 107 cm.
Attributed to a Kyoto workshop

Although an edict of 1876 rescinded the
traditional right of the samurai to wear
two swords, enamelers, lacquerers and
metalworkers continued to make elaborate
sets of sword fittings. Some of these were
perhaps intended for sale to Japanese
customers, but outsize *tachi* [slung swords]
such as these were designed to appeal to
the Western fascination with Japan's
traditional warriors and their weapons.

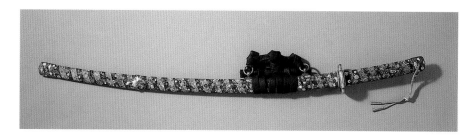

159
SWORD
About 1880–90
Cloisonné enamels worked in silver and
gilded wire; silk and leather cords
Length 95.3 cm.
Attributed to a Kyoto workshop

The decoration on the handle and scabbard
of this sword is loosely in the early style of
Namikawa Yasuyuki (see pages 254–5), but
is more than likely the product of another
workshop in Kyoto, possibly that of
Shibata, to whose work both the color-
scheme and the wirework on this piece bear
a close resemblance.

160
SWORD
About 1895–1900
Iron, with gold and silver
Length 109 cm.
Signed *Nihonkoku Kyoto no ju Komai
seizo* [manufactured by Komai of Kyoto
in Japan]
Produced by the Komai Company

This *tachi* [slung sword] is optimistically
decorated with seven different *mon* [crests]
of the Tokugawa (see pages 18–19) and
Imperial families.

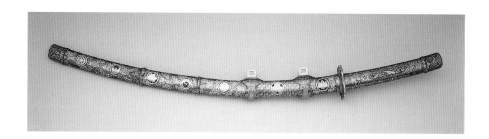

161
CABINET
About 1880–90
Wood, lacquered in *takamaki-e* and
hiramaki-e, with gold and silver;
silver fittings
24.5 × 27.3 × 17.5 cm.

The warbler perched on a branch of pine,
the two large gold characters on the doors,
and the overall design with the verandah of
a palace building at the left, immediately
identify the subject of this miniature cabinet
as Chapter 23, *Hatsune* [The First Warbler],
of *Genji monogatari* [The Tale of Genji], a
long novel written in the eleventh century
by the court lady Murasaki Shikibu. This
had been a very popular subject for lacquer
decoration since the 1630s, when a large
set of wedding furniture with *Hatsune*
motifs was ordered for the marriage of
the two-and-a-half-year-old daughter of
the third shogun, Iemitsu, to her second
cousin Tokugawa Mitsutomo. The action of
Chapter 23 opens on a particularly
auspicious calendrical occasion when the
cyclical day of the rat coincides with New
Year's Day. As is customary on the first *ne*
[rat] day of the year, the servants of Prince
Genji's daughter, the Akashi princess, set
out pine saplings, and her mother the
Akashi lady, now of advancing years,
sends baskets of gifts and an artificial bush
warbler on a pine branch, accompanied by
a thirty-one syllable *waka* poem. The first
two characters of this poem, *hatsu* and
ne, are applied in gold to the doors of the
cabinet. The insides of the doors and the
fronts of the drawers are decorated with
scenes from later chapters of *Genji*.

162
TRAY
About 1875–1900
Wood, lacquered in *kinji*, with encrustation
of shell, ivory, and other materials
20.5 × 30.3 cm.
Signed *Ekisei*
By Shibayama Ekisei (see numbers 69 and
195)

This tray depicts Momotaro, child hero of
the best-known of all Japanese fairy tales.
Momotaro [literally, "little peach boy"] was
found by the childless wife of a poor wood-
cutter, floating in a river in a huge peach.

She took the peach back to her husband and
the old couple cared for the foundling, who
developed formidable physical powers.
Eventually Momotaro decided to go to Oni-
gashima, the Devils' Island in the Inland Sea
off the coast of Shikoku, in order to conquer
the demons, seize their treasure and present
it to his adoptive parents. Here he is shown
castigating a pair of demons who are bringing him a *kusudama* [ceremonial bouquet].
Another of the demons weeps at the loss of
the treasure while their king looks on in
horror. The other treasures are already laid
out on a table in front of Momotaro.

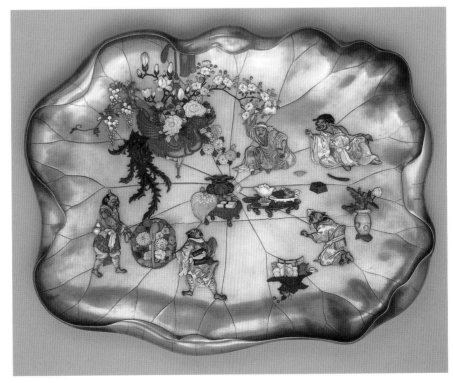

164
FIGURE OF KANNON
About 1900
Bronze, with gilding
Height 34.8 cm.
Signed *Taiun*
By Yamada Taiun (dates unknown)

This treatment of Kannon shows the influence
of classical European sculpture. Yamada Taiun
exhibited at the fifth and last Naikoku Kangyo
Hakurankai [National Industrial Exposition],
held in Osaka in 1903.

163
FIGURE OF KANNON
About 1880
Earthenware, painted and gilded
Height 75.3 cm.

This large figure depicts the *bodhisattva*
Kannon, one of the most popular of
Buddhist deities in both China (where she
is called Guanyin) and Japan. According to
the teachings of the Mahayana branch of
Buddhism, which developed from around
the first century, a *bodhisattva* is one who
has achieved six (later ten) perfections over
countless previous lives and stands on the
brink of Buddhahood, but elects to remain
in the world to offer help and protection to
mankind. Kannon has been depicted in
Japanese art since early times, and by
the Edo Period had become an object of
universal veneration.

165
FIGURE OF KANNON
About 1880
Silver, with copper and gold
Height 17.6 cm.
Signed *Ichiryu Tomotoshi* with a *kao*
[cursive monogram]
By Ichiryu Tomotoshi (1831–89)

For Ichiryu Tomotoshi, see number 47. This
model of Kannon, the goddess of mercy
(see number 163), carries a basket with a
fish, one of her emblems.

166

BOX
About 1875–1900
Wood, lacquered in *kinji*, *hiramaki-e*, and other techniques, with encrustation of shell, ivory, and other materials; ivory head and tusks
Height 23.0 cm.
Signed *Koichi*

A box in the form of the *bodhisattva* Fugen (see number 168) riding side-saddle on an elephant, the figure of Fugen lifting off to reveal a container in the elephant's body.

167

FIGURE OF KANNON
About 1890
Silver, with gold and *shakudo*
Height 13.0 cm.
Signed *Inshi Motonobu zo* [made by Inshi Motonobu]
Sealed *Ozeki* and *sei* [made by Ozeki]
By Yamada Motonobu (1847–1897)
Produced by the Ozeki Company

For the *bodhisattva* Kannon, see number 163.

168
Incense Burner
About 1890
Silver, with *shakudo*, *shibuichi*, gold,
malachite, coral, tiger's-eye, agate, and
nephrite; crystal ball
Height 37.1 cm.
Signed *Shoami Katsuyoshi sen* [carved by
Shoami Katsuyoshi]
By Shoami Katsuyoshi (1832–1908)

The white elephant is an animal of great
significance in Buddhism. It is the mount
of the *bodhisattva* Fugen, while another
bodhisattva, Monju, rides a lion-like
beast called a *shishi*. They are the
bodhisattvas of wisdom and are said to
have been born during the lifetime of the
historical Buddha. The elephant, one of the
animals present at the death and final
enlightenment of the Buddha, has a
saddle in the form of a lotus,
which, being symbolic of rebirth,
is the throne for all holy beings
in Buddhism. On the throne is a
cloud upon which rides a
coiled dragon, a messenger
of Buddhism representing
almighty power. The cloud
signifies that the dragon exists
in a realm beyond the heavens.
The dragon supports
a crystal ball, which
in popular legend
represents a jewel that
controls the tides, and can also be
seen as one of the Three Imperial
Regalia of Japan. In this case the crystal,
by its clarity and brightness, represents
the essence of Buddha's teaching, and it
is thus a replacement for the *bodhisattva*
who usually rides the elephant. The saddle-
cloth bears faces of the *shishi*, which guards
holy beings and whose roar expresses the
power of Buddha's law. Below the *shishi*
are, on one side, the *minogame*, turtles
trailing waterweed behind them, and on the
other a crane, both symbolizing longevity
and associated with Chinese immortals.
The phoenix forming a crown on the head
of the elephant is the most auspicious of
creatures, flying through the realm of
Buddhism and representing the joy of
Buddha's law. Stylized magic coats, from
among the auspicious objects associated
with the Seven Gods of Good Fortune, hang
from the caparison and alternate with bells
along the bottom edge of the saddle-cloth.
The ringing of bells is to dispel illusion,
and represents the spiritual awakening of
Buddhism.

169
TWO-FOLD SCREEN
About 1880
Hardwood lacquered in *hiramaki-e*
and *takamaki-e*, with shell, hardstones,
and ivory
Height 174.8 cm.

This screen depicts four *rakan* (see number
170).

170
VASE
Late 1880s
Earthenware, painted and gilded
Height 13.1 cm.
Signed *Meizan sei* [made by Meizan]
Made by the Yabu Meizan Factory

This vase depicts some of the *rakan*, disciples
of the Buddha, who were said in Japan to
be sixteen or five hundred in number. The
term *rakan*, or *arakan*, derives from the
Sanskrit *arhat*, meaning "one worthy of
respect". Although their true nature was
much debated during the early history of
Buddhism, *rakan* are generally regarded as
beings who have reached a point of spiritual
development just below that of a true
Buddha [enlightened one]. Their large gold
halos made them especially suitable for the
decoration of Satsuma ware, and they are
often depicted in earthenware produced by
the Yabu Meizan Factory (see also number
105). They are accompanied here by small
Chinese children, an idea with its origins in
late Ming-Dynasty (1368–1644) ceramic
decoration.

171
TRAY
About 1890
Wood, lacquered in *takamaki-e*, *kinji*,
and other techniques, with ivory details;
silver fittings
40.4 × 58.8 cm.
Signed *Hogisai Kako*

This tray depicts the sixteen *rakan* (see
number 170) and their emblems, including
a dragon, a tiger, a scroll, and a variety of
implements used in Buddhist ritual. They
are shown as usual with large earlobes, symbolic of their great wisdom. Nothing is
known of the artist, although a number of
pieces with the same signature are recorded.

172

GROUP

After 1881

Bronze, with gilding; crystal ball

99.0 × 80.0 cm.

Signed *Dai Nihon Teikoku Tokyo seizojin Otake Norikuni* [Tokyo, in the great Japanese Empire. Maker: Otake Norikuni], with a *kao* [cursive monogram]

By Otake Norikuni (*b.* 1852)

This group shows Susano-o, the Impetuous Male Deity (see number 174), receiving a sacred jewel from Haneakarutama no Mikoto, depicted here as a sea god festooned with dragons, fish scales, fins, and fish tails, his attendant standing at his side. Behind them, a two-horned *kirin* (see number 42) and various other creatures emerge from among the rocks. A pair of *gohei* [Shinto ritual banners] are attached to the branches of a tree in the background. A long in scription on the base explains the incident depicted here:

Susano-o no Mikoto was the child of Izanagi no Mikoto and the younger brother of Amaterasu Omikami. Their father determined that Amaterasu Omikami should rule the land of heaven and that Susano-o no Mikoto should rule the land of the Eight Great Islands. But Susano-o no Mikoto, dissenting, requested that he not rule the Eight Great Islands but go to the land of the underworld. His father told him to do as he wished. Susano-o no Mikoto thought: "Let me tell Amaterasu Omikami that I will go to the land of the underworld before I go." At that time there was a god called Haneakarutama no Mikoto, also called Kushiakarutama no Mikoto. He offered a beautiful jewel to [Susano-o no] Mikoto. This is the jewel called the *Mizuyasakani no Magatama*. Susano-o no Mikoto was highly delighted and, arriving back in the land of heaven, he gave it to Amaterasu Omikami. So

accounts of this appear in the *Nihongi* and the *Kogo shui*. Composed by Tomita Tetsunosuke (Junior, fifth rank); calligraphy by Katakura Akinori (Junior, seventh rank).

For further details of the Shinto creation myths, see page 140.

Another strikingly similar group, signed by Oshima Joun, was made for the second Naikoku Kangyo Hakurankai [National Industrial Exposition] held in 1881.[1] The connection between the two is obscure, as both makers were leading sculptors of the period and unlikely to copy the work of another (for Otake Norikuni, see number 231 and for Oshima Joun, see number 245). However, the judges of the 1881 exhibition criticized the lack of spirit and expression in the face of the human figure, so it is possible that Otake Norikuni, heeding the advice of the judges, produced a second version even more detailed and with a more animated, expressive figure receiving the jewel. Not only did he change the expression, but also the actual legend. Here Susano-o no Mikoto receives the sacred jewel from Haneakarutama no Mikoto, but in the version by Oshima Joun, it is Takenouchi no Sukune who is sent by the semi-mythical Empress Jingu to obtain a tide-controlling jewel from Ryujin, the dragon king of the sea. Two sets of drawings by Kawanabe Kyosai (1831–89) are closely related, if not actually preparatory, to this bronze or its related counterpart.[2] The marble-inlaid ebonized wood base is probably American.

1. Oliver Impey and Malcolm Fairley, *The Dragon King of the Sea* (Oxford, 1991), p.32.
2. Timothy Clark, *Demon of Painting: The Art of Kawanabe Kyosai* (British Museum, London, 1993), pp. 54–5.

173
Pair of Two-Fold Screens, see page 180.

173

PAIR OF TWO-FOLD SCREENS

About 1887–92
Hardwood, lacquered in *hiramaki-e* and
takamaki-e on a *kinji* ground, with ivory,
carved red lacquer, and shell
Each 230 × 210 cm.

The combination of Japanese and Chinese
mythology on different panels applied to
the same object is seen on other examples
of Shibayama-type encrustation such as the
vase, number 174. The figure brandishing
his sword over a dragon in the left-hand
panel of the "Japanese" screen is Susano-o,
the Impetuous Male Deity, and the design
of this panel appears to be loosely based on
a drawing by Kawanabe Kyosai, probably
dating from 1887.[1] The seated lady behind
Susano-o is Princess Kushiinada, whom he
married after intoxicating and slaying the
dragon; the design shows three pots of *sake*
[rice wine], one of them held by the dragon
in its claw. After he had killed the monster,
Susano-o found, in its tail, a sword which is

still revered as one of the Three Imperial
Regalia of Japan.

The right-hand screen depicts Benten,
one of the Seven Gods of Good Fortune
(see number 148). Although of Indian
origin, she had been thoroughly assimilated
into Japanese iconography during the Edo
Period, and in this instance her head-dress
is decorated with a *torii* [shrine archway],
symbolizing the Shinto religion. She is
shown with Hojo Tokimasa (1138–1215),
the influential father-in-law of Minamoto
no Yoritomo, founder of the Kamakura
shogunate (see pages 17–18). Tokimasa
used to visit Benten's shrine at Enoshima,
near Kamakura (see number 148), and on
one occasion the goddess appeared to him
and agreed to grant his prayer for prosperity, on the condition that he and his successors ruled with justice, failing which his
family would not last beyond the seventh
generation. She then vanished, leaving

behind three scales from her dragon, also
shown here. Tokimasa took the scales and
arranged them to form the *mon* [crest] of
the Hojo family. After Yoritomo's death,
Tokimasa's behavior became increasing
despotic and he was eventually exiled by
his own daughter. Although he had succeeded in setting up his family as regents
and eclipsed the power of the shoguns, his
successor the ninth regent Hojo Takatoki
(see number 156) was slaughtered along
with eight hundred and seventy of his family and retainers in 1333, and so Benten's
threat was eventually carried out.

The scenes on the "Chinese" screen,
depicting a Chinese princess or goddess
attended by a boy servant, have not been
precisely identified and may not refer to
any particular personality.

1. Timothy Clark, *Demon of Painting: The Art
of Kawanabe Kyosai* (British Museum,
London, 1993), p.53.

174

VASE

About 1880–90

Wood lacquered in *takamaki-e*, *kinji*, and *hiramaki-e*, with encrustation of shell, ivory, and other materials

65.8 × 60.7 × 15.8 cm.

Signed *Gyokkendo san* [produced by Gyokkendo] and *Nagata Toratsume saku* [made by Nagata Toratsume]

The two main panels on this vase depict, respectively, a Japanese and a Chinese goddess. The figure with rays emanating from her head is Amaterasu, the Sun Goddess, one of several deities born from clothing discarded by an earlier god, Izanagi, when he was defiled by the rotting body of his sister Izanami. Another god born in this way was Susano-o, the "Impetuous Male Deity". In the same variant of the story of Amaterasu and Susano-o as that depicted in number 172, Susano-o descends to the underworld where he is presented with a sacred jewel which he then gives to his sister, as shown on this panel. The jewel is, in fact, described in early texts such as the *Kojiki* (712), the *Nihongi* (720) and the *Kogo shui* (807) as a *magatama* [curved jewel] of the kind found in fifth- and sixth-century tombs in both Japan and Korea, but is often represented in Meiji art as a crystal. Since the scene on the other panel shows a Chinese goddess bestowing rather than receiving a jewel, it is possible that the figure in armor is not Susano-o but Amaterasu's grandson Ninigi, the supposed founder of the Japanese Imperial line, to whom she presented the Three Imperial Regalia of Mirror, Sword and Jewel when he descended to rule over Kyushu, Japan's southernmost main island.

The other panel depicts Seiobo, "The Royal Mother of the West", who ruled over a paradise in the Kunlun region of Central Asia and presented the Chinese emperor of the Western Han Dynasty, Wu Di (reigned 140–86 B.C.), with a peach which conferred immortality, shown here in a basket held in her right hand. The story of Seiobo is the subject of a medieval Japanese *No* play, and there was a revival of interest in the goddess when she became a favorite subject for congratulatory works of art commissioned for special occasions in late Ming-Dynasty China (1368–1644); such works, as well as representations of Seiobo in Chinese printed books, were imported to Japan.

Nothing is known of the Gyokkendo Company or Nagata Toratsume, joint makers of this piece, but its unusual shape, large size, and high quality suggest that it may have been intended for display at a major exhibition.

佐藤忠信吉野の
五重の塔に昇て
横川覺範と戰ふ

175
CABINET
1908–9
Wood, lacquered in *togidashi-e*, *takamaki-e*,
hiramaki-e and *nashiji*, with inlay of ivory,
bone and shell; silvered and gilded fittings
227 × 159 × 58.0 cm.
Produced by the Samurai Shokai Company

This sumptuously decorated cabinet was
purchased in 1909 from Samurai Shokai
(or Shokwai, see also number 202) by Baron
R. von Swaine of Schloss Theres, Hasfurt,
Unterfranken, Germany. The price was
1,000 yen, equivalent at that time to 2,050
marks. A letter of April 23, 1909, from
Samurai Shokai ("Wholesale and retail of
high art curios") assures the Baron that:

The cabinet is one of the most beautiful
ones to be found in Japan and we feel
sure that you will be perfectly satisfied
with it and it will become centre of the
admiration of those who know something about the arts. It is gold lacquer
and worked with the beautifully cut
inlaid mother of pearl design representing different remarkable events in our
history.

In 1910 the Samurai Shokai, whose
advertisement is reproduced on page 208,
supplied a cabinet (number 202) which
may have been intended for the Japan-
British Exhibition.

The mother-of-pearl designs incorporate
fourteen individually labeled stories from
Japanese history, which are described in
detail on pages 142–7. In keeping with
the warlike character of the rest of the
piece, the base is decorated with a band
of arrowheads.

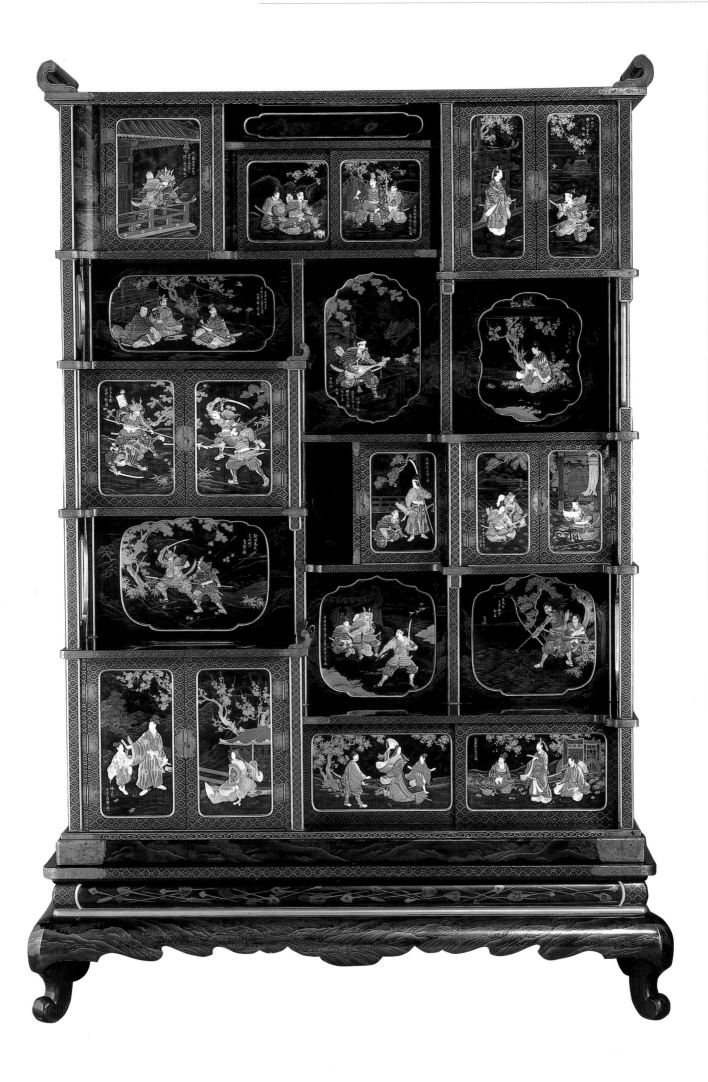

LACQUER

JAPANESE EXPORT
LACQUER BEFORE
THE MEIJI ERA

The hardened sap of the lacquer tree, *Rhus verniciflua*, was first used in Japan to protect the surface of everyday objects between about 4,000 and 3,000 B.C., and some surviving examples from this period even have simple decoration. It was not until the seventh and eighth centuries, however, that more complex methods of decorating lacquerware started to be developed as a result of growing patronage of luxury goods by the imperial family, the aristocracy, and the Buddhist priesthood. For more than a thousand years, lacquered objects would play a central role in Japanese life and culture, so much so that the cultivation of lacquer trees became an important economic activity requiring government encouragement and regulation. As early as A.D. 701, there were laws setting down the number of trees to be grown by varying sizes of household, and laying an obligation on lacquer-producing provinces to pay a tribute in kind to the central government. Possession of lacquer sap became a symbol of wealth: in 1567, for example, the general Takeda Shingen presented 1,000 buckets of lacquer to Oda Nobunaga (see page 171) on the occasion of the marriage of his son to the latter's daughter.[1]

By Nobunaga's time, the techniques of lacquer decoration, described in detail below, had reached a very high level of sophistication, and Europeans were having their first opportunity to appreciate the glossy black and gold finish that, in the West, would be called "Japan", just as porcelain came to be known as "China". Japanese lacquered chests and cabinets probably first reached the West in the third quarter of the sixteenth century, a few years after the arrival of the first Portuguese sailors and about seventy-five years before Japanese porcelain (see pages 18–19 and 330). The wares that were made for the new export market were quite different from those for Japanese buyers. Most were in European shapes, and the decoration was an exotic mixture of Japanese elements with motifs and patterns from China, Korea, and India, with lavish mother-of-pearl borders enclosing pictorial scenes or landscapes in gold lacquer. Japanese lacquered furniture made a striking addition to many European aristocratic and royal interiors during the seventeenth century, but it was never exported in anything like the same quantities as porcelain. Even though Japanese workshops introduced several new time-saving manufacturing methods, lacquerware, by its very nature, is not amenable to mass production. The trade reached a peak towards 1650, but from the 1680s the Japanese began to lose ground to cheaper Chinese imitations. Officially, the Dutch East India Company bought no lacquer after 1693, but as with porcelain, a small private trade continued until well into the nineteenth century. During the eighteenth century, antique Japanese lacquers (in other words, pieces that had originally been imported to Europe up to 200 years earlier) were avidly collected by the French aristocracy, who would order old pieces to be broken up and have the decorated panels incorporated into new styles of furniture. After the French Revolution (1789), the taste for "old Japan" was continued by the English millionaire, novelist, and collector William Beckford, who died in 1844, so that just a decade or so before Commodore Perry's arrival in 1853–4, a few enthusiasts in the West were still aware of lacquerware as a distinctive Japanese product. As we have seen, the official gifts to Perry included "... their famous lacquered ware, such as chow-chow boxes, tables, trays, and goblets" (page 22), and other examples of nineteenth-century Japanese lacquer are known to have reached the West during the 1850s. Silas E. Burrows, an American who arrived shortly after Perry's departure, received lacquerware among his official gifts, and there were cases of isolated trade with America as early as 1855, when the vessel *Caroline E. Foote* secured a shipment including items of lacquer work, and again in 1856, when an American ship stopped at Izu and bought lacquerware made in Shizuoka Prefecture.

CULTIVATION AND
APPLICATION

Because the techniques used to manufacture a piece of Japanese lacquerware are so different from anything in the Western craft tradition, they need to be described in some detail. It is difficult, however, to convey in words the almost miraculous transformation that occurs between the simple, agricultural process of lacquer-tapping and the final polishing of a high-quality decorated writing box or writing table such as catalogue number

Figure 1.
Hiramaki-e

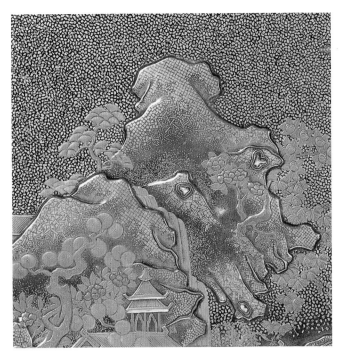

Figure 2.
Takamaki-e

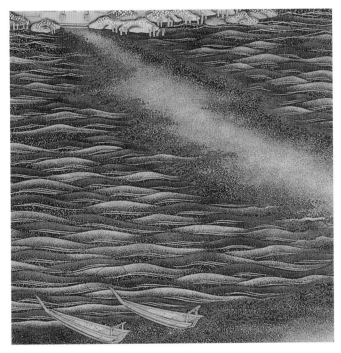

Figure 3.
Togidashi-e

Figure 4.
Nashiji

LACQUER

This section, devoted to the lacquerwares of the Meiji Era, features both pieces made in traditional techniques with traditional subject matter and more innovative work destined for the export market, including Shibayama ware, which is covered in further detail in the earlier section on Exotic Goods for Globetrotters.

176
WRITING TABLE AND BOX FOR WRITING UTENSILS
About 1900
Wood lacquered in *takamaki-e*, *hiramaki-e*, *kirikane* and *nashiji*; silver water-dropper and fittings
13.2 × 35.4 × 63.3 cm. (writing table);
5.2 × 23.0 × 25.3 cm. (box for writing utensils)

For the subject matter of this set, which shows views of Uji, a town near Kyoto, see number 151. The lavish use of *nashiji*, flakes of gold suspended in semi-transparent lacquer, and *takamaki-e* [built-up lacquer] is a continuation of the lacquer style associated in the Edo Period with wedding sets made for senior samurai and court weddings, but the addition of touches of color and the choice of an everyday subject such as tea-picking (based on an eighteenth-century picture book) draws on the tradition of miniature lacquers made for the urban merchant class. This juxtaposition of styles which had previously been mutually exclusive is characteristic of Meiji-Era lacquer.

177
BOX FOR WRITING UTENSILS AND BOX FOR WRITING PAPER

About 1900
Wood lacquered in *takamaki-e*, *hiramaki-e*, and *kirikane*; silver, gold and *shakudo* water-dropper; silver fittings
15.2 × 35.3 × 43.3 cm. (box for writing paper); 5.4 × 23.6 × 26.7 cm. (box for writing utensils)

The empty *ushiguruma* [aristocratic carriage drawn by oxen] suggests the presence nearby of a courtier, perhaps Prince Genji (see number 161), the hero of the eleventh-century novel *Genji monogatari* [Tale of Genji], and the boating scene inside the lid of the box for writing paper also alludes in general terms to the courtly life of the Heian Period (794–1185). These scenes are only loosely related to the designs on the box lids which depict a variety of plants including peonies, irises, hydrangeas, lilies, and Chinese bell-flowers. The slightly schematized design, while still basically traditional in appearance, represents a first stage in the transition to the new style seen in number 200.

178
BOX
About 1900
Wood lacquered in *takamaki-e*, *hiramaki-e*,
and *kinji*; silver fittings
14.5 × 21.3 × 26.2 cm.

The burnished gold ground called *kinji*
was a favorite with Meiji-Era lacquerers.
The overall style and disposition of the
decoration is similar to that on lacquer
boxes made for presentation by members
of the Imperial family (see number 372).

179
WRITING TABLE AND BOX FOR WRITING UTENSILS
About 1900
Wood lacquered in *takamaki-e*, *hiramaki-e*, *kirikane*, and *kinji*; silver and gold water-dropper and fittings
12.6 × 36.7 × 65.1 cm. (writing table);
5.0 × 24.7 × 27.7 cm. (box for writing utensils)

This set depicts pines and flowering cherry trees in Yoshino, a mountainous district to the south of Kyoto, celebrated for its magnificent cherry blossom. The box for writing utensils contains (from right to left): an inkstick holder, an ink-stone, a skewer (with cover) for piercing sheets of paper prior to binding, and a paper-knife and cover. The water-dropper (above the ink-stone), in the form of pine and cherry branches, would have been used to drip water onto the ink-stone. Using the special holder to keep his or her fingers clean, the writer would then have rubbed the solid inkstick in the water on the stone to produce liquid ink.

180

Set of boxes
About 1875–1900
Wood, lacquered in *takamaki-e, hiramaki-e,*
and *Gyobu nashiji*; with silver and shell
12.0 × 13.5 × 10.4 cm.

This complex set of nested boxes, whose
construction is typical of many Meiji-Era
pieces destined for the export market, is
decorated with *ema* [votive panels]. The
word *ema* is written with characters
meaning "painted horse", and *ema* are
supposed to have their origin in the
practice of dedicating painted animals,
instead of real ones, at Shinto shrines. In
fact *ema*, always made from wood and
usually with the distinctive roof-shaped
tops seen on some of these examples, can
be decorated with a wide range of subject
matter although the ones shown here are
rather more elaborate than most.

181

Set of Boxes
About 1875–1900
Wood, lacquered in *hiramaki-e, Gyobu
nashiji,* and shell
Height 5.8 cm.

182
SAKE CUP
About 1870
Tortoiseshell, lacquered in *takamaki-e*
and *hiramaki-e*
Diameter 43.5 cm.
Signed *Tanabe Shogyokusai* and sealed
Gensui

Lacquerwork on a tortoiseshell base is
thought to have been produced in Nagasaki
during the closing years of the Edo Period,
and was intended for the export market.
Such wares were frequently in the form of
boxes and covers, folding fans, dishes, and
outsize *sake* cups; the cups were decorative
rather than functional. Two comparable
examples of tortoiseshell in the
Victoria and Albert Museum,
London, were acquired in
1869 and 1872.

183

INCENSE BURNER
About 1875–1900
Hardwood, lacquered in *hiramaki-e*; with
shell, ivory, tortoiseshell, and hardstones
Height 8.9 cm.

For a pair of vases in similar style, see
number 133.

184

PAIR OF VASES
About 1875–1900
Carved red lacquer; panels of *kinji* lacquer
with encrustation of shell, ivory, carved red
lacquer, and other materials; black lacquer
bands inlaid with gold foil
Height 23.5 cm.
Sealed *Ozeki sei* [made by Ozeki]
Produced by the Ozeki Company

185

PLAQUE

About 1875–1900
Wood, lacquered in *hiramaki-e*, *takamaki-e*,
and *kinji*, with encrustation of shell, ivory,
and other materials; *shibuichi* rim
0.9 × 10.9 × 11.5 cm.
Signed *Nemoto zo* [made by Nemoto]

The shape of this plaque is based on that
of the *tsuba*, a metal plate that is fitted onto
a Japanese sword at the point where the
hilt meets the blade. Although this plaque
was never intended for use, the slot in the
center copies the slot for the sword blade
seen in real *tsuba*, while the smaller hole to
the side copies the holes pierced in many
tsuba for the handle of a small dagger,
kozuka, carried in the side of the scabbard.

186

DISH

About 1875–1900
Wood, lacquered in *hiramaki-e* and
takamaki-e, with encrustation of shell,
ivory, carved red lacquer, and other
materials
Diameter 45.0 cm.
Signed *Roshin*

The central circular panel portrays
two of the Seven Gods of Good
Fortune (see number 126) with
their attributes on either side of a
stream: Ebisu, with a sea-bream
hanging from his fishing rod, and
Bishamon, with a pagoda in his
left hand and a three-pointed
halberd in his right.

187

PAIR OF TUSK VASES
About 1885
Sections of tusk with encrustation of shell, ivory, coral, cloisonné enamels and silver, lacquered in *hiramaki-e, takamaki-e,* and *kirikane* towards the base; wood elephants lacquered in *kinji,* the undercloth and strappings encrusted with hardstones and silver, and embellished with cloisonné enamels; black lacquer stands with figured silk
Height 90.0 cm.
Signed in several places *Kaneko sei* [made by Kaneko]

One of the tusks shows the eighth-century Chinese Emperor Genso (in Chinese, Xuanzong) and his favorite concubine Yokihi (Chinese, Yang Guifei), the latter playing the flute. During the rebellion of An Lushan, an illiterate general trusted by the Emperor, Genso and his entourage were forced to flee the capital, but after only forty miles the imperial escort mutinied, killing the chief minister Yang Guozhong and demanding the death of Yang Guifei, who was strangled in order to placate them. This tragic epitome of princely infatuation has been much depicted in Japanese art and literature, and forms the subject of a *No* play in which Genso orders a magician to travel to paradise, where Yokihi declares her undying love.

This is an excellent example of the type of extravagant collaboration between skilled artists using the highest quality materials that is seen in many of the most elaborate ornamental works of the mid-Meiji Era. One of the several artists involved in its creation, in addition to Kaneko (see also number 190), whose signature appears on many of the different components, was probably Hiratsuka Mohei (see numbers 26, 45, and 56), an enameler specializing in translucent enamels on openwork silver.

188
TRAY
About 1875–1900
Silver filigree with cloisonné enamel
decoration, inset with four wood panels
lacquered in *kinji*, *takamaki-e*, and
hiramaki-e, and two ivory panels with
encrustation of shell and lacquer
4.6 × 23.8 × 29.4 cm.
Signed *Kaneko sei* [made by Kaneko]

This is another collaboration between
Kaneko (see numbers 187 and 190) and an
enameler, probably Hiratsuka Mohei.

189
DISH
About 1875–1900
Silver filigree with cloisonné enamel
decoration, inset with a wood panel
lacquered in *kinji* with encrustation of shell,
ivory, and other materials
4.3 × 24.6 cm.
Signed *Ryuetsu*

190
TRAY
About 1875–1900
Wood, with encrustation of shell, ivory, and
other materials on a *kinji* lacquer ground;
silver rim
2.3 × 19.3 × 11.7 cm.
Signed *Dai Nihon Tokyo Kaneko sei* [made
by Kaneko of Tokyo in great Japan]

For Kaneko, see numbers 187 and 188.

191
Vase
About 1875–1900
Wood, lacquered in *kinji* and *hirame*, with
encrustation of shell, ivory, and other
materials; silver fittings
Height 30.0 cm.
Signed *Shirashima*

192
Pair of Vases
About 1875–1900
Wood, lacquered in *takamaki-e*, *hiramaki-e*,
hirame, and *kinji*, with encrustation of
shell, ivory, and other materials; silver
fittings with cloisonné enamel details
Height 22.9 cm.

SEE BOTTOM RIGHT

193
Pair of Vases
About 1875–1900
Wood, lacquered in *kinji* with encrustation
of shell, ivory, and other materials; silver
fittings with cloisonné enamel details
Height 19.0 cm.

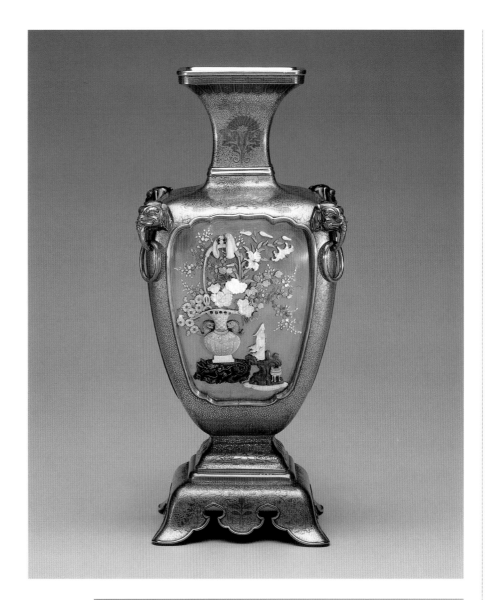

194
CABINET
About 1875–1900
Silver with cloisonné enamels; panels of
ivory and *kinji* lacquer with encrustation of
shell, ivory, and other materials; wood stand
17.9 × 16.1 × 7.5 cm.
Signed *Masatoshi*

Little evidence has come to light regarding
the organization of the Shibayama
workshops and very few of the signatures,
such as Masatoshi, found on Shibayama
pieces have been identified. The design on
the sides of this piece, with several
overlapping panels in different shapes, is
often seen in lacquer and metalwork of the
period. In his book *Art and Art Industries
in Japan*, published in 1878, the British
diplomat Sir Rutherford Alcock praised
such designs as quintessentially Japanese,
but although decoration within informally
arranged panels had been a hallmark of
Japanese decoration since the late sixteenth
century, it was not until the very end of the
Edo Period, when Japan had increasing
access to Western markets, that it was used
to the extent seen on this piece.

195

CABINET

About 1875–1900

Wood, lacquered in *nashiji* and *togidashi-e*, with encrustation of shell, ivory, and other materials; silver fittings

23.0 × 10.5 × 23.0 cm.

Signed *Shinryo*

By Shibayama Ekisei (dates unknown)

This very high quality cabinet is a rare example of a Shibayama work bearing an identifiable signature; the same signature appears on a similarly decorated cabinet in the Victoria and Albert Museum, London.[1] Shinryo Ekisei (see numbers 69, 162, and 197) is known to have won a prize for a decorative panel exhibited by the commissioner Ozeki Yahei at the first Naikoku Kangyo Hakurankai [National Industrial Exposition] of 1877. He is also recorded as having produced an object exhibited by Shibayama Senzo, who may have been associated with both this and the V&A cabinet.[2]

1. Joe Earle (ed.), *The Toshiba Gallery: Japanese Art and Design* [in the Victoria and Albert Museum] (London, 1986), cat. no. 190.
2. Tokyo-fu Kangyoka [Industrial Section of the Tokyo Prefectural Council], *Tokyo meikokan* [Almanac of Master Craftsmen in Tokyo] (Tokyo, 1879).

Detail of inside

196
CABINET
About 1875–1900
Silver inset with panels of ivory and *kinji*
lacquer with decoration in *hiramaki-e*
lacquer and encrustation of shell, ivory,
and other materials; the interiors of the
doors and the fronts of the drawers
lacquered in *hiramaki-e* and *takamaki-e* on
a dense *nashiji* ground
29.9 × 21.5 × 30.1 cm.
Signed *Masayoshi*

The design on the inside of the doors
shows wooden carriage wheels immersed
in water, a motif that dates back to a
famous lacquer box supposedly made in
the twelfth century. It is said to owe its
origins to the practice of immersing the
wheels of *ushiguruma* (aristocratic car-
riages drawn by oxen, see number 177)
to prevent them from drying out and
warping.[1]

1. Kyoto National Museum, *Maki-e, shikkoku
   to ogon no Nihonbi* [The Beauty of Black
   and Gold Japanese Lacquer] (Kyoto 1995),
   cat. no. 22.

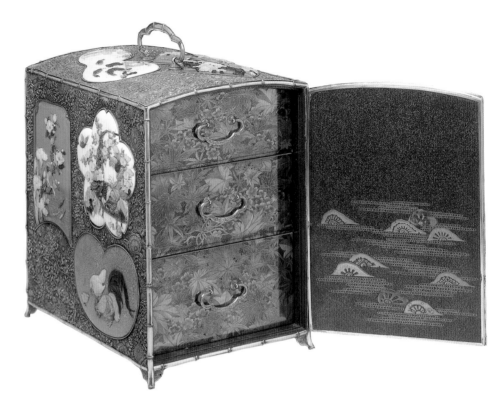

197
TRAY
About 1875–1900
Wood, lacquered in *hiramaki-e* and
takamaki-e, with encrustation of shell,
ivory, and other materials; silver edgings
2.6 × 42.5 cm.
Signed *Yasuyuki*
By Shibayama Ekisei (dates unknown)

For Shibayama Ekisei, see number 195.

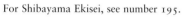

198
CABINET
About 1875–1900
Wood, lacquered in red lacquer,
Wakasa-nuri, *roiro*, and *takamaki-e*;
silver fittings
30.4 × 23.0 × 34.9 cm.
Style of Shibata Zeshin (1807–91)

For Shibata Zeshin, see numbers 34 and
391. The simulated metal *tsuba* [hand-
guards for swords] and *kozuka* [daggers]
are decorated with a variety of popular
subjects discussed elsewhere in this catalogue, including Hotei (see number 126),
a *sennin* (see number 141) with peaches,
Shoki with an *oni* [demon] (see number
137), Chokaro (see number 140), and a
rakan (see number 170) being pulled across
a river by two *oni*. The dagger blade and
some of the *tsuba* bear the signatures of
metalworkers but these were probably
added as an essential part of the design of
a typical *tsuba*, rather than referring to
specific artists. The decoration was applied
in an unusual technique whereby the usual
stages of lacquerwork, described on pages
185–6, were reversed. A negative model of
each sword-fitting motif was made in plaster
and the design was built inside the mold by
applying the various layers of lacquer in
reverse order. The lacquer decoration was
then released from the mold and applied to
the box.

199
SET OF FIVE BOXES
About 1910
Wood, lacquered in *takamaki-e* and
kuromaki-e [black lacquer decoration on
a black lacquer ground]
Each 4.6 × 10.1 × 15.3 cm.
Signed *Taisai*
By Koma Taisai (dates unknown)

The first character of the signature was also
used by Ikeda Taishin (1825–1903, see
number 392), the leading pupil of Shibata
Zeshin, and it is therefore likely that
Taishin was, in turn, Taisai's master.
Although we know little about Taisai's
life, a few examples of his work have
recently been published.

   This is an example of a new type of
lacquer design that made its appearance
in the early years of this century, where
plant forms are schematized and depicted
as though seen from close quarters but are
deprived of any naturalistic context.
Although something of this had been
seen in works of the so-called
Rimpa school of lacquerers
and painters in the earlier
Edo Period, the effect is
quite different
in the work of Taisai
and his contemporaries
and, in its pursuit of pure
design, shows the influence
of contemporary Western
movements such as *Art Nouveau*.

200
BOX FOR WRITING PAPER AND BOX FOR WRITING UTENSILS
About 1910
Wood, lacquered in *hiramaki-e*; silver edgings
14.7 × 31.5 × 39.5 cm. (box for writing paper); 5.0 × 23.7 × 27.0 cm. (box for writing utensils)
Signed *Kosai*
By Kosai (dates unknown, school of Shibata Zeshin)

The second character of Kosai's name was used by several pupils of Shibata Zeshin (see number 34). This is another example of the new style of lacquer decoration that is first seen around 1900.

201

BOX

About 1910

Wood, lacquered in *roiro* and *hiramaki-e*;
silver edgings; silk brocade lining
16.2 X 30.7 X 24.5 cm.
By Tsujimura Shoka (1867–1929)

This is another instance of the new lacquer
styles evolving at the end of the Meiji Era
that feature stylized close-up depictions of
plant forms, in this case *asunaro* [arbor
vitae, *Thujopsis dolabrata*]. A student of
Shirayama Shosai (see number 390),
Tsujimura Shoka was born in Odawara
and became a professor at Tokyo Art
School in 1905, receiving a gold medal at
St. Louis the previous year. This box was
exhibited at the great Japan-British
Exhibition held in London in 1910, where
it was awarded a gold medal.[1]

1. Office of the Imperial Japanese Government,
   *An Illustrated Catalogue of Japanese Old Fine
   Arts Displayed at the Japan-British Exhibition,
   London 1910* (Tokyo, 1910), cat. no. 247.

SAMURAI SHOKWAI.

No. 20, HONCHO, YOKOHAMA.

WITH a *MOST EXTENSIVE COLLECTION* of antique
PORCELAINS, BRONZES, SILVER, LACQUER
WARES, and EMBROIDERIES and NEW CURIOS
of every description, most cordially solicit the esteemed
visit and purchase by all ladies and gentlemen. ALL TRA-
VELLERS will find it to their advantage to send any purchases they may make to SAMURAI SHOKWAI, as we store,
pack, ship, forward, and make consular invoices, and represent all the principal merchants in the interior.

Advertisement for the Samurai Shokwai, from
Basil H. Chamberlain, *A Handbook for Travellers
in Japan* (London, Yokohama, Shanghai, Hong
Kong and Singapore, 1901), advertising supplement, p.17.

▶

202

CABINET

About 1910

Wood, lacquered in *hiramaki-e*, *takamaki-e*,
hirame, *nashiji*, and *Gyobu*; silver fittings
156 X 116 X 63.2 cm.
Produced by the Samurai Shokai Company

The sumptuous decoration of this cabinet
shows how traditional lacquer styles were
thriving at the very end of the Meiji Era
alongside more innovative work, such as
that seen in catalogue numbers 199–201.
An accompanying letter claims that the
cabinet was made in Japan for the Japan-
British Exhibition as a representative piece
of Japanese craftsmanship, but was not
finished in time for shipment to England.
It was purchased in Japan in 1910–11
from Samurai Shokai, Art dealers, Tokio,
Yokohama. The Samurai Shokai of
Kanagawa (i.e. Yokohama), recorded as
having won a gold prize for a group of
metalwork pieces shown at the Japan-
British Exhibition, was a well-known
company boasting "a most extensive
collection of antique porcelains, bronzes,
silver, lacquer wares, and embroideries
and new curios of every description".[1]

1. Basil H. Chamberlain, *A Handbook for
   Travellers in Japan* (London, 1901),
   advertising supplement, p.17.

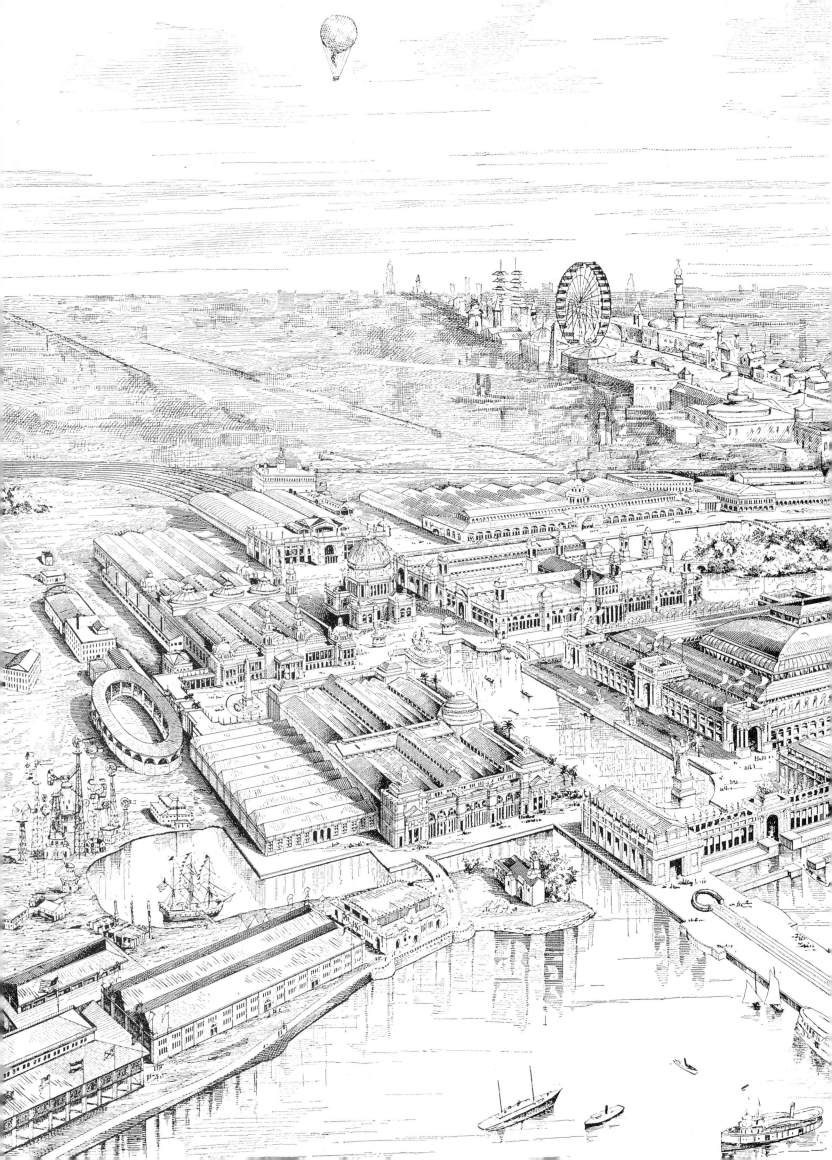

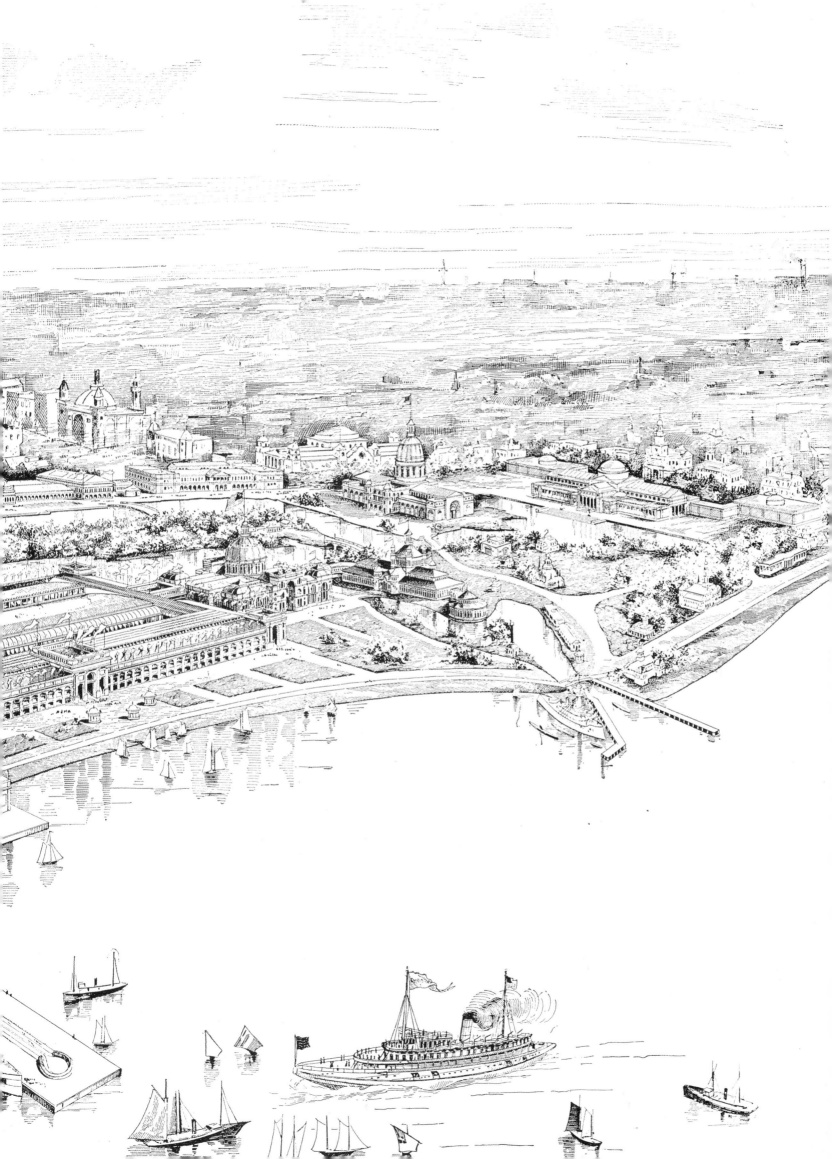

THE GOLDEN AGE:
FROM PHILADELPHIA TO PARIS, 1876–1900

THE NATIONAL
INDUSTRIAL
EXPOSITIONS

Following its success at Philadelphia, Japan took part in many of the international exhibitions that followed: Paris in 1878, 1889, and 1900, Amsterdam in 1883, New Orleans and Nuremburg in 1885, Barcelona in 1887, Chicago in 1893, St. Louis in 1904, and London in 1910. In addition, a total of five Naikoku Kangyo Hakurankai [National Industrial Expositions] were held in Japan: the first (1877), second (1881), and third (1890) in Tokyo, the fourth (1895) in Kyoto, and the fifth (1903) in Osaka, followed by a Kangyo Hakurankai [Industrial Exhibition] in Tokyo in 1907. These events in Japan were organized at irregular intervals to avoid clashes with the great world exhibitions, for which they served as a kind of testing ground, and their division of displays followed the international format, in particular its evolving distinction between "fine art" and "industrial art" or "art manufacture". The Industrial Expositions were an integral part of the government's project to consolidate its power and press ahead with a program of industrialization and radical social and economic reform. As nationwide events, they not only promoted competition by offering prizes to the most enterprising and innovative exhibitors, but also helped to foster a sense of shared Japanese national identity – something that had been largely absent during the Edo Period with its system of devolved feudal government and local loyalties. They were also among the earliest mass events of Japan's modern age. Even though there was no national transportation system, 454,168 people managed to attend during the three months of the first National Industrial Exposition, and 823,094 during the four-month run of the second Exposition.

We have already seen (page 94) how enterprises like the Ozeki Company promoted craft goods to foreign visitors, and they were equally active at exhibitions at home and abroad, participating fully in a symbiotic relationship with government which assisted their efforts by publishing design manuals and preparing detailed reports before and after each major event. These reports provided advice on the motifs that would find favor abroad, and the shapes and sizes that were most appropriate to Western interiors, while the carefully recorded remarks of the prize judges gave aesthetic guidance and noted, with approval or disapproval, emerging trends in design and technique. Once it became clear to administrators and entrepreneurs alike that it was the very "Japaneseness" of Japanese art and craft that made it so salable, the strongly Westernizing trends of the 1870s and 1880s were gradually reversed, and the government began to take active steps to promote traditional art-forms and find ways of adapting them to contemporary market conditions. This development was due in part to the influence of Ernest Fenollosa, a Harvard graduate who taught philosophy for eight years at the Imperial University. Leading craftsmen in metal and lacquer were commissioned to make copies of famous old pieces unearthed from the collections of Buddhist temples and Shinto shrines, an Imperial Museum was established in 1889, and the Tokyo Art School (later renamed Tokyo University of Arts) opened in 1887. Under the leadership of Fenollosa's pupil Okakura Tenshin, who was named principal of the School in 1890, it pursued a Japanizing agenda that also guided the officials who were in charge of the selection of exhibits for the 1893 Columbian World's Fair, held in Chicago.

"THE WHITE CITY"

As the four-hundredth anniversary of the discovery of America in 1492 drew near, there was a lot of discussion in the American press and in Congress as to how it could best be commemorated. It was finally decided that another great international exposition should be held, and by summer 1889 New York, Washington, St. Louis, and Chicago had all established committees to press their claims. In April 1890 Congress passed an act selecting Chicago for the site, but it was already clear that the project could not be completed in time for the anniversary year. The Columbian World's Fair or World's Columbian Exposition finally opened on May 1, 1893 and ran until October 31, although a dedication ceremony was held in late 1892 to preserve the historical justification for the event.

The Chicago Fair was the last and the greatest of the nineteenth century's international expositions (if 1900, when the great Paris Exposition Universelle was held, is taken as

PREVIOUS PAGE

Figure 1.

Panorama of the World's
Columbian Exposition, Chicago,
1893, from Hubert Howe Bancroft,
The Book of the Fair... (Chicago
and San Francisco, 1893), p.71.

the first year of the twentieth century). It covered 688 acres in Jackson Park on Lake Michigan, and attracted 27,539,000 visits – almost a quarter of the total number of people then living in the United States. On its busiest day, October 9 or "Chicago Day", 716,881 went through the turnstiles. Almost in defiance of the considerable social turmoil of the early 1890s – and a devastating depression in 1893 itself – the Fair was a supremely optimistic event, and everything about it was on a grand scale. The Manufactures and Liberal Arts Building, for example, covered over eleven acres of exhibition space and rose to a height of 212 feet, reachable by giant Otis elevators which took visitors up to the flat roof to gaze out over the vast site. The official pavilions, with their celebration of industry, commerce, and technology, were supplemented by the attractions of the "Midway Pleasance", with a host of "native villages" and bazaars from around the world, including Japan, as well as fixed observation balloons ($2 per ascent), and a giant wheel 250 feet in diameter built by a Mr. G. W. G. Ferris of Pittsburg which could carry 2,160 people at a time in 36 cars.

Despite, or perhaps because of, Chicago's reputation as a brash go-ahead city, already in 1890 the site of the first skyscrapers designed by Louis Sullivan, the buildings of the fair were designed in a conservative style that was officially called "Neo-classical florentine" and unified by a gigantic architectural order with arches sixty feet high. Although the internal structures of the largest pavilions were industrial and utilitarian, reflecting the latest developments in iron and steel technology, they were completely disguised by exterior walls made from "staff", a malleable mixture of plaster, cement, and fiber. Powered sprayers – one of many inventions that owe their origin to the Fair – were used to paint the buildings white to resemble marble, and at night they were lit by electricity, giving rise to the popular designation, "The White City", in contrast to "The Black City", a nickname previously applied to Chicago because of its industrial grime.

Sullivan, appalled by the historicist approach of the Fair's principal architect, Daniel H. Burnham, and planner, Frederick Law Olmsted, wrote: "thus architecture died in the land of the free and the home of the brave ... the damage wrought by the World's Fair will last for half a century." But although Olmsted's giant colonnades, lagoons, arches, domes, and piazzas may seem to us an incongruous setting for an event that was, in essence, a celebration of everything modern and industrial – even futuristic – they made a tremendous impression on visitors. The many detailed photographs of the event, preserved in a host of guidebooks and albums, still convey something of the grandeur of the Fair and its pivotal place in the development of American industry, commerce, and popular culture.[1]

The exhibits sent by the Japanese to Chicago in 1893 are often seen as the apogee of the Meiji decorative style, and the selection of works illustrated on pages 220–51 shows the decorative art of the period at its most accomplished and distinctive. By this date, twenty years of government and imperial patronage had enabled masters such as Miyagawa Kozan in porcelain, Yabu Meizan in earthenware, Namikawa Sosuke in enamel, and Suzuki Chokichi in bronze to improve on the techniques they had inherited from the Edo

THE PHOENIX PALACE

Figure 2.
The Ho-oden and the Manufactures and Liberal Arts Building at the World's Columbian Exposition, Chicago, 1893, from Hubert Howe Bancroft, *The Book of the Fair...* (Chicago and San Francisco, 1893), p.484.

Figure 3.
The Ho-oden at the World's Columbian Exposition, Chicago, 1893, from Hubert Howe Bancroft, *The Book of the Fair...* (Chicago and San Francisco, 1893), p.913.

Period and take their art to hitherto undreamed levels of perfection. Just as at Philadelphia in 1876, the Japanese exhibits were among the most highly praised for the delicacy and finish of the metal and ivory work, the bronzes, the pottery, and the porcelain.

Following the promulgation of the Constitution in 1889, the Imperial Diet (congress) held its first session in March 1890, and even though no official invitation had yet been received, it proposed that provision should be made for Japanese participation in the Chicago Fair. In November the government formally applied to the Diet for 630,000 yen. This was passed by a unanimous vote, and six months later a Preliminary Exhibition Bureau was established in the Ministry of Agriculture and Commerce, with an advisory council made up of leading figures from industry and commerce. A network of related associations was set up throughout the country and the response was overwhelming: the government had originally expected to ship 1,000 tons of exhibits, three times the amount sent to the 1889 Paris Exposition, but the initial bids totaled 7,000 tons. Eventually this was reduced to a final figure of 1,750 tons, still more than five times the Philadelphia total.[2]

The Japanese authorities quickly set about obtaining as much display space as possible, just as they did for Philadelphia. Despite the size of the Fair site, the American organizers found themselves under enormous pressure from competing claims of the participating nations. However, Japan succeeded once again in securing a generous settlement that included 40,000 square feet in the Manufactures and Liberal Arts Building, 2,850 square feet in the Palace of fine Arts, and substantial spaces in the Educational, Women's, Horticultural, and several other major buildings, as well as 40,000 square feet on Wooded Island, a spit of land located in a lagoon near the United States Government Building. The intention had been for the island to be a haven of peace from the hubbub of the Fair, but the Japanese were allowed to use it for the construction of the Ho-oden [Phoenix Palace], an adaptation of the eleventh-century Ho-odo [Phoenix Hall] at Uji, a town south of Kyoto. The change of name symbolized the fact that the architecture of the building had also been altered for didactic purposes, so that its three main components could give visitors an idea of the style of three different periods. The north wing was Fujiwara or Late Heian Period (980–1185), based on both the original building at Uji and the Imperial Palace in Kyoto, with rounded posts, hinged shutters and blinds, and a display of historic bronzes, arms, armor, lacquerware, and pottery. The south wing reflected the Ashikaga or Muromachi Period (1333–1568), and was based on the famous Ginkakuji [Silver Pavilion] in Kyoto, with square posts and sliding screens. The interior of the central hall was a reproduction of a seventeenth-century castle, with modern wall paintings by students from Tokyo Art School.

The land around the Phoenix Palace was landscaped and planted in Japanese style, although the effect of a pocket of Eastern understatement set in the heart of the bombastic neoclassicism of the rest of the Fair may have been blunted by the presence on Wooded Island of the Hunter's Cabin, a monument to Davy Crockett and Daniel Boone! The Palace was presented to the City of Chicago and was one of the few structures to survive the Fair by more than a few months (most were soon looted or burned down), but it too eventually succumbed to a fire and was demolished in 1946. During the half century that it survived, however, it had a significant influence on American architects, in particular Frank Lloyd Wright, who collaborated with Louis Sullivan on some of the buildings of the Fair and began to work independently in 1893.[3]

Although the exotic building on Wooded Island, the seventh largest national pavilion in the Fair, was the most prominent Japanese contribution to the overall appearance of "The White City", many other aspects of Japanese life were displayed in addition to the main displays of modern arts and crafts in the Manufactures and Fine Arts buildings. There were exhibits of gardening, rice, tea, tobacco, razors, safes, and buttons, as well as photographs of railroad lines and statistics on education, life insurance, and crime, with the aim of parading Japan's efforts to catch up with the advanced nations of the West.[4]

"A NEW ORDER OF THINGS"

Japan was the only Asian nation granted a place in the prestigious setting of the Palace of Fine Arts, and even managed to get the amount of space allotted to it doubled in the course of the Fair. Because so many of the other Japanese displays were concerned with state-of-the-art industrial and social developments, care was taken to ensure that the exhibits selected for this honor were of the very highest quality and could be easily distinguished from the more commercial wares on view elsewhere. The Japanese commissioners were aware that their paintings and sculptures were unlikely to make as great an impression on the American public as their porcelain, cloisonné enamel, textiles, and metalwork. As a result, they made a great effort to persuade their hosts that the three separate areas eventually given to Japan in the Palace of Fine Arts should be used in a completely different way from the spaces occupied in the same building by America and the European nations. A contemporary commentator noted that:

Figure 4.
The entrance to the Japanese exhibit in the Palace of Fine Arts at the World's Columbian Exposition, Chicago, 1893. Photograph courtesy of New York Public Library.

> Recognizing the radical differences between Japanese art and that of the western world, the authorities of the Art Department of the Columbian Exposition did not bind Japanese art exhibitors exclusively to the rigid classification established for other nations, but urged that the exhibit be made thoroughly national in character – exactly such an exhibit as would be formed under a classification devised for an art exhibition to be held in Japan.[5]

If the official figures are to be believed, the effect of this concession was that no fewer than 270 of the 291 exhibits from all nations that gained admission to the Palace of Fine Arts, despite being defined as "decorative art", were Japanese. This is in complete contrast to the statistics for painting and sculpture, which show that only 24 out of 1,013 sculptures and 55 out of 7,357 paintings were Japanese.[6] Although other records of the Fair suggest slightly larger numbers of Japanese paintings and sculptures, there is no doubt that "works of decorative art" predominated in the Japanese display. Another commentator wrote that "the Japanese collection contained few pictures. It was largely made up of bronzes, carving in wood and ivory, lacquer, and embroideries."[7] The distinction between Art and Industrial sections had become a significant issue in Japan as early as 1881 when, for example, the cloisonné enamels of Namikawa Sosuke (see pages 254–5) were shown in the Art section at the second Naikoku Kangyo Hakurankai [National Industrial Exposition], while all other cloisonné artists who exhibited did so in the Industrial sections. The achievement of exhibition in the Art sections was perceived as mark of enhanced status and this must have made the selection process at Chicago an extremely delicate task, especially given the huge discrepancy in the spaces available: the area available in the Manufactures and Liberal Arts Building was fourteen times greater than that allotted in the Palace of Fine Arts. Another complicating factor was the dual purpose of the former building which, as its name implied, could include Remington typewriters and J.S. Bach's clavichord under the same roof! Even the knowledgeable Captain Frank Brinkley, who saw the "Works of Art" (his phrase) selected for Chicago at a preview in Tokyo, was unable to predict the ultimate division of some of the exhibits. He was confident that the pair of colossal cloisonné enamel vases and censer submitted by Suzuki Shirozaemon (see catalogue number 225 for one of the vases) would be excluded from the Palace of Fine Arts because "it is hard to wed politics with art",[8] but in fact they were prominently displayed there under a canopy on the ground floor at the west end of the East Court, and singled out for attention by Hubert Howe Bancroft in his massive *Book of the Fair*:

> From Shirozayemon Suzuki come the three largest pieces of cloisonné that have ever been fashioned. Two of them are vases and the third an incense-burner, the former nearly nine feet high, designed for exhibition and costing more than two years of labor. Their figures of birds and animals are symbolic of the seasons and the virtues, and are also of national significance. On the top are red and white stripes inlaid with silver stars, with chrysanthemums and other floral devices emblematic of the friendship existing between Japan and the United States.

Figure 5.
Japanese bronzes in the Manufactures and Liberal Arts Building at the World's Columbian Exposition, Chicago, 1893 from Hubert Howe Bancroft, *The Book of the Fair...* (Chicago and San Francisco, 1893), p.223.

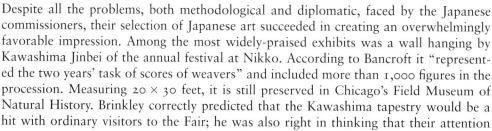

Despite all the problems, both methodological and diplomatic, faced by the Japanese commissioners, their selection of Japanese art succeeded in creating an overwhelmingly favorable impression. Among the most widely-praised exhibits was a wall hanging by Kawashima Jinbei of the annual festival at Nikko. According to Bancroft it "represented the two years' task of scores of weavers" and included more than 1,000 figures in the procession. Measuring 20 × 30 feet, it is still preserved in Chicago's Field Museum of Natural History. Brinkley correctly predicted that the Kawashima tapestry would be a hit with ordinary visitors to the Fair; he was also right in thinking that their attention would be drawn by a famous set of twelve hawks from the atelier of Suzuki Chokichi (see pages 64–5) that are now in the Imperial Collection. For the purposes of this catalogue, it is particularly interesting that a generalist like Bancroft should have been so struck not only by the huge cloisonné enamel vase, but also by two other pieces in the Khalili Collection that are almost certain to have been shown at Chicago. He mentions "Otake [Norikuni]'s bronze rooster, perched on a hollow stump, with a hen and chickens below, the feathers are wonderfully wrought, especially in the rooster's sweeping tail" (see catalogue number 231), as well as a porcelain vase by Miyagawa Kozan, "wave-patterned and with figures of dragons under the glaze" (see catalogue number 221), another work strongly commended by Brinkley.[9]

Brinkley was especially pleased with the selection of ceramics, noting that only a few objects were included in the Fine Art section and that the rest, in particular the "Yokohama School" (see pages 90–115), were relegated to the Manufactures Building – even though the division of the displays sometimes meant that leading artists exhibited in both buildings. Brinkley also praised the Japanese artists for their success in applying their skills to the creation of new types of product, a process already described on pages 64–7 in connection with metalwork: "the talent is there, just as abundantly as ever, and the only perplexity is to find directions in which it can be usefully exercised." He was less encouraging about sculpture in wood, ivory, and cast metal, where he thought that "the exporters in the Settlements", [i.e. Yokohama, Kobe, and other ports] had "exercised a vitiating influence", but he did have some good words to say about Takamura Koun's horse-chestnut wood carving of a baboon, characteristically described inaccurately by Bancroft as a gorilla carved from cherrywood.

204
PLATE
About 1890
Earthenware, painted and gilded
Diameter 37.2 cm.
Sealed *Dai Nihon Meizan sei*
[made by Meizan of great Japan]
Made by the Yabu Meizan
Workshop

205
PLATE
About 1890
Earthenware, painted and gilded
Diameter 27.7 cm.
Signed *Yabu Meizan*
Made by the Yabu Meizan Workshop

206
VASE
1890s
Earthenware, painted and gilded
Height 40.5 cm.
Signed *Kinkozan zo* [made by Kinkozan]
Made by the Kinkozan Workshop

207
VASE
About 1890
Porcelain, painted in underglaze blue,
brown, and green, and yellow enamel
Height 59.0 cm.
Signed *Kozan sei* [made by Kozan]
Made by the Miyagawa Kozan Workshop

The form of this exceptionally large vase is
based on Chinese porcelain of the Kangxi
Period (1662–1723). After the mid-1880s,
Chinese models, especially the porcelains
of the Qing Dynasty (1644–1912), became
an important source of design inspiration
for ceramics produced at the Miyagawa
Kozan Workshop.

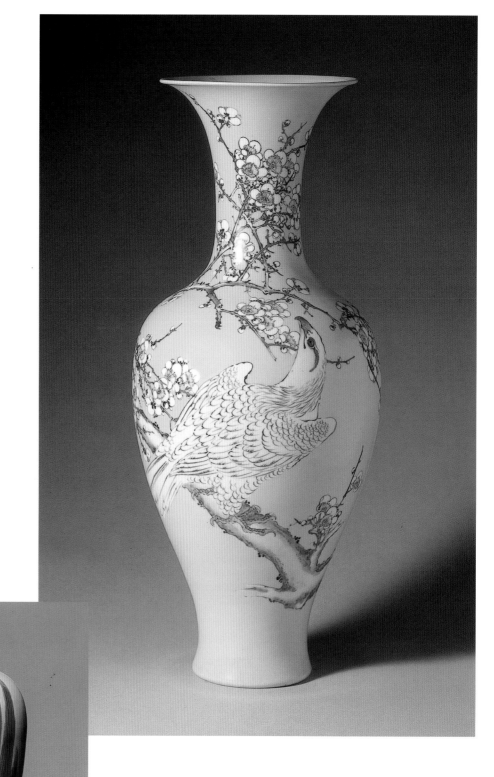

208
VASE
1890s
Porcelain, painted in underglaze blue on a
yellow enamel ground
Height 17.5 cm.
Signed *Makuzu-gama Kozan sei* [made by
Kozan at the Makuzu kiln]
Made by the Miyagawa Kozan Workshop

209
VASE
1890s
Porcelain, painted in underglaze red and
yellow on a pale green ground
Height 24.0 cm.
Signed *Makuzu-gama Kozan sei* [made by
Kozan at the Makuzu kiln]
Made by the Miyagawa Kozan Workshop

210
VASE
1890s
Porcelain, decorated in low relief on an
underglaze green ground
Height 49.1 cm.
Signed *Makuzu-gama Kozan sei* [made by
Kozan at the Makuzu kiln]
Made by the Miyagawa Kozan Workshop

211
VASE
About 1900–10
Porcelain painted in underglaze blue
Height 42.5 cm.
Signed *Makuzu Kozan sei* [made by
Makuzu Kozan]
Made by the Miyagawa Kozan Workshop

This striking vase is similar to one exhibited
by Kozan in the Paris Exposition of 1900.

212
VASE
About 1890
Porcelain, painted in underglaze blue
and black
Height 54.1 cm.
Signed *Arita Fujisaki sei* [made by Fujisaki
of Arita]
By Fujisaki Tahei (dates unknown)

The design on this vase depicts *chidori*
[literally, "thousand-birds"] in flight above
turbulent foaming waves. These birds,
creatures more of the imagination than of
nature, have been a favorite motif since the
Heian Period (794–1185). Fujisaki, who
worked in the porcelain center of Arita in
the southern island of Kyushu, won prizes
at Paris in 1900 and at the fifth Naikoku
Kangyo Hakurankai [National Industrial
Exposition] (1903).

213
TEAPOT
About 1900
Porcelain painted in underglaze blue
Height 22.1 cm.
Signed *Makuzu Kozan sei* [made by
Makuzu Kozan]
Made by the Miyagawa Kozan Workshop

A teapot of similar form was exhibited at
the Paris Exposition of 1900.

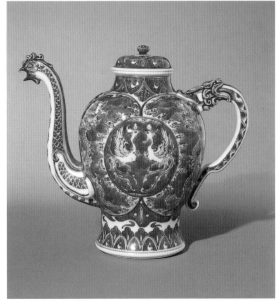

214
VASE
About 1890
Cloisonné enamels worked in silver wire;
silver rim and foot
Height 13.3 cm.
Signed *Kyoto Namikawa* [Namikawa
of Kyoto]
Made by the Namikawa Yasuyuki Workshop

The use of silver for the mounts becomes
more common in Namikawa Yasuyuki's
work after this period; silver mounts are
seen on the pair of double gourd vases by
Namikawa, decorated with butterflies,
acquired from the World's Columbian
Exposition in Chicago by the Tokyo
National Museum in 1893. At the third
Naikoku Kangyo Hakurankai [National
Industrial Exposition] (1890), Namikawa
Yasuyuki exhibited a "small flower-vase
with slender neck decorated with chrysanthemums",[1] which was perhaps similar to
this piece. Most cloisonné enamel was
shown in the Industrial section; only
Namikawa Yasuyuki, Namikawa Sosuke,
and three other artists exhibited in the
Art section.

1. Suzuki Norio and Sakakibara Satoru, *Nihon
   no shippo* [Japanese Cloisonné Enamel]
   (Kyoto, 1979), p.238.

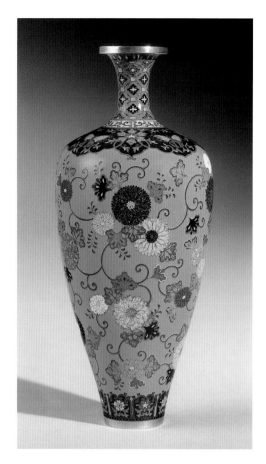

215
VASE
About 1890
Cloisonné enamels worked in silver and
gold wire
Height 22.2 cm.
Signed *Kyoto Namikawa* [Namikawa of
Kyoto]
Made by the Namikawa Yasuyuki Workshop

A more muted version of this formal leaf
pattern is seen on a double gourd vases
acquired by Tokyo National Museum in
1893.

216
PAIR OF VASES
Early 1890s
Cloisonné enamels worked in silver wire;
wood stands
Height 31.1 cm.
Signed *Kyoto Namikawa* [Namikawa of
Kyoto]
Made by the Namikawa Yasuyuki Workshop

These vases, particularly large for the work of Namikawa Yasuyuki, would presumably have been made either for a special presentation or for a major exhibition. It can only be suggested that this may have been the World's Columbian Exposition in Chicago in 1893, though they do not closely resemble the vases bought by the Tokyo National Museum from that exhibition. Quite possibly this marks the point at which Namikawa began to change his style to a more overall pictorial style, such as

was remarked upon by the judges of the fourth Naikoku Kangyo Hakurankai [National Industrial Exposition] in 1895. The pair are complete with original lacquered wood stands carved with scroll feet and six supports; designs for similar stands are recorded in *Kyo shippo mon'yo shu* [A Collection of Designs for Kyoto Enamels], an undated selection of Namikawa designs.[1]

1. Yoshida Mitsukuni and Nakahara Kenji, *Kyo-shippo mon'yo shu* [A Collection of Designs for Kyoto Enamels] (Kyoto, 1981), p.35.

217
PANEL
1890s
Musen enamels
36.0 × 53.5 cm.
Attributed to the Ando Jubei Workshop

During the 1890s, the snow-capped cone
of Mount Fuji was a favorite subject for
pictorial enamel panels; a very similar
panel by Namikawa Sosuke was exhibited
in the World's Columbian Exposition in
Chicago in 1893 and illustrated in a booklet published by Sosuke in 1896.[1] The mirror-like surface suggests the work of Ando
Jubei, though this is not certain.

   1. Anon., *S. Namikawa, Inventor of Cloisonné
      Without Wires, Member of Board of Imperial
      Artists, Decorated with Medal of Green
      Ribbon* (Undated pamphlet, latest dated
      quotation Feb. 9, 1896).

▶

218
CABINET
About 1885–95
Hardwood and carved red lacquer with
cloisonné enamel
213 × 136 × 62.0 cm.
Attributed to the Namikawa Sosuke and
Honda Workshops

The enamel panels on this grand piece of
furniture are evidently the work of two
different artists, working in wholly unrelated
styles. The upper doors and the lower tier
of drawers, here attributed to Honda, are
in the formal style from which Namikawa
Sosuke (and Namikawa Yasuyuki) had at
this date broken free. The upper doors
have borders of patterns unrelated to the
central scene, while the other doors have
no borders and are worked in styles that
minimize the wire instead of emphasizing
it. The doors of the central and lower
sections are here attributed to Namikawa
Sosuke, and it is interesting to see him
working in three styles; the blue-gray-
ground doors in *shosen* and *musen* are
typical of his oeuvre (see for example,
catalogue number 264). The yellow-green-
ground sliding doors are very much in the
style of the Shijo artist Watanabe Seitei
(1851–1918), using the scratchy, almost
scribbled, wirework that apparently only
Namikawa could do.

219
Incense Burner
About 1890
Iron; with gold, silver, and *shibuichi*
Height 18.6 cm.
Sealed *Mitsutaka*
By Kajima Ikkoku II (1846–1925)

For Kajima Ikkoku II, see number 87. He
won the *hojo* [certificate of merit] at the
third Naikoku Kangyo Hakurankai
[National Industrial Exposition] of 1890.

220
Box
About 1890–1900
Iron with gold, *shibuichi*, and *shakudo*;
silver liner
6.5 x 11.0 cm.
Signed *Shomin* with a seal
By Unno Shomin (1844–1915)

221

VASE

About 1893

Porcelain, painted in underglaze blue and red on a deeply incised and enameled ground

Height 37.6 cm.

Signed *Dai Nihon Kozan sei* [made by Kozan of great Japan]

Made by the Miyagawa Kozan Workshop

This piece accords very closely with the description given by Captain Frank Brinkley of a vase exhibited by Kozan at Chicago in 1893:

> [The] noble vase covered from neck to base with a deeply incised diaper of wave pattern. The diaper is graded

above and below with perfect skill, and the potter has contrived that the glaze in the depressed portions shall show white, while on the surface it has a delightful green hue. Round the neck the diaper passes into the more open form of curling wave crests, and here the chisel has been used so strongly that the interstices of the design are semi-transparent, imparting an idea of lightness and delicacy that cannot be too much praised. Round the body are twined two dragons, one in liver-red, the other in a deep rich blue, the colors being under the glaze. This grand vase goes to Chicago

under the name of Miyagawa Kannosuke.[1]

Kannosuke is an error for Hannosuke, the given name of Miyagawa Hanzan (1859–1940), Miyagawa Kozan's adopted son and heir who had a strong influence on the increased sophistication of works of the Kozan workshop in the early 1890s. This is probably the earliest documented piece attributed to him.

1. Frank Brinkley, *Artistic Japan at Chicago: A Description of Japanese Works of Art Sent to the World's Fair* (Yokohama, 1893), p.30.

222
VASE
1890s
Porcelain, painted in yellow and white
enamels on a coral ground
Height 32.5 cm.
Signed *Makuzu-gama Hanzan sei* [made by
Hanzan at the Makuzu kiln]
Made by the Miyagawa Kozan Workshop

It is particularly rare to find a work actually
signed by Miyagawa Hannosuke (Hanzan,
later Makuzu Kozan II, see page 331). The
style of this piece is typical of the later
Meiji-Era movement towards more open
styles of decoration.

223
JAR
About 1895
Cloisonné enamels worked in silver wire
Height 23.8 cm.
Signed *Kyoto Namikawa* [Namikawa of
Kyoto]
Made by the Namikawa Yasuyuki Workshop

This new style or phase of Namikawa's work
was identified by the judges of the fourth
Naikoku Kangyo Hakurankai [National
Industrial Exposition] in 1895, who commented:

> Yasuyuki has been good at making pieces
> of cloisonné with designs of dragon,
> phoenix, colorful birds and flowers, and
> similar traditional subject matter, using
> intricate wirework. However, in this exhi-
> bition there are fewer such pieces and the
> designs have changed; here flowers of the
> four seasons, with birds of exquisite color-
> ing, are set on to a black background
> color, forming a picture far beyond a mere
> pattern. But he seems still to adhere to the
> traditional methods of depiction, not
> attempting to imitate brushwork as do
> some other persons. He places great
> emphasis on fine wirework and on a flaw-
> less surface with no pitting or bubbles,
> achieved through painstaking study of
> glazing and firing. For this he has been
> awarded the first prize.[1]

1. Suzuki Norio and Sakakibara Satoru, *Nihon
   no shippo* [Japanese Cloisonné Enamel]
   (Kyoto, 1979), p.247.

224
PANEL
About 1893
Cloisonné and *musen* enamels
74.5 × 37.0 cm.
Signed *Hokusai Taito hitsu* [painted by
Hokusai Taito]
Attributed to Kawade Shibataro (dates
unknown) after a design by Katsushika
Hokusai (1760–1849)

This panel, depicting Hotei (see number
126) on his sack unrolling a scroll which
falls down towards a *karako* [Chinese boy],
corresponds with the description of a panel
exhibited at the World's Columbian
Exposition, Chicago (1893): "Hotei (a god
of fortune) with a child. Panel", after the
name of Kawade Shibataro.[1]

1. Department of Publicity and Promotion,
   *World's Columbian Exhibition, Revised
   Catalogue, Department of Fine Arts* (Chicago,
   1893), cat. no. 79a.

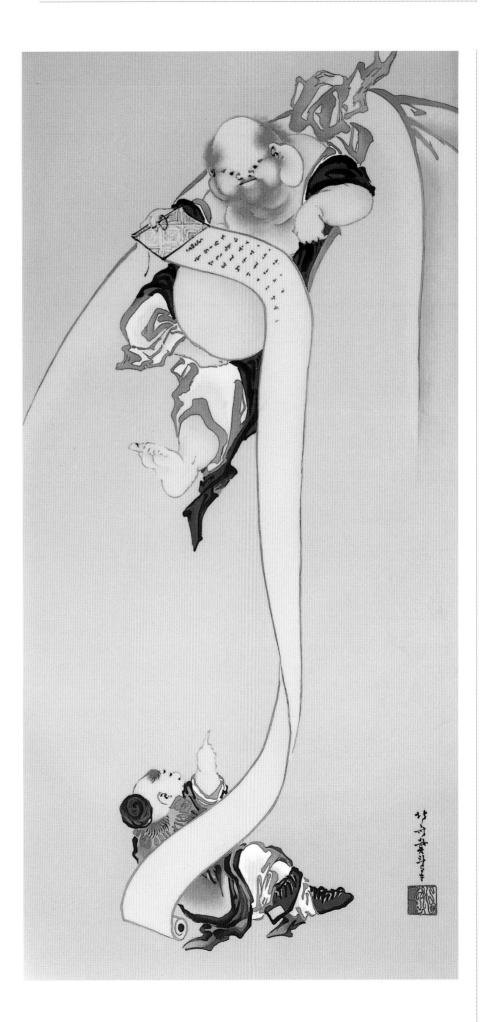

225
VASE
About 1893
Cloisonné enamels worked in silver wire
Height 172 cm.
By Suzuki Shirozaemon (dates unknown)
Designed by Araki Kanpo (1831–1915)

This vase originally formed part of a
three-piece garniture made for the World's
Columbian Exposition in Chicago (1893).
In the catalogue, the vases of the garniture
are described as being eight feet, eight inches
(264 cm.) tall, "the largest examples of
cloisonné enamel ever made".[1] The construction of this vase suggests that there is a
section missing between the main body of
the vase and its foot, though this might not
account for the great difference in size noted
here. It seems probable that the carved
wooden pedestals, as described in the catalogue, were included in the measurement.

The catalogue is at pains to explain the
iconography, and to credit the artists:

> The designs on the vases were the idea of
> Mr. Shin Shinwoda, Special Counsellor
> for Arts of the Japanese Commission to
> the World's Columbian Exposition.
> Their manufacture was undertaken by
> Mr. Shirozayemon Suzuki, of Yoko-
> hama, with the co-operation of Mr.
> Seizayemon Tsunekawa, at Nagoya. The
> original design was painted by Mr.
> Kanpo Araki, of Tokyo, and the black
> ink sketch on the copper was made by
> Kiosai Oda, of Nagoya. The men directly
> in charge of making the vases were
> Gisaburo Tsukamoto and Kihio ye
> Hayashi, of Toshima ... The bronze
> American eagle [on the censer] was
> made by Yukimune Sugiura, of Tokyo.
> The general design represents the sea-
> sons of the year ... and the two eagles,
> autumn; while on the reverse ... a winter
> scene is portrayed. The same design also
> symbolizes three virtues – wisdom, hon-
> esty and strength, symbolized respective-
> ly, by the dragon, chickens and eagles.

> Another idea conveyed by the front
> design is, that the dragon typifies China;
> the two eagles, Russia; the group of
> chickens, the Corean Islands, and the
> rising sun, the Empire of Japan; while
> the bronze eagle on the cover of the
> censer is the American eagle.

> The silver stars inlaid on the horizontal
> red and white stripes ... are emblematic
> of the American stars and stripes ...

"Shin Shinwoda" (Shioda Shin or Masashi,
1837–1917), one of the most important art
administrators and educators of the Meiji
Era, took part in on-the-spot preparations
for the Vienna (1873) and Philadelphia
(1876) and was instrumental in setting up
the influential Ryuchikai Art Association in
1879.[2] He is recorded as responsible, as
"the well-known art designer", for the
concept of the pair of screens by Ando
Jubei exhibited at the Liège Exposition in
1905 (see number 310). "Kanpo Araki"
(Araki Kanpo, 1831–1915), who made the
original design, was a celebrated *Nihonga*
[Japanese-style painting] artist, and a
member of the Art Committee of the
Imperial Household and of the Royal
Society of Arts in London. The description
quoted above gives a remarkable insight
into the care devoted to the design of
exhibition wares by the Japanese authorities.
It also makes clear the number of artists
and master craftsmen, to say nothing of the
skilled workers, involved in the making of
such a piece.

1. Department of Publicity and Promotion,
   *World's Columbian Exhibition, Revised
   Catalogue, Department of Fine Arts* (Chicago,
   1893), pp. 392 and 393, cat. no. 375.
2. Tokyo National Museum, *Chosa kenkyu
   hokokusho Onchi zuroku* [Research Report on
   the *Onchi zuroku*] (Tokyo, 1997), p.47.

226

PAIR OF VASES
About 1890–95
Cloisonné and *musen* enamels; *shakudo*
rims and feet
Height 38.5 cm.
Signed with the *Sakigake* seal of Namikawa
Sosuke
Made by the Namikawa Sosuke Workshop

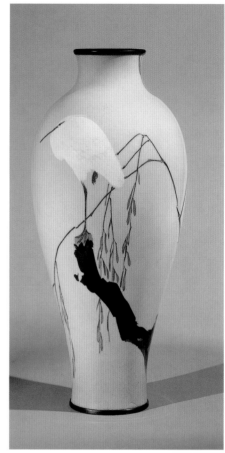

227

INCENSE BURNER
About 1895
Iron, with gold, copper, bronze, and *shakudo*
Height 15.3 cm.
Signed *Chishinsai Katsunobu* and sealed
Chishin
By Ishikawa Katsunobu (*b.* 1869)

Ishikawa Katsunobu was born in Mito. He
was apprenticed to Namekawa Sadakatsu
(see number 228) in 1882, becoming an
independent artist in 1890, and working in
Tokyo. His teacher, Sadakatsu, exhibited a
"Globular iron censer carp and turtle top",
probably similar to this piece, at the World's
Columbian Fair in 1893.[1] Captain Frank
Brinkley describes it thus:

> ... it is in the purest style, the decoration
> consisting of carp chiseled in high relief,
> the lid surmounted by a tortoise.
> Nothing could be simpler or less ornate.
> But each of the carp is alive. Only a
> Japanese master can carve such things
> out of iron ...[2]

Ishikawa Katsunobu exhibited two pieces
at the Paris Universal Exposition in 1900.[3]

1. Department of Publicity and Promotion,
   *World's Columbian Exhibition, Revised
   Catalogue, Department of Fine Arts* (Chicago,
   1893), part x, department k, p.158, cat. no.
   340.
2. Frank Brinkley, *Artistic Japan at Chicago: A
   Description of Japanese Works of Art Sent to
   the World's Fair* (Yokohama, 1893), pp. 3–4.
3. Tokyo Kokuritsu Bunkazai Kenkyujo [Tokyo
   National Research Institution of Cultural
   Properties] (ed.), *Meijiki bankoku hakurankai
   bijutsuhin shuppin mokuroku* [Catalogues of
   Objects Exhibited at International Expositions
   in the Meiji Era] (Tokyo, 1997), Q168, R818.

228

PAIR OF VASES
About 1895
Silver, with *shibuichi* and *shakudo*
Height 34.7 cm.
Signed *Tadakatsu* and *Sadakatsu*, sealed
Ittokusai
By Namekawa Sadakatsu (1848–after 1900)

Like many other leading Meiji-Era metal-workers, Namekawa Sadakatsu was born in Mito. He started his own business at the age of twenty-five and moved to Tokyo, where he stayed with and studied under Unno Shomin (see numbers 395–6). He exhibited in Chicago in 1893 and Paris in 1900, and in the third and fourth Naikoku Kangyo Hakurankai [National Industrial Expositions] in 1890 and 1895, where he won a *hojo* [certificate of merit] and a *myogisho* [technical excellence prize]; as well as in the Varied Industries section at St. Louis in 1904.

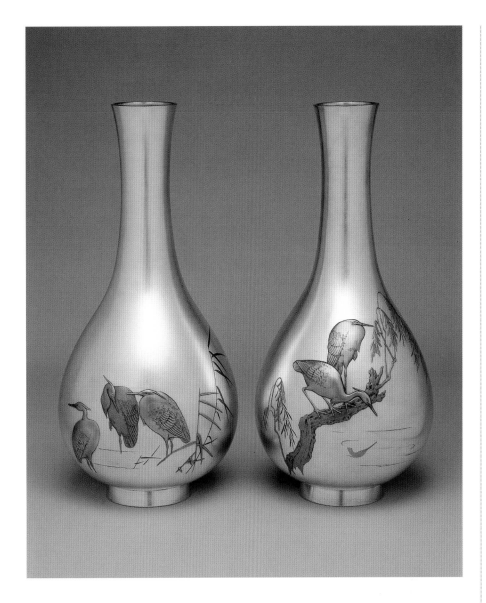

229

BOX
About 1895
Lacquer, with an inset panel of silver with *shibuichi* and gold
6.2 × 16.0 × 11.3 cm.
Signed *Shukyo*, with a seal *Shin*
By Tsukada Shukyo (1848–1914)

For Tsukada Shukyo, see number 398. He seems to have made a specialty of cigar and cigarette boxes, showing examples of similar size to the present piece in 1895, 1910 and 1914; that shown in 1895 also has lacquered sides.[1]

1. "Works of Living Artists Exhibited at the Spring Exhibition (1895) of the Japan Art Association", *Magazine of Japanese Art* (Tokyo, 1895), vol. 2, no. 3.

A corner of the Japanese Section of the
Manufactures and Liberal Arts Building
at the World's Columbian Exposition,
Chicago, 1893, from *The Graphic History
of the Fair...* (Chicago, 1894), p.146.
Courtesy of the Chicago Historical Society.

230
INCENSE BURNER
1870s
Bronze, the eyes in gilt and *shakudo*
410 × 132 cm.
Signed *Dai Nihon Tokyo imonoshi Hayashi Harusada kore o tsukuru* [this was made by the master bronze-caster Hayashi Harusada of Tokyo in great Japan]

This immense *koro* [incense burner], the tallest object in the Khalili Collection, is one of the most ambitious surviving examples of the great flowering of the bronze-caster's art that occurred during the early years of the Meiji Era. Consisting of thirteen major components, many of them, in turn, made from several separate castings, it brings together a wide variety of motifs, chiefly from Chinese legend. As well as the flute- and drum-playing demons and the easily recognizable eagle and dragon, the low-relief decoration on the sides of the container features three other creatures, the *kirin*, with the body of a deer, the hooves of a horse, the tail of an ox, and a single horn on its head; the *ho-o* [phoenix]; and the *shishi*, a lion-like creature. The two smaller beings on the side of the bowl are the Chinese sage Kinko (see also number 79), who is always shown riding on the back of a carp, and Kannon, the most popular of the *bodhisattva*, saintly Buddhist beings who renounce their own enlightenment, remaining on earth to relieve the sufferings of mankind (see number 163).

Despite the ambitious scale of this bronze, there is no mention of its maker, Hayashi Harusada, in any of the records of exhibitions held in Japan, Europe, or America during the Meiji era. It is all the more fortunate, therefore, that a little known popular guide to the World's Columbian Exposition includes an illustration that shows visitors to the Manufactures and Liberal Arts Building admiring a very similar and equally large bronze (see opposite). It is tempting to imagine that the Japanese figure in the foreground might be Hayashi Harusada himself.[1]

1. [Anon.], *The Graphic History of the Fair, Containing a Sketch of International Expositions, A Review of Events Leading to the Discovery of America, and a History of the World's Columbian Exposition, Held in the City of Chicago, State of Illinois, May 1 to October 31, 1893* (Chicago, 1894), p.146.

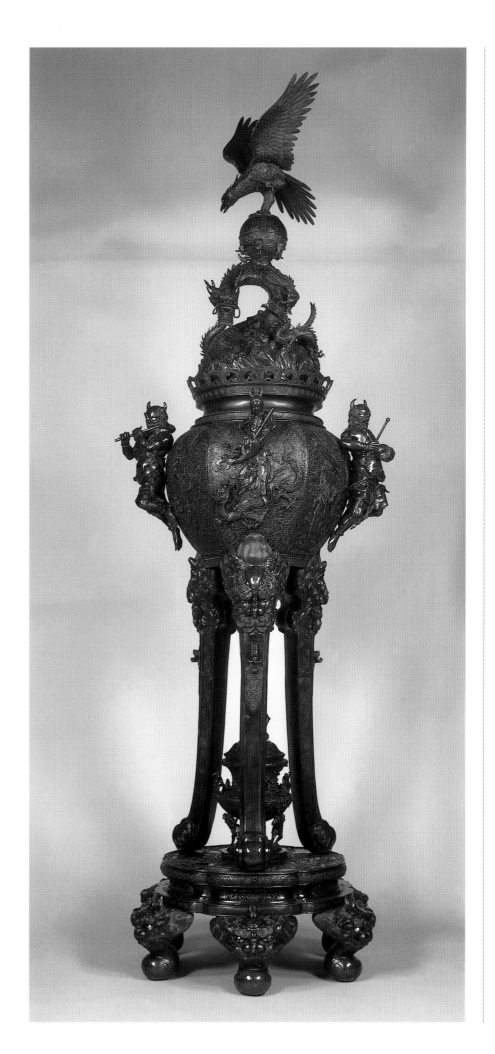

231
Group
About 1893
Bronze, with gold and *shakudo*
Height 126.5 cm.
Sealed *Toyo Nihonkoku Tokyo
Nihonbashi-ku Sukiya-cho bijutsu seisakujo
Maruki kojo no in* [seal of the Maruki
Workshop, the art workshop in Sukiya
Street, Nihonbashi Ward, Tokyo, Japan,
East Asia]
By Otake Norikuni (*b.* 1852)
Produced by the Maruki Company

The Maruki Company, of which little
appears to be recorded, made or commissioned fine quality bronze and ivory works.
Otake Norikuni (see also numbers 31 and
172) learned from his father Otake Eijiro,
whom he succeeded in 1871. This bronze is
reputed to have been exhibited at the
World's Columbian Exposition in Chicago
(1893). The name of the company is not
recorded in the catalogue, but the artist
Otake Norikuni is listed as exhibiting a
cockerel group.[1] A further figure of a single
cockerel of markedly similar appearance
was exhibited by Otake Norikuni at the
Paris Exposition of 1900[2] and another version of this group, with the same seal, is in
the collections of the National Museums of
Scotland.

1. Department of Publicity and Promotion,
   *World's Columbian Exhibition, Revised
   Catalogue, Department of Fine Arts* (Chicago,
   1893), part x, department k, group 139,
   no. 12, Otake Norikni [sic].
2. *Bijutsu gaho, Daini rinji zokan bijutsu gaho;
   Pari hakurankai shuppin kumiai seisakuhin*
   [Extra Issue no. 2 of Fine Arts Magazine
   Containing Illustrations and Descriptions of
   Products of the Paris World Exposition
   Exhibitor's Union] (Tokyo, 1900), unpaginated.

232
FIGURE OF AN EAGLE
About 1890–1900
Bronze, with gilding and *shakudo*
Height 235 cm. (overall); 152 cm. (bird)

A similar bird stood at the entrance to the
Japanese exhibit in the Fine Arts Pavilion
at the World's Columbian Exposition held
in Chicago in 1893 (see fig. 4, p.215).

233
FIGURE OF AN EAGLE
About 1890–1900
Bronze, with gilding and *shakudo*;
wood stand
Height 116 cm. (overall); 45.0 cm. (bird)
Signed *Gyoko saku* [made by Gyoko]
By Akasofu Gyoko (dates unknown)

For Akasofu Gyoko, see numbers 93
and 234.

234
FIGURE OF A HAWK
About 1890–1900
Silvered bronze with gilding and *shakudo;*
lacquered stand with gilding
Height 96.0 cm. (overall); 24.0 cm. (bird)
Signed *Gyoko saku* [made by Gyoko]
By Akasofu Gyoko (dates unknown)

For Akasofu Gyoko, see numbers 93
and 233.

235
**INCENSE BURNER IN THE FORM
OF A HAWK**
About 1893–94
Silver, with gold and *shakudo;* lacquer
stand mounted in silver
Height 68.3 cm. (overall); 34.2 cm. (bird)
Signed *Takachika* and sealed *zo* [made]
By Sano Takachika (dates unknown)

This is a good example of the extent to
which the "incense burner" shape had
become something of a formality by the
mid-Meiji Era; the term is used here simply
because the bird's back is detachable. A
gold and silver group of a heron and crow
on a bronze stump by Sano Takachika (see
also numbers 61, and 328–9) was exhibited
in the 1894 Nihon Bijutsu Kyokai [Japan
Art Association] exhibition. This piece
bears a strong resemblance to the famous
set of twelve hawks exhibited by Suzuki
Chokichi (see number 1) at the World's
Columbian Fair, Chicago, in 1893.[1]

1. Tokyo National Museum, *Umi o watatta Meiji
   no bijutsu* [World's Columbian Exhibition of
   1893 Revisited] (Tokyo, 1997), cat. no. 81.

236
VASE
Late 1890s
Porcelain, painted in underglaze blue on a
molded ground
Height 28.2 cm.
Signed *Makuzu-gama Kozan sei* [made by
Kozan at the Makuzu kiln]
Made by the Miyagawa Kozan Workshop

237
VASE
Late 1890s
Porcelain, painted in yellow enamel on a
coral red ground
Height 37.2 cm.
Signed *Makuzu-gama Kozan sei* [made by
Kozan at the Makuzu kiln]
Made by the Miyagawa Kozan Workshop

238
VASE
Late 1890s
Porcelain, painted in underglaze red, blue,
blue-gray and green on a yellow ground
Height 47.0 cm.
Signed *Makuzu-gama Kozan sei* [made by
Kozan at the Makuzu kiln]
Made by the Miyagawa Kozan Workshop

The range of underglaze colors applied to
this vase demonstrates the ever-increasing
technical sophistication of Makuzu wares
in the years between the Chicago (1893)
and the Paris (1900) expositions.

239
VASE
1890s
Porcelain, painted in underglaze blue on a
yellow ground
Height 37.0 cm.
Signed *Dai Nihon Seifu zo* [made by Seifu
of great Japan]
By Seifu Yohei III (1851–1914)

Seifu Yohei III (see page 333) showed
six pieces at the fourth Naikoku Kangyo
Hakurankai [National Industrial
Exposition] of 1895, where he was the
only artist to win a *meiyo shohai* [prize of
honor]; he also showed at Chicago in 1893
and Paris in 1900.

240

DOUBLE-GOURD VASE
1890s
Porcelain, painted in white slip and
underglaze copper-red
Height 23.2 cm.
Signed *Tozan sei* [made by Tozan]
By Ito Tozan (1846–1920)

The somewhat exaggerated form and
less-than-perfect technical decoration would
suggest a date earlier than 1900, when this
artist's works, as illustrated in the Fine Arts
Catalogue of the Paris Exposition, show a
more advanced style. Ito Tozan was born in
Awata, Kyoto; like many other Kyoto potters, he seems to have made both porcelain
and earthenware. He exhibited frequently,
winning prizes at Amsterdam (1883), Paris
(1889), Chicago (1893), the fourth Naikoku
Kangyo Hakurankai [National Industrial
Exposition] (1895), Paris (1900), and the
fifth Naikoku Kangyo Hakurankai [National
Industrial Exposition] (1903). In 1895, he
won a *nito myogi shohai* [second prize for
technical excellence] for an earthenware
flower vase with a design of a group of
butterflies. He was awarded the Green
Ribbon in 1899, and was made a *Teishitsu
Gigeiin* [Imperial Artist] in 1917, three
years before his death.

241

BOX
About 1900
Cloisonné enamels; silver rims
8.3 × 20.3 × 15.2 cm.
Nagoya school, perhaps by Kumeno Teitaro
(1865–1939)

This box is tentatively attributed to Kumeno
Teitaro, on account of a description by
Harada of a similar piece:

> ... a cigarette-box, made by Kumeno
> Teitaro of Nagoya, about three and a
> half inches long and a little less wide, lit-
> erally covered with tiny butterflies, most
> delicate wire being used to give form to
> two sets of wings and a pair of antennae
> for each butterfly. At an arm's length the
> box appears to be covered simply with
> shapeless dots, and it is only by a closer
> examination that thousands of butter-
> flies of perfect shapes and beautiful col-
> ors can be appreciated. How the minute
> work has been done is still a mystery to
> many of his friends.[1]

1. Jiro Harada, "Japanese Art and Artists of
   Today – VI. Cloisonné Enamels", *The Studio*
   (June 1911), p.275.

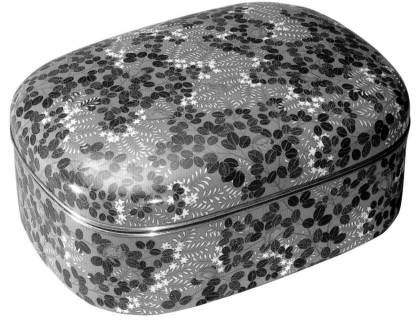

242

BOX FOR WRITING UTENSILS AND BOX FOR WRITING PAPER
About 1875–1900
Wood, lacquered in *takamaki-e*, *hiramaki-e*, *togidashi-e*, *nashiji*, and *roiro*; gilt metal water-dropper, silver fittings and edgings
4.5 × 21.5 × 25.0 cm. (box for writing utensils); 15.0 × 32.0 × 38.7 cm. (box for writing paper)
Signed in two places *Homin*
By Uematsu Homin (1845–1902)

Uematsu Homin was a leading representative of the late Edo-Period style of lacquering associated with the merchant class. He and his son Hobi collaborated on a pair of boxes shown at the Paris Exposition of 1900.[1]

The design on the lids refers to a dream of Yukiyoshi, a famous calligrapher of the Sesonji school, which flourished in the Kamakura Period (1185–1333). Yukiyoshi once wrote the characters for a tablet adorning the gateway to a certain temple in Omi. Years later, when he was confined to bed with a serious illness, a heavenly being appeared to him in a dream saying that the tablet, which had fallen into a state of disrepair, had been restored and that someone would soon come to ask him to write on it again.

1. Tokyo Kokuritsu Bunkazai Kenkyujo [Tokyo National Research Institution of Cultural Properties] (ed.), *Meijiki bankoku hakurankai bijutsuhin shuppin mokuroku* [Catalogues of Objects Exhibited at International Expositions in the Meiji Era] (Tokyo, 1997), Q360.

243
INCENSE BURNER
About 1900
Cloisonné enamels worked in silver wire
Height 45.7 cm.

The overall shape of this incense burner, with its bracket handles and attached stand of almost High Victorian elaboration, can be compared to a piece in the John R. Young Collection attributed to Ando,[1] and to an incense burner by Ando illustrated by Harada in 1911.[2] The wirework is extremely good, using the techniques of sculpting and tapering wire that seem to have begun in about 1899.

1. Oliver Impey and Malcolm Fairley, *The Dragon King of the Sea: Japanese Decorative Art of the Meiji Period from the John R. Young Collection* (Ashmolean Museum, Oxford, 1991), cat. no. 15.
2. Jiro Harada, "Japanese Art and Artists of Today – VI. Cloisonné Enamels", *The Studio* (June 1911), p.273.

244
CHARGER
About 1900
Bronze, with *shakudo*, copper and gilding; silver rim
Diameter 99.0 cm.
Signed *Yukimune kore o sen* [this was engraved by Yukimune], with a seal *Sugiura*
Engraved by Sugiura Yukimune

For Sugiura Yukimune, see numbers 7 and 8. The treatment of the crows on this out-size dish, which was most probably made for exhibition, closely resembles a study of a crow perched on a skull by Sugiura Yukimune shown at the Paris Universal Exposition in 1900.[1]

1. *Bijutsu gaho, Daini rinji zokan bijutsu gaho Pari hakurankai shuppin kumiai seisakuhin* [Extra Issue no. 2 of Fine Arts Magazine Containing Illustrations and Descriptions of Products of the Paris World Exposition Exhibitor's Union] (Tokyo, 1900), unpaginated.

245
ORNAMENT
About 1900
Bronze, silver, gilding, *shibuichi*,
and *shakudo*
13.1 × 48.7 cm.
Signed *Joun saku* [made by Joun]
By Oshima Joun (1858–1940)

This is an example of the mutual cross-fertilization of styles in the late Meiji Era. Earlier Meiji decorative art had been a factor in the development of *Art Nouveau* in Europe and America; in fact the very term *Art Nouveau* comes from the name of a shop, *L'Art Nouveau*, opened in Paris by Samuel Bing, a dealer who specialized in Japanese artifacts. Here we see the sinuous curves of mature Western *Art Nouveau* redeployed in Japan for the creation of a piece probably made for overseas exhibition or sale (see below). The highly versatile Oshima Joun, the son of a cast-metal worker, Oshima Takajiro, succeeded to the family business in 1877. By 1879, he had eleven assistants and was working with the Sanseisha Company of Tokyo on a great bronze figure of the Dragon King of the Sea, made for the second Naikoku Kangyo Hakurankai [National Industrial Exposition] of 1881 (see number 172 for a very similar group). He taught at Tokyo Art School from 1887 until 1932. A similar but slightly larger group of five carp was exhibited in the Paris Exposition of 1900[1] and another group of carp was exhibited in the Japan-British Exhibition of 1910, where it is listed under the name of the exhibitor Yezawa Kingoro,[2] whereas in the unpaginated Japanese edition it is under the name of Oshima Joun. Joun was praised for his renditions of carp by Harada in 1911.[3]

1. *Bijutsu gaho, Daini rinji zokan bijutsu gaho; Pari hakurankai shuppin kumiai seisakuhin* [Extra Issue no. 2 of Fine Arts Magazine Containing Illustrations and Descriptions of Products of the Paris World Exposition Exhibitor's Union] (Tokyo, 1900), unpaginated.
2. Office of the Imperial Japanese Government Commission to the Japan-British Exhibition, *An Illustrated Catalogue of Japanese Modern Fine Arts Displayed at the Japan-British Exhibition, London, 1910* (Tokyo, 1910), p.184.
3. Jiro Harada, "Metal-Work", *The Studio* (Feb. 1911), p.101.

ENAMEL

A NEW ART FORM

In Japanese cloisonné enameling, different areas of colored glass paste, separated from one another by thin strips of copper, gold, or silver ribbon (*cloisons,* placed edgeways and attached to a copper base, are fired at about 1550–1650° F. until the paste melts and fuses. Because the glass shrinks when it is fired, the process of application followed by firing has to be carried out more than once; just as in lacquering (see page 186), the best finish is achieved by gradually building up the surface in thin layers. Japanese enameling is also similar to Japanese lacquerwork in the importance attached to the final polishing, which is carried out with a range of different materials including stones, charcoal, and pulverized horn. Sometimes the enamels are built up in relief (*moriage*, see catalogue numbers 274 and 308), or the copper base can be engraved with designs which remain visible when covered with translucent or transparent enamel (*tomei shippo* or *tsuki jippo*, see catalogue numbers 284–6).

Although versions of cloisonné enameling have been known in the West for nearly two millennia and in China from about the fourteenth century, it made little headway in Japan until a few decades before the beginning of the Meiji Era. The Japanese are thought to have used enamels since about 1600, but only for the partial decoration of smaller metal objects such as sword-fittings or the recessed handles of sliding wood and paper screens. Most of this earlier enameling was not true cloisonné, but rather the simpler "champlevé" [literally, "raised field"] technique, in which the enamel pastes are placed in hollows carved into the metal base. One family of enamelers, the Hirata, did use true cloisonné techniques to decorate sword-fittings, and the delicacy of their craftsmanship, with minute gold wire *cloisons* and translucent rather than opaque enamel pastes, often laid over a ground of gold foil, was perhaps a foretaste of the miraculous results that would be achieved in the Meiji Era. Looking at the jewel-like delicacy of Hirata work, one can well understand why the Japanese refer to enameling as *shippo*, literally the "seven treasures" referred in Buddhist texts which can include gold, silver, glass, lapis lazuli, agate, coral, and shell. But even the Hirata family confined itself to the manufacture of small areas of decoration that were applied to still smaller metal objects. For most of the Edo Period, vessels with all-over enameling do not seem to have been made in Japan, and although Chinese enameled wares were presumably imported, no attempt was made to copy them.

Suddenly, towards the middle of the nineteenth century, cloisonné enamel vases, bowls, and plates began to be manufactured. By the 1880s Japanese enamels were already one of the wonders of the world, and during the first decade of the twentieth century they outstripped anything that had been achieved before in the medium. Another twenty years on, Japanese enameling was in decline, and today it would be impossible to reproduce the achievements of the great craftsmen whose masterpieces are illustrated on the following pages. This rapid rise and fall, perhaps an extreme example of the trajectory followed by Meiji-Era decorative art as a whole, is partly explained by the very fact that the craft of cloisonné enameling had no strong cultural or technical roots in Japan. In the case of ceramics and lacquer, when foreign demand for the best quality goods had started to decline, it was possible to compensate by reorienting production towards an elite, conservative domestic market that had remained largely unaffected by the stylistic upheavals of the late nineteenth and early twentieth centuries. No such market existed for cloisonné beyond the occasional order for presentation vases from corporations or the Imperial Household Agency, and the Agency seems to have stockpiled a large number of earlier pieces which it retained, often for many years, until they were needed for some formal occasion. Another factor in the decline of cloisonné enameling may have been the very novelty and unpredictability of the technique. Throughout the Meiji Era, the leading masters vied to improve the quality of pastes and refine firing techniques so as to achieve larger areas of colored enamel unsupported by *cloisons*. The proportion of rejects must have risen as these technical experiments became ever more ambitious and more risky, contributing to the very high price of the best pieces that survived the rigorous quality control of the most prestigious workshops. Of course, this must have happened to a certain extent in ceramics (one extreme example is described on page 333), but even a bold technologist like Miyagawa Kozan, working in the relatively well-established medium of porcelain, was probably able to predict the results of his experiments with reasonable accuracy. Tireless enamel innovators like Namikawa Sosuke and Namikawa Yasuyuki, on the other hand, were in completely uncharted territory, often with more expensive raw materials than their competitors in other media. Unlike porcelain, even those pieces that emerged undamaged from repeated firings then had to be laboriously polished, a process that could take weeks in the case of larger items.

According to tradition, the Japanese "re-invention" of cloisonné enameling took place in 1838 and is credited to one man, a metal gilder called Kaji Tsunekichi (b. 1803) who was inspired by the chance purchase of a Chinese cloisonné dish. Kaji decided to make a copy of the dish, and is supposed to have sought help from a potter who understood the similar techniques involved in applying enamel colors over glazed porcelain. This technology, known in Japan since the seventeenth century (see page 330), may have played a part in the early development of Japanese enamels on metal, and in fact Namikawa Sosuke, one of the two great Namikawas discussed in detail below, produced enameled porcelains early in his career. There is no way of knowing whether the story of Kaji Tsunekichi is even partly true, but it does seem that the earliest Japanese cloisonné vessels surviving today, with dark-colored, rough enameling, were made in the 1850s, or perhaps a little earlier, in a crude imitation of Chinese prototypes. Kaji's work is said to have been noticed by Tokugawa Keisho, a relative of the shogun and *daimyo* of the area around Nagoya. In about 1850, Tokugawa retained Kaji to make cloisonné wares, and Nagoya would be one of the three main centers of the enamel industry in the Meiji Era, the others being the old and new capitals, Kyoto and Tokyo. If traditional accounts are to be believed, Kaji taught his skills, under conditions of strict confidentiality, to a certain Hayashi Sogoro (d. 1896), who in turn passed on some of the secrets to Tsukamoto Kaisuke (1828–87). To help preserve the mysteries of the craft, Kaisuke and his fellow pupil Tsukamoto Gisaburo were made to find out for themselves what raw materials their master had used for his glass pastes. In the case of the blue pastes, vital for copying the predominantly blue background of Chinese cloisonné, it turned out that Hayashi had made them by recycling crushed blue medicine-bottles. Up to the 1860s there are still many gaps in our information regarding the identity of the founding fathers of Japanese enameling, but we are on firmer historical ground with Hayashi Kodenji, Tsukamoto Kaisuke's pupil. Hayashi Kodenji (see catalogue numbers 275–9) became independent in 1862; together with Ando Jubei (see catalogue numbers 273–4), he would dominate the Nagoya enameling industry until the end of the Meiji Era.

Just as the first examples of Japanese porcelain made in the seventeenth century (see page 330) are based on Chinese examples, so the first Japanese enameled vessels made in the 1850s and 1860s look at first glance like clumsy versions of their contemporary Chinese counterparts. This is hardly surprising, given that the Chinese already had some four centuries' experience of enameling and had worked for four centuries in such a conservative style that, to the untrained eye, there is not a lot of difference between works of the fifteenth century and those of the nineteenth century. Among the earliest examples of Japanese cloisonné in a Western collection are a kettle and a tiered box acquired at the 1867 Paris Exposition by the South Kensington Museum in London (now the Victoria and Albert Museum). Although purchased as "antique", these two pieces were probably new, or nearly new, and they demonstrate that Japanese enamels had still not broken free of Chinese models. Blue backgrounds predominate, and there are large numbers of *cloisons*, serving not so much as a design feature but simply to hold the enamel pastes in place during the difficult firing process. The cracked and pitted surface is a far cry from the almost superhuman, mirror-like perfection of later work, and the colors are still opaque, even muddy.

After this slow start, the Japanese enamelers of the Meiji Era were quick to exploit the new medium, so much so that only six years after the Paris show the Nagoya Cloisonné Company, founded in 1871 by Muramatsu Hikoshichi and Tsukamoto Jin'emon, the elder brother of Kaisuke, won a first prize at the Vienna Exhibition in 1873. In 1875 Tsukamoto Kaisuke and his two sons moved from Nagoya to Tokyo, where they joined

Figure 1.

The studio of Namikawa Yasuyuki before 1903, photograph from Ponting, *In Lotus-land Japan* (London, 1910), opposite p.239.

the German Heinrich Ahrens Company and engaged a German chemist and polymath, Gottfried Wagener (1831–92) as their technical consultant – Wagener was one of many foreign experts who were invited to Japan to assist in the process of industrial and social reform. Wagener spent the last twenty-four years of his life in Japan, advising craftsmen, building the first modern seismograph, and, as we have already seen, playing a crucial role in shaping Japan's contribution to the 1873 Vienna World Exhibition (see pages 30–1). He was also involved in preparations for the 1876 Philadelphia Exhibition and the first and second National Industrial Expositions in 1877 and 1881. For three years until 1878, Wagener provided Tsukamoto with technical know-how that he had acquired from his time in the Paris workshop of Dumas. Although the exact nature of his advice is not recorded, Wagener had previously worked as adviser on glazes and colors to the porcelain factories in Arita and it is likely that he helped apply this expertise to the manufacture of enamels, including more sophisticated chemical compounds which – crucially for cloisonné – could withstand expansion and contraction during firing without leaving tell-tale cracks. This development helped put enamels in the forefront of design development during the later Meiji period, since it made it possible to break free of the mannered wirework of the Chinese tradition and develop a new and essentially Japanese pictorial style. Wagener made a further contribution to this process by helping develop the so-called *shosen* [minimized wires] enameling in which the wires, generally very thin, are still visible but are used to delineate or emphasize part of the design as in a drawing, without necessarily forming a cell. Although both *shosen* and the related *musen* (apparently wireless, although not really so) techniques would later be trumpeted by Namikawa Sosuke his own inventions, Wagener wrote that:

> the most admired enamel pictures without any visible wires [go] back
> to the training which these masters received in the German company ...
> the technically admired qualities of delicate shading or strong contrasts
> between two colors, without any visible wire, are due solely to manual
> ability and little tricks.[1]

THE TWO NAMIKAWAS

Wagener's advice was a critical factor in the careers of the two most famous enamelers of the Meiji Era, Namikawa Yasuyuki (1845–1927) of Kyoto and Namikawa Sosuke (1847–1910) of Tokyo. Despite their identically pronounced surnames (which are, however, written with quite different Chinese characters), the two men were unrelated, an odd fact which only served to heighten Western amazement at the seemingly miraculous output of their respective factories. Wagener is known to have come into direct contact with Namikawa Yasuyuki in the course of his experiments with enamels, and when the Ahrens Company closed, its workers were taken on by Muramatsu Hikoshichi in Nagoya and Namikawa Sosuke in Tokyo. The influence of European chemical technology was thus felt in all three of the great enamel-producing centers of Meiji Japan. Sosuke and Yasuyuki were very different personalities. Sosuke was always keen to promote his technical inventions, his advertising constantly boasting, as we have seen, of his *shosen* and *musen* enamels, "first manufactured in 1889",[2] even though several commentators were doubtful that he had actually discovered a way of dispensing with *cloisons* altogether. Yasuyuki seems to have been altogether more conservative and retiring, though no less dedicated. His (or, more accurately, his employees', since both Yasuyuki and Sosuke were entrepreneurs rather than craftsmen) painstakingly precise method of working enables us to trace the development of his techniques and style with some accuracy. The first tentative chronology for Yasuyuki's enamels was recently mapped out by the two editors of the Khalili Collection catalogues and their research has provided us with a framework for dating enamels by other leading workshops.[3]

In the early unsigned enamel vase (see catalogue number 246) attributed to Namikawa Yasuyuki, we see the first signs of the struggle to break free of the technical restrictions imposed by this difficult medium. Translucent enamels are used alongside opaque ones, although they are not perfectly controlled, and a partially successful effort is made to reduce the reliance on wires to hold the enamels in place. The colors are different from those usually seen in Chinese cloisonné, but many of the motifs are closely copied from Chinese models. In another unsigned vase, perhaps made about five years later, and identifiable as Yasuyuki's work because the design appears in a pattern book associated with his workshop, the wirework is already more delicate, the colors are more even, and the surface can take a high polish. A similar piece was exhibited at Nuremburg in 1885. The magnificent pair of vases with wooden stands (see catalogue number 216), which probably date from the 1890s and must surely have been intended for exhibition, represent the culmination of Namikawa's early style and prefigure the growing pictorialism of his later work. The prestige of cloisonné enameling at this time is reflected in the large number of pieces that were shown at the fourth National Industrial Exposition, held in 1895, and particularly in the proportion admitted to the Fine Art section, where twelve exhibitors showed a total of twenty-one pieces; in the Industrial section, 134 exhibitors showed 970 pieces.

Yasuyuki's gold and silver wirework, which had always been very carefully worked, became increasingly delicate during the 1890s. Towards the end of the decade he started to shape and taper the wire, as in catalogue number 255, and by about 1905 (see catalogue number 305), he was able to use it just as painter would use ink, for example, to trace the outline of a bamboo stem. One of the finest works by Namikawa Yasuyuki in the Khalili Collection, a tiny incense burner dating from about 1910 and included in the section on Artists to the Imperial Household (see catalogue number 385), is in effect, a painting in enamel. The complicated borders of the 1880s and 1890s have been almost completely eliminated, and the sculpted gold and *shakudo* play as important an expressive role as do the muted enamels.

In 1891, Mary Crawford Fraser, wife of the British Ambassador, visited the third National Industrial Exposition and afterwards made some notes in her diary which summed up the differences between the work of Namikawa Yasuyuki of Kyoto and Namikawa Sosuke of Tokyo:

> The enamels are many and beautiful, and there is no shadow of doubt that modern enamel in every way surpasses the old. There are two very distinct styles in the modern enamel, the Kyoto makers preferring to work in the true cloisonné, where the design is laid on in gold or copper wire in geometrical (or at any rate purely decorative) patterns of bewildering fineness ... The Tokyo enameler works on different lines, and produces panels which look like fine paintings on porcelain, or monochrome vases and dishes ...[4]

We have seen how Namikawa Yasuyuki would later become less "bewildering" and "geometrical" and would strive for more painterly effects. His rival Namikawa Sosuke, by contrast, had already, by 1891, been making enamels in a distinctive pictorial style for the best part of ten years, often in collaboration with the painter and designer, Watanabe Seitei (1851–1918, see catalogue number 257). Recent discussion of Japanese enamels has tended to focus closely on technical changes and, in particular, on the technical difference between the works of the two Namikawas. It is worth remembering, however, that both of them were moving in much the same stylistic directions during the last decades of the Meiji Era. Both of them transcended the Chinese origins of their craft, improved it with European technology, and added the vital Japanese qualities of infinite patience and meticulous attention to detail. Their work, alongside that of Makuzu Kozan in porcelain, did much to fix a particular idea of "Japanese design" in the Western consciousness during the early years of the present century.

NOTES

1. Quoted in Gunhild Avitabile, "Gottfried Wagener (1831–1892)", in Oliver Impey and Malcolm Fairley (eds.), *The Nasser D. Khalili Collection of Japanese Art* (London, 1995), vol. 1, p.104.
2. Basil H. Chamberlain, *A Handbook for Travellers in Japan* (London, 1901), advertising supplement, p.41.
3. See Oliver Impey and Malcolm Fairley, "Japanese Cloisonné Enamel", in Oliver Impey and Malcolm Fairley (eds.), *The Nasser D. Khalili Collection of Japanese Art* (London, 1994), vol. 3, pp. 20–48.
4. Mary Crawford Fraser, *A Diplomat's Wife in Japan* (Edited by Hugh Cortazzi; New York and Tokyo, 1982), pp. 156–7.

ENAMEL

The enamels selected for this section, which charts the extraordinarily rapid development of the art of cloisonné enameling in Meiji-Era Japan, are mostly arranged by place of manufacture, starting with the work of Namikawa Yasuyuki of Kyoto, continuing with the unrelated Namikawa Sosuke of Tokyo, and concluding with the many workshops that operated in Nagoya.

246
VASE
1870s
Cloisonné enamel worked in gilt metal wire; gilt metal mounts
Height 24.2 cm.
Attributed to the Namikawa Yasuyuki Workshop

This is one of the early unsigned works of Namikawa and among the earliest recorded. The colors combine opaque, transparent, and clear enamels on a colored ground in a way the artist was to perfect later. At this stage, the control of the transparent colors is far from perfect. To overcome this, he has added many tight scrolls around the foot and the neck which serve to hold the enamel on the body, but around the blade motifs there are larger areas with no wire. This must be an attempt to obviate the necessity for wire, but here it is a failure, for the color is filled with small cracks that are certainly unintentional.

247
JAR
About 1890
Cloisonné enamels worked in silver and gilt
copper wire; gilt bronze rims, foot and finial
Height 15.5 cm.
Signed *Kyoto Namikawa* [Namikawa of
Kyoto]
Made by the Namikawa Yasuyuki Workshop

248
VASE
About 1895
Cloisonné enamels worked in silver wire;
silver rim and foot
Height 18.2 cm.
Signed *Kyoto Namikawa* [Namikawa of
Kyoto]
Made by the Namikawa Yasuyuki Workshop

A similar, but smaller, pair of vases was
acquired by Tokyo National Museum from
the World's Columbian Exposition of 1893
in Chicago.

249
VASE
About 1900–03
Cloisonné enamels worked in silver wire; silver rims, foot, and finial
Height 22.9 cm.
Signed *Kyoto Namikawa* [Namikawa of Kyoto]
Made by the Namikawa Yasuyuki Workshop

This vase marks three new departures in the work of Namikawa. Firstly, there is only one scene: that is, the vase has a "front" and a subsidiary "back", though the back is still much decorated. Secondly, the silver wire has not been simply cut in ribbons, as before, but has been tapered and sculpted to depict as well as to outline. Thirdly, the vase is much lighter that its predecessors. After this time, the work of Namikawa Yasuyuki is always comparatively light in weight, presumably because better techniques enabled him to achieve the same effects with thinner colors, a copper body, and fewer firings. This vase can be dated to before 1903, as it is visible, actually being worked on in Namikawa Yasuyuki's studio, in a photograph published in 1903.[1]

1. Herbert Ponting, "The Work of a Japanese Craftsman: A Little Workshop Producing Marvellous Cloissonné [sic] ware", *World's Work*, vol. 5, no. 4 (Feb. 1903), pp. 180–2.

250
INCENSE BURNER
About 1900
Cloisonné enamels worked in gold wire; silver rims and foot
Height 11.8 cm.
Signed *Kyoto Namikawa* [Namikawa of Kyoto]
Made by the Namikawa Yasuyuki Workshop

This is a striking example of Namikawa Yasuyuki's ability to shade enamel colors into one another, a technique he developed in the late 1890s. Many of his later works also demonstrate a mastery of carefully controlled color gradation, but the method is different from that employed here. In the later pieces, the gradation of the ground color is not used pictorially and does not attempt to place the design proper in real space.

251
VASE
About 1900–05
Cloisonné enamels worked in silver wire; silver rim and foot
Height 17.3 cm.
Signed *Kyoto Namikawa* [Namikawa of Kyoto]
Made by the Namikawa Yasuyuki Workshop

The depiction of the wisteria is extraordinarily naturalistic within the canons of the style of *Nihonga* [Japanese-style painting] followed by Namikawa Yasuyuki. The use of wire as an entity in itself, where it does not enclose enamel, is visible here for the first time, the tendrils tailing off into sprigs of wire.

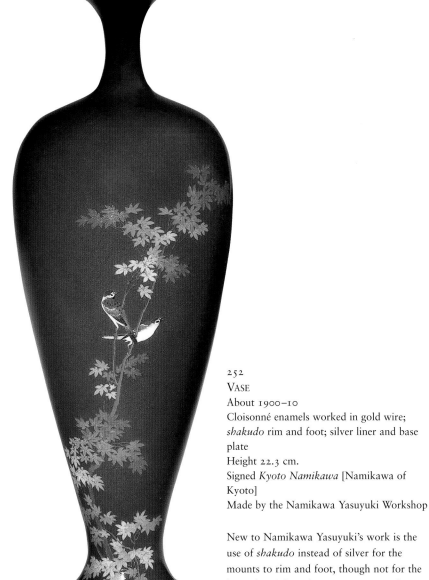

252
VASE
About 1900–10
Cloisonné enamels worked in gold wire; *shakudo* rim and foot; silver liner and base plate
Height 22.3 cm.
Signed *Kyoto Namikawa* [Namikawa of Kyoto]
Made by the Namikawa Yasuyuki Workshop

New to Namikawa Yasuyuki's work is the use of *shakudo* instead of silver for the mounts to rim and foot, though not for the base plate. The color, too, appears to be a new one, a rich deep plum shade.

253
BOX
About 1905–10
Cloisonné enamels worked in silver wire; gilt metal rims, feet and base
3.6 × 7.8 × 5.5 cm.
Signed *Kyoto Namikawa* [Namikawa of Kyoto]
Made by the Namikawa Yasuyuki Workshop

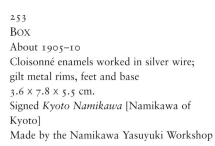

254
VASE
About 1905–10
Cloisonné enamels worked in gold and silver wire; *shakudo* rim and foot; silver base plate
Height 24.5 cm.
Signed *Kyoto Namikawa* [Namikawa of Kyoto]
Made by the Namikawa Yasuyuki Workshop

The leaves and stems are depicted in the most advanced technique in sculpted and tapered wire, the narrow tendrils tapering off from thinning green enamel to silver wire alone.

255
INCENSE BURNER
About 1903–10
Cloisonné enamels worked in silver wire; silver rims, base, and feet
Height 8.6 cm.
Signed *Kyoto Namikawa* [Namikawa of Kyoto]
Made by the Namikawa Yasuyuki Workshop

Namikawa Yasuyuki tended to use green (as here), brown, or blue for the ground color on his later pieces. Landscape was never a common subject matter for enamelers, since depiction of landscape on this small scale poses several problems in miniaturization; one is the illustration of leaves of trees. It is interesting to see here the first use of end-sections of silver wire to depict leaves: the wire has been cut to the required cross-section in ribbons.

256
VASE
About 1905-10
Cloisonné enamels worked in silver wire;
silver rim and foot
Height 17.7 cm.
Signed *Kyoto Namikawa* [Namikawa of
Kyoto]
Made by the Namikawa Yasuyuki Workshop

The startling, almost abstract, depiction of
the hydrangea is enhanced by the use of
metal squares and other shapes to give an
effect akin to that of *kirikane* in lacquer,
while the leaves are comparatively naturalistic. The white ground (a late ground color),
entirely plain at the back, increases the
sense of modernism and novelty.

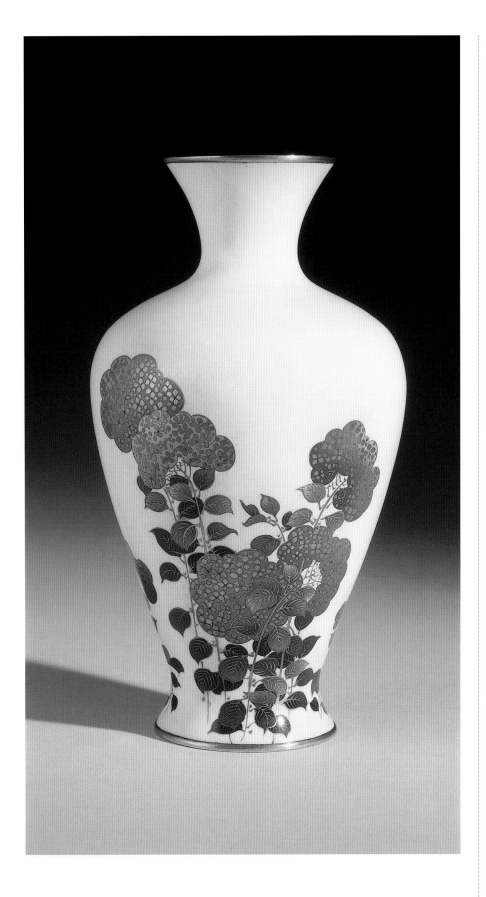

257
TRAY
About 1890
Musen and cloisonné enamels worked in
silver wire
Width 29.7 cm.
Signed *Seitei*
Attributed to the Namikawa Sosuke
Workshop, from a design by Watanabe
Seitei (1851–1918)

This is one of several enamels from the
Namikawa Sosuke Workshop, both signed
and unsigned, that are based on designs by
the painter and book illustrator Watanabe
Seitei. Around the edge of the tray, not
concealed by the metal rim, is a key-fret
border, presumably present for technical
reasons only, as it does not enhance the
design. Namikawa was later able to
dispense with such borders altogether.

258
TRAY
About 1890–95
Musen and cloisonné enamels; *shakudo* rim
Width 27.7 cm.
Signed *Seitei*
Sealed *Sakigake*
Made by the Namikawa Sosuke Workshop

Namikawa Sosuke seldom used a matte
ground; when he did, it was apparently in
order to evoke the atmospheric effect of an
ink painting, even though there is some
color on this piece.

259
TRAY
1890–1895
Musen and cloisonné enamels worked in
silver and gold wire
Width 29.7 cm.
Sealed *Sakigake*
Made by the Namikawa Sosuke Workshop

Namikawa Sosuke was certainly signing his
work by 1893, for a pair of vases datable
to that year in the British Museum, London,
is signed by him. The tray is assigned to
this relatively early period on account of
the pitted quality of the white enamel
(apparently a difficult color), a defect
which Namikawa had overcome by 1895,
the year of the fourth Naikoku Kangyo
Hakurankai [National Industrial
Exposition]. The shading on the bodies of
the birds and the restrained use of gold
wire might suggest a later date, but comparison with later pieces demonstrates that
there were technical as well as aesthetic
advances after this piece was made.

260
VASE
About 1890–95
Cloisonné enamels worked in silver wire;
copper alloy rim and foot
Height 18.9 cm.
Sealed *Sakigake*
Made by the Namikawa Sosuke Workshop

261
VASE
About 1895
Translucent cloisonné enamels on a silver
body; silver rim and foot
Height 16.0 cm.
Sealed *Sakigake*
Made by the Namikawa Sosuke Workshop

The first recorded use of *tomei shippo*, the
use of transparent enamel over a decorated
metal body, by Namikawa Sosuke was in
1893, when he made two such vases for
the twenty-fifth wedding anniversary of the
Emperor and Empress; these are illustrated
in Namikawa Sosuke's 1896 booklet.[1] The
Empress wrote a special commendation of
these pieces. The difference between this
technique and that of Namikawa's favored
shosen and *musen* could hardly be more
marked. It seems likely that he would have
made such wares only to special order.

1. Anon., *S. Namikawa, Inventor of Cloisonné
   Without Wires, Member of Board of Imperial
   Artists, Decorated with Medal of Green
   Ribbon* (Undated pamphlet, latest dated
   quotation Feb. 9, 1896).

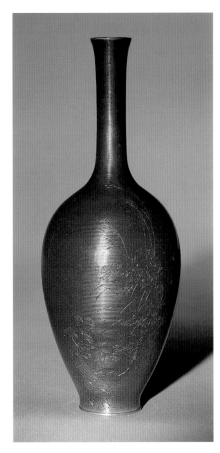

262
VASE
About 1890–95
Musen and cloisonné enamels worked in
silver wire; copper alloy rim and foot
Height 51.3 cm.
Sealed *Sakigake*
Made by the Namikawa Sosuke Workshop

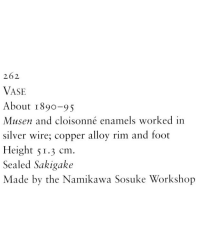

263
PLAQUE
About 1890
Cloisonné enamels
46.0 × 33.8 cm.
Signed and sealed *Seitei*
Made by the Namikawa Sosuke Workshop
after a design by Watanabe Seitei (1851–1918)

264
PANEL
About 1896
Musen enamels
37.4 × 52.0 cm.
Signed and sealed *Seitei* with a *kao*
[cursive monogram]
Made by the Namikawa Sosuke Workshop
from a design by Watanabe Seitei
(1851–1918)

This panel was exhibited in Kyoto in spring
1896.[1]

1. [Anon.], "Works of Living Artists
   Exhibited at the Spring Exhibition
   (1896) of the Japan Art Association",
   Magazine of Japanese Art (Tokyo, 1896).

265
VASE
About 1895–1901
Musen enamels; *shakudo* rim and foot
Height 30.5 cm.
Sealed *Sakigake*; inscribed in gold lacquer
Jamuzu-kun ni okuru Meiji sanjuyonnen
jugatsu Sakuma Kozaburo [Presented to
Mr James by Sakuma Kozaburo, October
Meiji 34 (1901)]
Made by the Namikawa Sosuke Workshop

Unusually in the work of Namikawa
Sosuke, there is no visible use of wire at
all, apart from in the signature. A large
enamel panel with similar decoration of
cherry trees in mist, worked in the same
techniques, was exhibited at the fourth
Naikoku Kangyo Hakurankai [National
Industrial Exposition] in 1895 and is
illustrated in Namikawa Sosuke's 1896
booklet.[1] Thus, in the seven intervening
years, either there was no change in
Sosuke's depiction of this type of scene or
else the vase was made earlier and the
inscription added separately in 1902; this
latter possibility appears the more likely.

1. Anon., *S. Namikawa, Inventor of Cloisonné*
   Without Wires, Member of Board of Imperial
   Artists, Decorated with Medal of Green
   Ribbon (Undated pamphlet, latest dated
   quotation Feb. 9, 1896).

266
VASE
About 1900
Musen and cloisonné enamels; copper alloy
rim and foot
Height 22.6 cm.
Sealed *Sakigake*
Made by the Namikawa Sosuke Workshop

267
TRAY
About 1900
Musen and cloisonné enamels; *shakudo* rim
Width 29.8 cm.
Sealed *Sakigake*
Made by the Namikawa Sosuke Workshop

The white enamel is clear and not pitted.
The use of the wire merely as a hint, rather
than as a depiction, is particularly
noticeable here.

268
TRAY
About 1900
Musen and cloisonné enamels; *shakudo* rim
Width 27.6 cm.
Sealed *Sakigake* and with an unread seal
Made by the Namikawa Sosuke Workshop
after an unknown artist

269
TRAY
About 1900
Musen and cloisonné enamels; *shakudo* rim
30.8 x 26.0 cm.
Sealed *Sakigake* and *Korin*
Made by the Namikawa Sosuke Workshop
after a design by Ogata Korin (1658–1716)

Almost certainly Sosuke was working
from a sketch attributed to or a print
after the great Rimpa artist Ogata Korin
(1658–1716). The technique of dripping wet
paint on to wet paint, typical of the Rimpa
artists, is here brilliantly captured in *musen*
[wireless enamels].

270
VASE
About 1900–10
Musen and cloisonné enamels; *shakudo* rim
and foot
Height 29.2 cm.
Sealed *Sakigake*
Made by the Namikawa Sosuke Workshop

271
VASE
About 1900–10
Musen enamel; *shakudo* rim and foot
Height 35.8 cm.
Sealed *Sakigake*
Made by the Namikawa Sosuke Workshop

272
VASE
About 1900–10
Musen and cloisonné enamels worked
in gold and silver wire; copper alloy rim
and foot
Height 22.6 cm.
Sealed *Sakigake*
Made by the Namikawa Sosuke Workshop

273
INCENSE BURNER
About 1900–05
Cloisonné enamels worked in gold and
silver wire; silver rim and foot; carved
wood stand
Height 22.9 cm.
With the silver wire seal of Ando Jubei
Made by the Ando Jubei Workshop

This superb incense burner amply
demonstrates the great variety of styles
available from the Ando Company.

274
BOX
About 1910
Moriage enamel; silver rims; silk brocade
lining
7.6 × 17.8 × 13.7 cm.
With the silver wire seal of Ando Jubei
Made by the Ando Jubei Workshop

A box in this technique by Ando was
exhibited at the Japan-British Exhibition
(London, 1910).[1]

1. Office of the Imperial Japanese Government
   Commission to the Japan-British Exhibition,
   *An Illustrated Catalogue of Japanese Modern
   Fine Arts Displayed at the Japan-British
   Exhibition, London, 1910* (Tokyo, 1910),
   no. 180.

275

PAIR OF VASES

About 1900

Cloisonné enamels worked in silver wire;
silver rims and feet; wood stands

Height 14.9 cm.

Signed *Aichi Hayashi Ko* [Hayashi Ko(denji)
of Aichi]

Made by the Hayashi Kodenji Workshop

276

VASE

About 1900–05

Cloisonné enamels worked in silver wire

Height 30.7 cm.

Signed *Nagoya Hayashi saku* [made by
Hayashi of Nagoya], and with the stamped
lozenge seal of Hayashi Kodenji

Made by the Hayashi Kodenji Workshop

277
JAR
About 1900–05
Cloisonné enamels worked in gold and silver
wire; silver rims and foot; wood stand
Height 21.5 cm.
Signed *Nagoya Hayashi zo* [made by
Hayashi of Nagoya] and with the stamped
lozenge seal of Hayashi Kodenji
Made by the Hayashi Kodenji Workshop

Namikawa Yasuyuki had mastered the
technique of tapered and sculpted wire
by 1899, and other factories rapidly
followed suit. It is interesting to note the
extraordinary difference in style between
Hayashi's bird vase, catalogue number 279,
and his better-known and more intricate
examples. Hayashi was also known for his
tsuiki enamels, demonstrating the great
diversity of product of one of the larger
commercial companies.

278
PLATE
About 1910
Cloisonné enamel worked in silver and gold
wire; silver rim and foot
Diameter 18.5 cm.
Marked with the Hayashi lozenge seal
Made by the Hayashi Kodenji Workshop

279
VASE
About 1910
Musen enamels with silver beaks and eyes;
silver rim and foot
Height 62.0 cm.
Signed *Dai Nihon Hayashi Kodenji zo*
[made by Hayashi Kodenji of great Japan]
Made by the Hayashi Kodenji Workshop

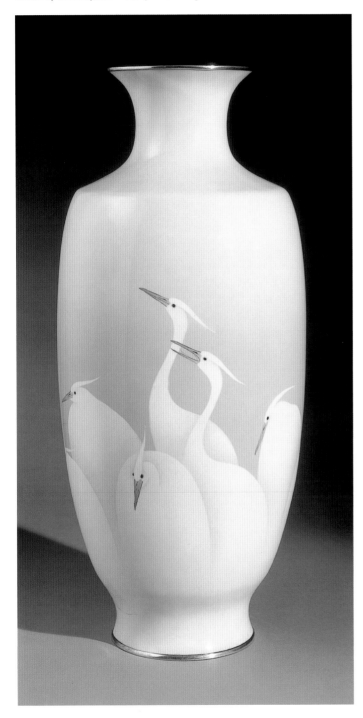

280
VASE
About 1905
Plique-à-jour enamels worked in silver wire
Height 15.3 cm.
Attributed to the workshop of Hattori Tadasaburo

281

JAR

About 1900–05

Cloisonné enamels worked in silver wire; silver rims and foot, gilt metal base

Height 32.0 cm.

Signed *Aichi Hayashi saku* [made by Hayashi of Aichi] and with the lozenge-shaped mark of Hayashi Kodenji

Made by the Hayashi Kodenji Workshop

282

VASE

About 1900–05

Cloisonné enamels worked in gold and silver wire; silver rim and foot; gilt metal base

Height 9.5 cm.

Signed *Nagoya Hayashi zo* [made by Hayashi of Nagoya] around the lozenge-shaped Hayashi mark

Made by the Hayashi Kodenji Workshop

290
LAMPSHADE
About 1905
Plique-à-jour enamels worked in silver wire;
silver rims
Height 20.9 cm.

291
VASE
About 1900
Musen enamels; silver mounts
Height 36.7 cm.
Sealed *Hattori*

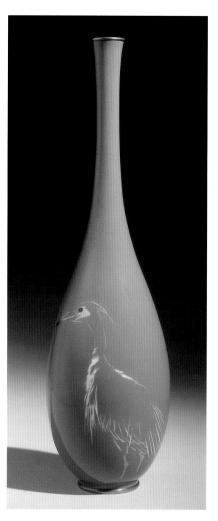

▶
293
VASE
About 1900
Cloisonné enamels worked in silver wire;
gilt metal rim and foot
Height 24.3 cm.
Stamped mark *Kume*
Made by the Kumeno Teitaro Workshop

292

HANGING FLOWER VASE
About 1900–10
Musen enamels; silver mounts
Height 30.0 cm.
Attributed to Gonda Hirosuke (1865–1937)

This unusual shape is first seen in eighteenth-
century bronzes. The attribution to Gonda
is based on the container's similarity to
pieces exhibited by him at Paris in 1900.[1]

1. *Bijutsu gaho, Daini rinji zokan bijutsu gaho;
   Pari hakurankai shuppin kumiai seisakuhin*
   [Extra Issue no. 2 of Fine Arts Magazine
   Containing Illustrations and Descriptions of
   Products of the Paris World Exposition
   Exhibitor's Union] (Tokyo, 1900), unpaginated.

The Japanese section in the Palace of Fine Arts was in the West Pavilion next to the Bulgarian, Portuguese, and Italian displays, and covered 6,800 square feet compared to 2,850 at Chicago. The official record suggests that there were about 250 exhibits which a rigorous selection procedure had whittled down from the 713 originally submitted. The display eventually included 64 Japanese-style paintings, 28 Western-style paintings, 39 sculptures, and about 120 examples of decorative art including metalwork, lacquer, carving in ivory, bamboo and horn, ceramics, enamels, and textiles, as well as a small selection of designs for craft items and architecture. Before these works left Japan, 3,000 artists were invited by the government to visit the collection in Tokyo. As we have already seen, the ceramic entrepreneur Yabu Meizan (see pages 116–9 and catalogue numbers 95–105, 108–113, 116, 118–125) played a prominent part in the preparations. On August 15, 1903, he was appointed one of five Directors of the Louisiana Purchase Exposition Japan Exhibits Association, and he left Japan just eight days before the attack on Port Arthur, arriving at St. Louis on February 20. Meizan's adopted son Yabu Tsuneo worked as senior manager of the exhibit in the Palace of Fine Arts, and Meizan was permitted to show two pieces in this prestigious setting: a flower-shaped bowl with figures, now in the Walters Art Gallery (Baltimore) and another bowl with figures, birds, flowers, and a landscape. Apart from brief mentions in the records of prize-winners and long lists of names, there is no detailed documentation of the wares displayed in other buildings of the Fair, but it is interesting that at this late date, even in the Fine Arts section, Meizan made little or no concession to the prevailing design trends discussed below. This did not, however, prevent him from both winning a gold medal in the Art Manufactures section and achieving his best-ever exhibition sales.

As well as Yabu Meizan's bowls, the illustrated catalogue of the Japanese exhibits in the Art Palace shows three vases by Kinkozan, the Kyoto "Satsuma" potter (see page 119 and catalogue numbers 114–5), that are in completely new style and techniques, with relief carving and the so-called *yohen* [transmutation] glazes also seen at an earlier date on the porcelain of Miyagawa Kozan (see catalogue number 86). These changes were part of an evolution in the design of ceramics and some other decorative arts that had started in the mid-1890s and intensified in the light of critical comments made at the Paris Exposition of 1900. In 1901, the Nihon Zuan Kai [Japan Design Association] was established in order to stimulate the improvement of design, and a committee summed the problem up by noting that a few of the Paris exhibits – for example those by Kozan – had been highly praised, but going on to say:

> However ... there are several areas demanding urgent improvement. These may be summarized in three points: firstly, the careful preparation of materials and the distribution of each kind of material; secondly, the improvement of the manufacturing process; thirdly, the shapes and designs.[14]

These remarks concerned Japan ceramics, but the criticism of shapes and designs might equally have been applied to many of the other media on display in Paris. While Yabu Meizan seems to have ignored adverse criticism, for example the comments of Maeda Kasetsu (see page 218) which could have been made with him specifically in mind, a glance at the list of prize-winners at St. Louis makes it clear that the some of the most successful exhibitors had understood the need to rein in their decorative instincts and refine their shapes. Namikawa Sosuke in enamels, Miyagawa Kozan in porcelain, and Shirayama Shosai in lacquer – all represented in the Khalili Collection – won Grand Prizes for *Bijutsu seisaku genpin* [original art works], and their work certainly did move towards a greater simplicity and emphasis on form rather than surface decoration. This is particularly true in the case of enamels. Most of the technical improvements that occurred in the newly-discovered medium during the Meiji Era came about precisely because of the artists' determination to make their designs more open and more pictorial. At first, dense wirework was needed to hold the enamels on to the body during firing, but Namikawa Sosuke and his namesake Namikawa Yasuyuki succeeded in either reduc-

DEVELOPMENTS IN JAPANESE DESIGN

Figure 3.
In the Japanese Garden at the Louisiana Purchase Exposition, St. Louis, 1904. Photograph courtesy of the Missouri Historical Society.

Figure 4.
Replica of the Yomeimon Gate at Nikko installed in the Palace of Varied Industries, St. Louis, 1904. Photograph from Buel, *Louisiana and the Fair...* (St. Louis, 1904). Courtesy of New York Public Library.

A LESSON FOR UNCLE SAM

Figure 5.
The Japanese Section of the Palace of Fine Arts at the Louisiana Purchase Exposition, St. Louis, 1904. Photograph from *Exhibition of the Empire of Japan*. Courtesy of the Missouri Historical Society.

ing their dependence on wire or actually using it as an integral part of a pictorial design (see catalogue numbers 305–310).

Another Grand Prize winner at St. Louis who had moved decisively towards pictorialism was Kawashima Jinbei II. Born into a family of Kyoto silk-weavers, he traveled to Europe in 1886, touring textile factories in France and Germany and admiring the tapestry-hung state rooms of the great royal and ducal palaces. Jinbei was especially impressed by France's Gobelins tapestry workshops and made a careful study of their manufacturing techniques, convinced that Japanese weavers, like their European counterparts, could create large-scale designs based on famous Old Master paintings, but with the difference that the originals would be Japanese rather than Western. The first fruits of his research, a series of tapestries in the Imperial Palace completed in 1888, were destroyed by bombing in 1945, but one of his earliest datable larger works – a completely new departure in the history of Japanese textiles – is a copy of a painting by Hara Zaisen, itself based on seventeenth-century depictions of the *inuoimono*, a kind of ritualized dog-hunt. As mentioned earlier (page 216), Jinbei made an impressive contribution to the Chicago World's Fair, and his display at St. Louis was even more ambitious, consisting as it did of entire rooms hung with tapestries based on a famous series of scroll paintings by the eighteenth-century painter Ito Jakuchu.[15]

By pressing ahead with design reform while maintaining or even improving the technical qualities of their wares, the leading Japanese exhibitors ensured that the critical reaction to the Japanese exhibits was generally favorable, if not as ecstatic as it had been at Chicago. But the recovery from Japan's failure at Paris was due to more than just aesthetic factors. The growing realization that Japan was likely to emerge triumphant from the Russo-Japanese War meant that the country's social and moral qualities came to be praised as much as its ingenious workmanship. Because China was officially exhibiting for the first time (at Chicago there had only been a private display in the Midway Pleasance),[16] Japan also had an opportunity to show off her superiority to the Asian neighbor she had already humiliated in battle.

Like the Columbian World's Fair, the Louisiana Purchase Exhibition was celebrated in a number of multi-volume local publications such as J.W. Buel's ambitiously titled *Louisiana and the Fair: An Exposition of the World, Its People and Their Achievements*. Buel, whose semi-official middle-of-the-road opinions can probably be taken as a fair summary of informed reaction to the Japanese presence at St. Louis, commented that "in the manufacture of silk fabrics, satins, damasks, screens, fans, iron-ware and lacquered goods [the Japanese] are unapproachable" and "In the applied arts, in carvings, bronzes, pottery, decorative work, the Japanese are almost unequaled". Although this catalogue is confined to the decorative arts, it is worth noting that while Buel was quick to praise Japanese "deftness" he was much less

295
PLATE
About 1900–10
Porcelain, painted in underglaze blue and
yellow enamel on a coral-red ground
Height 38.7 cm.
Signed *Makuzu-gama Kozan sei* [made by
Kozan at the Makuzu kiln]
Made by the Miyagawa Kozan Workshop

296
BOWL
About 1910
Porcelain painted in underglaze black
and pink
Diameter 28.5 cm.
Signed *Makuzu-gama Kozan sei* [made by
Kozan at the Makuzu kiln]
Made by the Miyagawa Kozan Workshop

297
BOWL
About 1910
Porcelain painted in underglaze blue
Diameter 39.2 cm.
Signed *Makuzu-gama Kozan sei* [made by
Kozan at the Makuzu kiln]
Made by the Miyagawa Kozan Workshop

298
VASE
About 1900–10
Porcelain painted in underglaze blue
Height 60.0 cm.
Signed *Makuzu-gama Kozan sei* [made by
Kozan at the Makuzu kiln]
Made by the Miyagawa Kozan Workshop

299
VASE
About 1910
Porcelain painted in underglaze blue
Height 52.7 cm.
Signed *Makuzu Kozan sei* [made by
Makuzu Kozan]
Made by the Miyagawa Kozan Workshop

This vase was exhibited at the Japan-British
Exhibition, London (1910), and is illustrated
in *The Studio* (June 1910, p.287), where
Shugio Hiromichi described the vase as:

> a beautiful specimen of blue and white
> porcelain. It is a perfect piece both artis-
> tically and technically, very simple in line,
> and classic in shape, and quite artistic in
> the design of the matchless chrysan-
> themums, the pride of our country.

300
VASE
About 1910
Porcelain painted in underglaze blue
Height 60.5 cm.
Signed *Makuzu Kozan sei* [made by
Makuzu Kozan]
Made by the Miyagawa Kozan Workshop

301
VASE
About 1900–10
Porcelain painted in underglaze green, black, yellow, and modeled in low relief
Height 29.7 cm.
Signed *Makuzu Kozan sei* [made by Makuzu Kozan]
Made by the Miyagawa Kozan Workshop

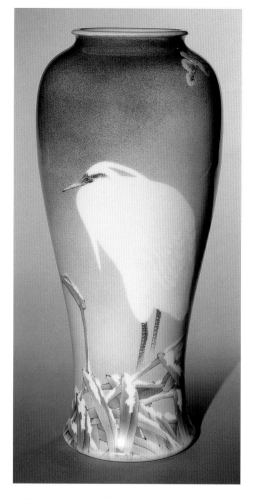

302
VASE
About 1910
Porcelain, modeled and enameled
Height 31.1 cm.
Impressed mark *Makuzu*
Made by the Miyagawa Kozan Workshop

A smaller version of this delightful porcelain fantasy was acquired by the Victoria and Albert Museum, London, after the Japan-British Exhibition of 1910 (inv. no. C.244-1910).

303
VASE
About 1900
Cloisonné enamels worked in silver wire;
silver rims, foot and finial
Height 23.5 cm.
Signed *Kyoto Namikawa* [Namikawa
of Kyoto]
Made by the Namikawa Yasuyuki
Workshop

304
Jar
About 1900–05
Cloisonné enamels worked in gold wire;
silver rims and feet
Height 7.0 cm.
Signed *Kyoto Namikawa* [Namikawa
of Kyoto]
Made by the Namikawa Yasuyuki
Workshop

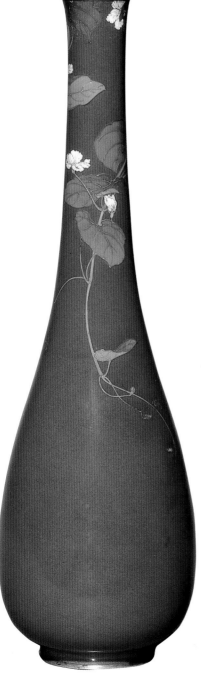

306
Vase
About 1905–10
Cloisonné enamels worked in silver wire;
silver rim and foot
Height 35.1 cm.
Signed *Kyoto Namikawa* [Namikawa
of Kyoto]
Made by the Namikawa Yasuyuki
Workshop

305
Brush Pot
About 1903–10
Cloisonné enamels worked in silver wire;
silver rim and foot
Height 11.1 cm.
Signed *Kyoto Namikawa* [Namikawa
of Kyoto]
Made by the Namikawa Yasuyuki
Workshop

At the fifth Naikoku Kangyo Hakurankai
[National Industrial Exposition] (1903),
Namikawa Yasuyuki exhibited a single
piece for which he won a second prize. It
was described by the judges as a:

> Gold-wired cylindrical brush pot with
> bamboo design. The few delicate bam-
> boos look as if they were brush strokes
> on the dark purple ground, and each leaf
> is carved as if it were a brush stroke.

Apart from the ground color, and the use of
gold, this description might almost fit the
present piece. However, the judges continue:

> ... the work is carefully done to his usual
> standard, but it seems unnecessary to
> have placed the butterfly beside the
> bamboo ...[1]

1. Suzuki Norio and Sakakibara Satoru, *Nihon
no shippo* [Japanese Cloisonné Enamels]
(Kyoto, 1979), p.251.

307
Pair of Vases
About 1900–10
Cloisonné enamels worked in gold wire;
shakudo rims and feet, silver base plates
and liners
Height 27.6 cm.
Signed *Kyoto Namikawa* [Namikawa
of Kyoto]
Made by the Namikawa Yasuyuki
Workshop

308
VASE
About 1905
Moriage enamel; silver mounts
Height 40.2 cm.
With the silver wire seal of Kawade
Shibataro
Made by Kawade Shibataro (dates
unknown) at the Ando Jubei Workshop

A pair of vases of similar design were
included in the Louisiana Purchase
Exposition of 1904,[1] and others on a dark
green ground were exhibited by Kawade at
the Universal and International Exposition
in Liège (1905), and illustrated in the
ensuing auction catalogue. The credit for
the invention of the *moriage* "heaped-up"
enamel technique is often given to Shibataro,
one of the most skilled enamelers working
in the Ando Jubei Workshop. *Moriage*-
decorated pieces were first exhibited in Japan
at the fifth Naikoku Kangyo Hakurankai
[National Industrial Exposition] in 1903,
and internationally at the Louisiana
Purchase Exposition, St. Louis, in 1904.
Hattori Tadasaburo (see numbers 291,
315, and 367) is also sometimes credited
with the invention of *moriage*, but only
Kawade's pieces are listed in the fifth
National Industrial Exposition catalogue
as being in *moriage* technique.

1. Kwanjiro Yamashita, *The Illustrated
   Catalogue of Japanese Fine Art Exhibits in
   the Art Palace at the Louisiana Purchase
   Exposition, St. Louis, Mo., U.S.A.* (Kobe,
   1904), p.80.

309
PAIR OF VASES
About 1905
Moriage and *musen* enamels worked in
silver wire
Height 93.2 cm.
With the silver wire seal of Kawade
Shibataro within the Ando seal
Made by Kawade Shibataro (dates
unknown) at the Ando Jubei Workshop

These massive vases are similar to a pair
made for the Universal and International
Exposition in Liège of 1905, having the
same borders and the same shape.[1]

1. Ch. Desoer (ed.), *Catalogue Officiel de
   la Section Japonaise, Exposition
   Universelle et Internationale de Liège*
   (Brussels, 1905), no. 123, Gr. xv, cl. 94.

310
PAIR OF SCREENS
About 1900–05
Wood, inset with panels of *musen* and
cloisonné enamels; the wood frame with
flambé transparent enameled copper, shell
and lacquer; the reverse lacquered in
takamaki-e and *hiramaki-e*; cloisonné
enamel mounts
Height 93.2 cm.
Made by the Ando Jubei Workshop

These magnificent screens were made by
the Ando Company for the Liège Universal
and International Exposition of 1905, where
the Ando name plate and trademark were
placed on the exhibition stand and are
visible in a photograph in the catalogue.[1]
They were subsequently offered for sale at
an auction held by Robinson and Fisher in
Willis's Rooms in London on December 5,

1905, where they were fully described and
illustrated:

MAGNIFICENT TWO-FOLD SCREEN,
framed of Teakwood, with cloisonné
ornaments in joints, wire and wireless
cloisonné panels, representing four
Seasons, are fitted on one-piece MUL-
BERRY, which is thoroughly carved and

tastefully inlaid with ivy leaves of mother-o'-pearl. This grand specimen, which took the artist over five years for its completion, was designed by the well-known art designer, SHIODA, and the pictures in panels were specially drawn by eight celebrated artists of today.

It is not known whether the two screens were actually separated in 1905; they certainly were by 1987, when one of the pair was exhibited in Los Angeles at the County Museum of Art (attributed to Namikawa Sosuke). There is no indication on the screens as to the identity of the "eight celebrated artists of today". The "well-known art designer, SHIODA" is

Shioda Shin, an influential figure in the enamel industry (see number 225).

1. Ch. Desoer (ed.), *Catalogue Officiel de la Section Japonaise, Exposition Universelle et Internationale de Liège* (Brussels, 1905), P.202.

311
PAIR OF VASES
About 1905–10
Moriage enamels worked in silver wire;
sentoku [a form of brass] handles, silver
rims and foot-rims; silvered bronze liners
Height 32.5 cm.
With the silver wire seal of Kawade
Shibataro within the Ando seal
Made by Kawade Shibataro (dates
unknown) at the Ando Jubei Workshop

312
PLATE
About 1910
Cloisonné enamels worked in silver wire;
silver rim and foot
Diameter 21.5 cm.
With the seal of Kawade Shibataro within
the Ando seal; paper label in English *J.
Ando, Cloisonné Wares, Tokyo, Japan*
Made by Kawade Shibataro (dates
unknown) at the Ando Jubei Workshop

A somewhat similar plate is illustrated in
the catalogue of the 1910 Japan-British
Exhibition in London.[1] This plate is
accompanied by the original wood box
inscribed *nanasun seiyobanazara* [seven-
sun (1 *sun* = about 1.2 inches) European
flower plate].

1. Office of the Imperial Japanese Government
   Commission to the Japan-British Exhibition,
   *An Illustrated Catalogue of Japanese Modern
   Fine Arts Displayed at the Japan-British
   Exhibition, London, 1910* (Tokyo, 1910),
   no. 178.

313
VASE
About 1905–10
Moriage enamels; silver rim and foot
Height 32.3 cm.
With the silver wire seal of Ando Jubei
Made by the Ando Jubei Workshop

314
VASE
About 1910
Musen enamels; silver rim and attached
silver foot
Height 35.3 cm.
With the engraved seal of Ando Jubei
Made by Kawade Shibataro (dates
unknown) at the Ando Jubei Workshop

This superb vase was exhibited at the 1910
Japan-British exhibition in London and is
illustrated in the catalogue;[1] in the Japanese
edition of the catalogue, it is listed as the
work of Kawade Shibataro. It is very
similar in technique to the panels in
catalogue number 310.

1. Office of the Imperial Japanese Government
   Commission to the Japan-British Exhibition,
   *An Illustrated Catalogue of Japanese Modern
   Fine Arts Displayed at the Japan-British
   Exhibition, London, 1910* (Tokyo, 1910),
   no. 175.

315
PAIR OF VASES
About 1905
Moriage enamels; silver rims and feet
Height 36.9 cm.
Signed *Hattori zo* [made by Hattori]

For other works by the Hattori family, see
catalogue numbers 291 and 367. At the
Louisiana Purchase Exposition in St. Louis
in 1904, some vases with *moriage* were
exhibited under the name "Hattori
Isaburo", and Hattori Tadasaburo exhibited
two vases with *moriage* at the Japan-British
Exhibition in London in 1910.

316
Pair of Vases
About 1905–10
Cloisonné enamels worked in silver wire;
silver rims and feet
Height 45.4 cm.
Signed *Dai Nihon Aichi Hayashi Ko*
[Hayashi Ko(denji) of Aichi in great Japan]
Made by the Hayashi Kodenji Workshop

317
BOX FOR WRITING UTENSILS AND BOX FOR WRITING PAPER
About 1910
Wood lacquered in *hiramaki-e* and *roiro*;
silver water-dropper
4.7 × 20.5 × 24.6 cm. (box for writing
utensils); 14.3 × 21.3 × 27.5 cm. (box for
writing paper)

SCULPTURE

Figurative *okimono* [ornaments] and other pieces feature in several other sections of the catalogue, but this small group has been brought together to illustrate some aspects of the Western-influenced style of sculpture that emerged in the mid-Meiji Era.

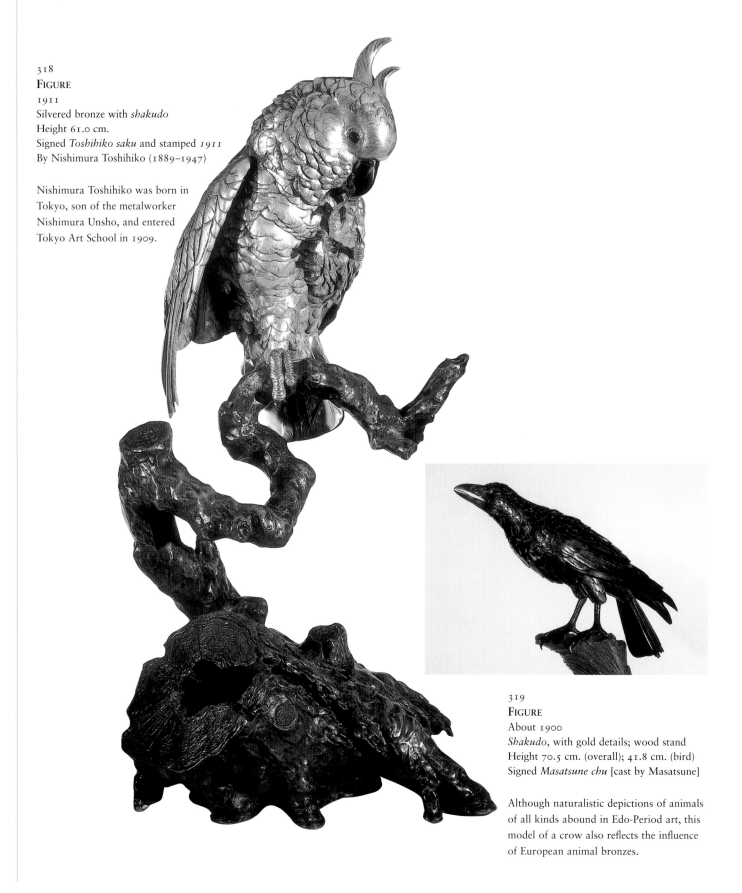

318
FIGURE
1911
Silvered bronze with *shakudo*
Height 61.0 cm.
Signed *Toshihiko saku* and stamped *1911*
By Nishimura Toshihiko (1889–1947)

Nishimura Toshihiko was born in Tokyo, son of the metalworker Nishimura Unsho, and entered Tokyo Art School in 1909.

319
FIGURE
About 1900
Shakudo, with gold details; wood stand
Height 70.5 cm. (overall); 41.8 cm. (bird)
Signed *Masatsune chu* [cast by Masatsune]

Although naturalistic depictions of animals of all kinds abound in Edo-Period art, this model of a crow also reflects the influence of European animal bronzes.

320
FIGURE
1899
Silver; bronze base
32.8 x 32.2 cm.
Signed on the base *Meiji tsuchinoto-i
Yoshimori saku* [made by Yoshimori in the
tsuhinoto-i year (1899) of Meiji]
By Unno Yoshimori II (Bisei, 1864–1919)

A very similar piece, also by Unno
Yoshimori, was awarded a First Class Gold
Medal at the Spring Exhibition of the Japan
Art Association in 1896 and purchased by
the Imperial Household.[1] The subject is an
archer practicing *yabusame*, an ancient
form of ceremonial archery on horseback,
and according to the 1896 catalogue
description, the artist made himself a pupil
of "a well-known master ... and familiarized
himself thoroughly with all [*yabusame's*]
technical points, including the dress &c.
used in connection with this ceremony".

1. [Anon.], "Works of Living Artists Exhibited at
   the Spring Exhibition (1896) of the Japan Art
   Association", *Magazine of Japanese Art*
   (Tokyo, 1896).

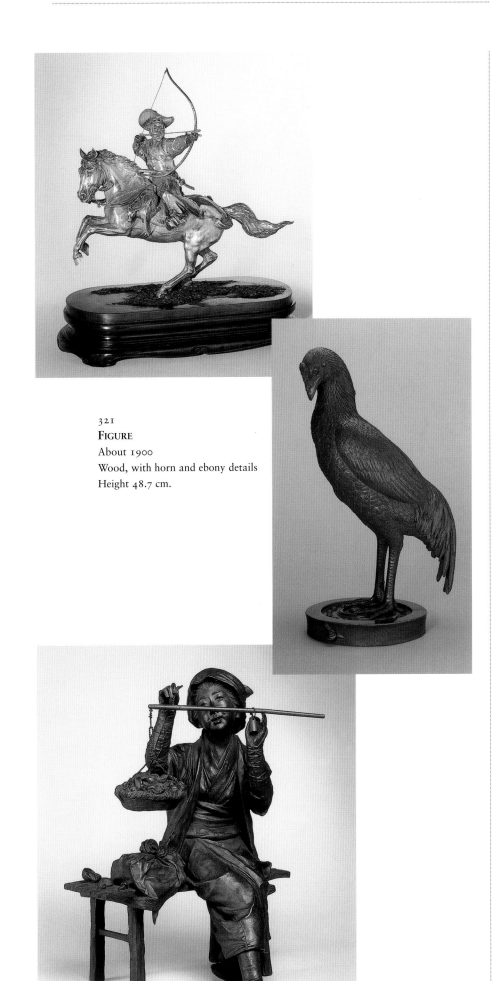

321
FIGURE
About 1900
Wood, with horn and ebony details
Height 48.7 cm.

322
FIGURE
About 1900
Bronze
53.5 x 40.2 cm
Signed *Kaniya Kuniharu saku* [made by
Kaniya Kuniharu]
By Kaniya Kuniharu (1869–after 1910)

Kaniya Kuniharu was one of the foremost
craftsmen in cast bronze of the Meiji Era.
He had been taught by two particularly
eminent artists, Takamura Koun (1852–
1934) and Otake Norikuni (see numbers
31, 172, and 231). Koun, a master of wood
sculpture, had been appointed professor of
sculpture at the founding of the Tokyo Art
School in 1889; his style was also continued
by Kaniya's pupil Watanabe Haruaki (see
number 325). Kuniharu himself was one of
the founding members of the Tokyo Chukin
Kai [Tokyo Cast Metal Association] in
1907 with Oshima Joun (see numbers 48
and 245). He exhibited at both national
and international exhibitions, including the
Paris Exposition of 1900.

323
FIGURE
About 1900–10
Cast bronze
Height 58.5 cm.
Signed *Udagawa Kazuo saku*
[made by Udagawa Kazuo]
By Udagawa Kazuo (dates unknown)

Udagawa Kazuo exhibited from 1900 until
1910.[1] Similar but not identical groups
were shown at the Louisiana Purchase
Exhibition (1904)[2] and the Japan-British
Exhibition (1910); the same model was
also executed in a combination of wood
and ivory.[3]

1. Tokyo Kokuritsu Bunkazai Kenkyujo [Tokyo
   National Research Institution of Cultural
   Properties] (ed.), *Meijiki bankoku hakurankai
   bijutsuhin shuppin mokuroku* [Catalogues of
   Objects Exhibited at International Expositions
   in the Meiji Era] (Tokyo, 1997), P142, etc.
2. Kwanjiro Yamashita, *The Illustrated Catalogue
   of Japanese Fine Art Exhibits in the Art Palace
   at the Louisiana Purchase Exposition, St. Louis,
   Mo., U.S.A.* (Kobe, 1904).
3. Shibuya Kuritsu Shoto Bijutsukan [The Shoto
   Museum of Art], *Nihon no zoge bijutsu –
   Meiji no zoge chokoku o chushin ni* [History
   of Japanese Ivory Carving – Gebori Okimono
   and Shibayama of Meiji Period] (Tokyo,
   1996), pp. 105 and 175.

324
FIGURE
About 1900–10
Cast bronze with ivory and iron; wood
stand
Height 99.0 cm.
Signed *Udagawa Kazuo saku*
[made by Udagawa Kazuo]
By Udagawa Kazuo (dates unknown)

For this artist, see number 323.

331
FIGURE
About 1900
Bronze
Height 31.2 cm.
Signed *Mukai Katsuyuki zo* [made by
Mukai Katsuyuki]
By Mukai Katsuyuki (dates unknown)

This delicately modeled figure is illustrated
in the catalogue of the Japanese section of
the Paris Exposition of 1900, where it is
said to represent a woman of the Genroku
Period (1688–1704).[1] Mukai also exhibited
a male and female peacock at the
Louisiana Purchase Exhibition (1904).[2]

1. *Bijutsu gaho, Daini rinji zokan bijutsu gaho;*
   Pari hakurankai shuppin kumiai seisakuhin
   [Extra Issue no. 2 of Fine Arts Magazine
   Containing Illustrations and Descriptions of
   Products of the Paris World Exposition
   Exhibitor's Union] (Tokyo, 1900), unpaginated.
2. Tokyo Kokuritsu Bunkazai Kenkyujo [Tokyo
   National Research Institution of Cultural
   Properties] (ed.), *Meijiki bankoku hakurankai*
   bijutsuhin shuppin mokuroku [Catalogues of
   Objects Exhibited at International Expositions
   in the Meiji Era] (Tokyo, 1997), S155, T822.

332
FIGURE
About 1910
Bronze
Height 65.5 cm.
Cast mark *Kaku-u sei* [made by Kaku-u]

This accomplished study by an unknown
artist shows just how thoroughly the con-
ventions of Western academic sculpture had
been assimilated by the end of the Meiji Era.

TEXTILES

This section covers a small group of textiles from the second half of the Meiji Era. Although few can be attributed with confidence to a particular company, it is likely that all of them were made in Kyoto.

333

HANGING
About 1895–1900
Silk embroidery
Approximately 260 x 320 cm.
Signed *Nuishi Maeda* [embroiderer Maeda]

One of the earliest datable large textiles of the middle Meiji Era is that made at the Kyoto workshop of Kawashima Jinbei II (1853–1910), exhibited at the third 1890 Naikoku Kangyo Hakurankai [National Industrial Exposition] of 1890, subsequently presented by the Meiji Emperor to the Russian Tsar Nikolai during his visit to Japan in the following year and exhibited in Wilmington, Delaware in 1998.[1] Like many examples of that date, it is copied directly from a painting; the most famous of these, depicting a festival at Nikko, made a great impression at the World's Columbian Fair in 1893, one guidebook commenting: "One piece of tapestry, representing 'The Gate of Nikko during a Festival', contains hundreds of figures, and required four years for its completion. This exhibit must be seen to be appreciated".[2] It was later purchased by the Chicago Museum of Natural History. Starting in about 1893, however, a number of large hangings were manufactured in either *tsuzure nishiki* [handwoven brocade] or jacquard tapestry with designs which appear to have been conceived with the textile medium more specifically in mind.[3] Nothing is known at present about Maeda, the embroiderer whose name appears on this piece.

1. Kawashima Textile Museum and Osaka Municipal Museum, *Tekisutairu ato 100 – Kindai Nihon no shitsunai soshoku ori mono* [100 Years of Textile Art: Japanese Decorative Textiles in Recent Times] (Kyoto, 1994), cat. nos. 4 and 6; State Hermitage Museum and the State Archives of the Russian Federation, *Nicholas and Alexandra* (exhibition catalogue, London, 1998), cat. no. 305.
2. Rand McNally & Co., *A Week At the Fair, Illustrating the Exhibits and Wonders of the World's Columbian Exposition* (Chicago, 1893).
3. Tokyo National Museum, *Umi o watatta Meiji no bijutsu* [World's Columbian Exhibition of 1893 Revisited] (Tokyo, 1997), cat. no. 36.

334
PANEL
About 1900–10
Silk embroidery
64.0 × 67.0 cm.

An embroidered hanging of lions was shown
in 1903 at the fifth Naikoku Kangyo
Hakurankai [National Industrial Exposition].
The exhibitors were Iida Shinshichi of the
well-known textile firm of Takashimaya
(now a leading department store) and
Yamada Hinkichi, both of Kyoto.[1]

1. Tokyo National Research Institution of
   Cultural Properties, *Naikoku Kangyo
   Hakurankai bijutsuhin shuppin mokuroku.*
   [Catalogues of Objects Exhibited at the
   National Industrial Expositions] (Tokyo,
   1996), V823, V849.

335
PANEL
About 1900–10
Silk embroidery
32.5 × 55.0 cm.
Labeled in English *Purveyor to H.I.J.M.'s
Household, S. Nishimura, Kyoto, Japan,
Manufacturer of High Class Embroideries,
Fancy Cut-Velvets and Silk Goods in
General* and with Japanese addresses in
both Kyoto and Tokyo

The well-known firm of Nishimura
Sozaemon (see also number 341) exhibited
a tiger wall hanging at the fifth Naikoku
Kangyo Hakurankai [National Industrial
Exposition] in 1903.[1]

1. Tokyo National Research Institution of Cultural
   Properties, *Naikoku Kangyo Hakurankai bijut
   suhin shuppin mokuroku.* [Catalogues of
   Objects Exhibited at the National Industrial
   Expositions] (Tokyo, 1996), V834.

336
PANEL
About 1900–10
Silk embroidery
51.0 X 87.0 cm.

This remarkable evocation of the sea was
originally dyed in rich blues (visible behind
the frame) which have now faded to
browns, creams and grays.

▶

337
HANGING
About 1895–1910
Silk embroidery; the border woven silk
271 X 218 cm. overall; 230 X 174 cm.
excluding border

Around 1900 a number of Kyoto factories,
especially that of Kawashima Jinbei,
produced large textile hangings inspired by
the European custom of decorating formal
rooms with large tapestries (see page
288). The main subject-matter of this
embroidery, a *ho-o* bird, is seen on late
sixteenth-century Japanese screens made
for the interiors of palaces and castles; at
that time the *ho-o* was favored as a motif
because in early Chinese writings its
appearance is said to herald the arrival
of a virtuous monarch. This hanging thus
combines elements of both European
and Japanese elite interior design of the
sixteenth century, but in a distinctly early
twentieth-century mode of expression.

338
PANEL
About 1900–10
Silk embroidery
38.0 x 51.0 cm.

An embroidered panel of a dog or dogs
was shown by Terajima Rokunosuke at the
fifth Naikoku Kangyo Hakurankai
[National Industrial Exposition] in 1903.[1]

1. Tokyo National Research Institution of Cultural
   Properties, *Naikoku Kangyo Hakurankai bijut
   suhin shuppin mokuroku.* [Catalogues of
   Objects Exhibited at the National Industrial
   Expositions] (Tokyo, 1996), V854.

339
PANEL
About 1900–10
Silk embroidery
45.0 × 67.0 cm.

340
PANEL
About 1900–10
Silk embroidery
45.0 × 67.0 cm.

341
PANEL
About 1910
Silk embroidery; framed
62.0 × 88.0 cm.
With the trade label of Nishimura
Sozaemon

The treatment of the trees closely resembles
an embroidered panel of hunting by Mount
Fuji, thought to be a preparatory work for
a *tsuzure nishiki* [handwoven brocade],
made in 1909 by Kawashima Jinbei II (see
page 288) for the Karinoma room of the
Akasaka Detached Palace, after a painting
by Asai Chu (1856–1907); Nishimura
Sozaemon, whose label appears on this
piece, also worked on the Detached Palace.[1]
He exhibited embroideries with landscape
scenes as early as 1893, was a prizewinner
at the Paris Universal Exposition of 1900,
and showed several embroideries at the
Japan-British Exhibition in 1910.

1. Kawashima Textile Museum and Osaka
   Municipal Museum, *Tekisutairu ato
   100 – Kindai Nihon no shitsunai soshoku ori
   mono* [100 Years of Textile Art: Japanese
   Decorative Textiles in Recent Times] (Kyoto,
   1994), cat. nos. 20 and 24.

342
PANEL
About 1900–10
Silk embroidery
63.7 × 43.5 cm.

This panel appears to be based on a
European genre painting, probably a
Spanish work produced by one of the late
nineteenth-century ateliers specializing in
picturesque scenes for tourists.

353
INCENSE BURNER
About 1900–10
Porcelain, painted in underglaze blue on a
yellow ground
Height 23.0 cm.
Signed on the base and inside the cover
Makuzu Kozan sei [made by Makuzu Kozan]
Made by the Miyagawa Kozan Workshop

354
VASE
About 1910
Porcelain, painted in underglaze blue
and yellow
Height 30.5 cm.
Signed *Makuzu Kozan sei* [made by
Makuzu Kozan]
Made by the Miyagawa Kozan Workshop

355
VASE
About 1910
Porcelain, painted in underglaze blue on a
yellow ground
Height 39.5 cm.
Signed *Makuzu Kozan sei* [made by
Makuzu Kozan]
Made by the Miyagawa Kozan Workshop

356
VASE
About 1910
Porcelain, painted in underglaze yellow and
black on a pink ground
Height 24.1 cm.
Signed *Shofu*
By Shofu Kajo (1870–1928)

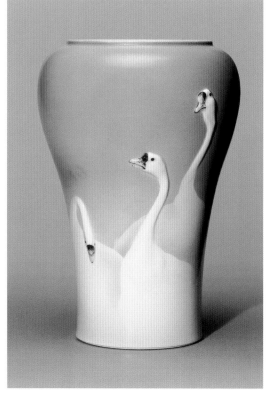

357
JAR
About 1890
Porcelain; painted in underglaze green,
brown, and white
Height 29.7 cm.
Signed *Inoue Ryosai*
By Inoue Ryosai (*b.* 1827)

Inoue Ryosai was born in 1827, starting work originally in Seto and moving to Edo (Tokyo) in 1866. He won a *kamon shohai* [flower prize] at the first Naikoku Kangyo Hakurankai [National Industrial Exposition] in 1877, and in 1878 exhibited for the Kiritsu Kosho Kaisha in Paris. At the third Naikoku Kangyo Hakurankai in 1890, he won a *santo myogi shohai* [third prize for technical excellence] for a celadon flower vase carved with an antique flower pattern. At the fourth Naikoku Kangyo Hakurankai in 1895, it was his son-in-law Jihei who exhibited, though Ryosai was again exhibiting at the fifth in 1903, where he won a second prize.

358
VASE
About 1900–10
Porcelain; painted in underglaze black,
brown, green, and yellow
Height 30.0 cm.
Signed *Inoue Ryosai*
By Inoue Ryosai (*b.* 1827)

The decoration reflects that on a jardinière
exhibited in Paris in 1900 by the Royal
Copenhagen Porcelain Factory which is
probably the earlier of the two.[1] The overall
design repeats and therefore must be sten-
ciled, but the actual decoration is done with
a brush. This is an interesting combination
of Eastern and Western techniques.

1. Arthur Hayden, *Royal Copenhagen Porcelain*
   (London, 1911)

359
VASE
About 1900
Porcelain, painted in underglaze green
Height 61.4 cm.
Signed *Nishiura yaki* [Nishiura ware]
By Nishiura Enji (dates unknown)

According to the catalogue of the Liège
exhibition of 1905, Nishiura Enji worked
at Tajimicho, Gifu, making faiences, and
had won medals at St. Louis in 1904 and
other exhibitions.[1]

1. Ch. Desoer, (ed.), *Catalogue Officiel de la
   Section Japonaise, Exposition Universelle et
   Internationale de Liège* (Brussels, 1905), p.166.

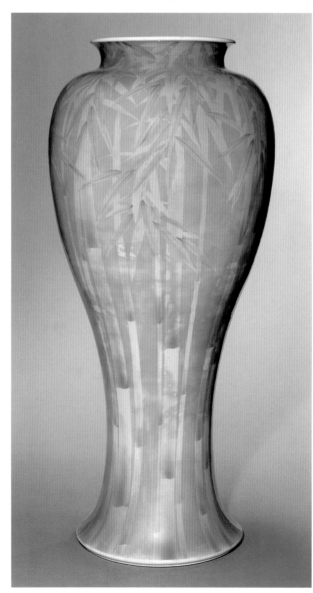

360
VASE
About 1910–15
Porcellaneous ware with enameled
decoration, modeled in relief
Height 35.6 cm.
Signed *Makuzu*
Made by the Miyagawa Kozan Workshop

This unusual piece is made in the shape of
a formal presentation jar for fine tea.

361
VASE
About 1900
Porcelain; painted in underglaze blue,
black, yellow, and aubergine
Height 46.5 cm.
Signed *Kato Hanju sei* [made by
Kato Hanju]
By Kato Hanju (dates unknown)

This artist won a third prize at the last
Naikoku Kangyo Hakurankai [National
Industrial Exposition] held in 1903.

362
VASE
About 1910
Porcelain, painted in underglaze orange and
black on a ground graduated from pale
blue to cream
Height 39.3 cm.
Signed *Yugyokuen Toju sei* [made by
Yugyokuen Toju]
By Kato Yutaro (1851–1915)

Kato Yutaro worked at Seto before moving
to Tokyo. He first exhibited at the second
Naikoku Kangyo Hakurankai [National
Industrial Exposition] in 1881 and won
prizes at the third, fourth, and fifth
Naikoku Kangyo Hakurankai. He also
exhibited at Paris (1900) and London
(1910), where he showed a bowl with
decoration similar to the present example,
wrongly included in the cloisonné enamel
section of the English edition of the catalogue.[1] This is an understandable error, as
there is a close link in style with that of
moriage enamel, which was particularly
popular at around this time. The scales of
the fish worked in relief could easily have
been mistaken for *moriage* enamel of the
type perfected by Ando Jubei or Hattori
Tadasaburo (see number 287).

1. Office of the Imperial Japanese Government
   Commission to the Japan-British Exhibition,
   *An Illustrated Catalogue of Japanese Modern
   Fine Arts Displayed at the Japan-British
   Exhibition, London, 1910* (Tokyo, 1910),
   p.163.

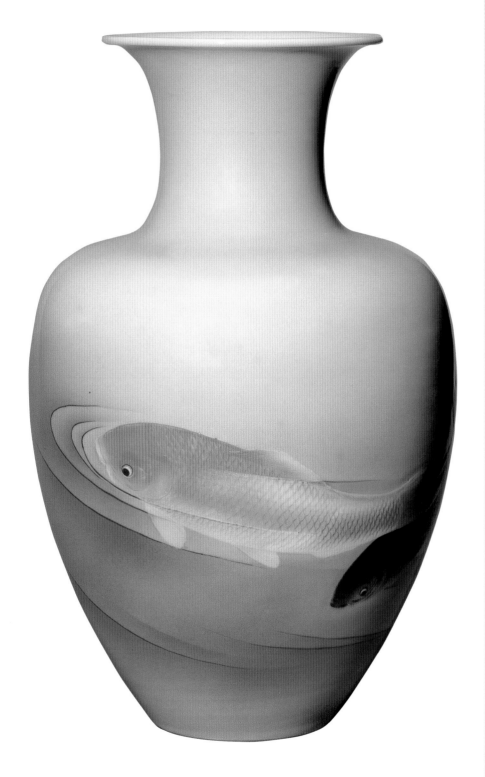

ARTISTS TO THE IMPERIAL HOUSEHOLD

EMPEROR AND ARTIST

It is not easy to determine the Meiji Emperor's personal artistic tastes. The evidence suggests that in painting he enjoyed works that reflected the humorous aspects of Edo-Period art, including several scrolls depicting a hundred different aspects of the popular deities, Otafuku and Hotei (see catalogue number 126); he also owned figurines of *tanuki* [Japanese raccoons].[1] When the imperial family showed their preferences in public they often leaned towards the decorative arts, particularly those in elaborate and expensive styles that had already become old-fashioned in Western eyes. At the first National Industrial Exposition of 1877, Miyagawa Kozan (see pages 330–3) achieved fame by virtue of the fact that the emperor actually touched a high-relief decorated vase of his – the vase was in a style that would be sharply criticized some years later by the journalist and connoisseur Captain Frank Brinkley. In the course of a series of imperial visits to the Japan Art Association exhibition in 1889, the emperor bought thirty-eight pieces, the empress dowager seventeen, and the Imperial Household Department thirty-nine; only ten of these were paintings. This large-scale personal patronage was beneficial in the short term, but in the longer term it had some of the same disadvantages as state sponsorship of the decorative arts: it favored the labour-intensive and costly at the expense of the affordable and, in Western eyes, well designed. Imperial buying, like state commissions, contributed to the adverse criticism of Japanese work at the 1900 Paris Exposition. Since these exhibition purchases came about as a result of actual visits by members of the imperial family, it is reasonable to assume that personal preferences played at least some part in their selection. In most cases, however, commissions from the Imperial Household, just like those from other parts of the Meiji administration, were probably decided upon by bureaucrats. Such commissions reflected the same policy of support for the traditional arts that lay behind the organization of the National Industrial Exhibitions, the effort to present Japanese art at international expositions, and the formation of the semi-public Kiritsu Kosho Kaisha Company.

Just as it impossible to know what the Emperor may have thought of the pieces ordered in his name, there is little evidence as to how the Imperial Household Department was viewed by the artists who worked for it. As early as 1869, the lacquerer Shibata Zeshin is said to have been commissioned to decorate thirty chairs with gold *maki-e*, and in 1872 he was asked to do the lacquerwork on a riding crop used by the emperor on an official visit to the western part of Japan. The painter Kaburagi Kiyokata, whose father was a friend of Zeshin, recalled that Zeshin was initially reluctant to carry out official instructions even though the order for the riding-crop was passed on to him by one of the highest officials of the government. After a lifetime working through dealers and for individual clients, the idea of state sponsorship must have taken some getting used to, but in time Zeshin seems to have become an enthusiastic participant in the official process of national renewal. Younger artists, who had less experience of the traditional organization of the arts in Japan, probably found it easier to adapt to the new way of doing things.

Another artist who carried out imperial commissions very early in the Meiji Era was Zeshin's friend, the metalworker and sword-fitting maker Kano Natsuo (see catalogue number 394), who made a mounting for the *suiryuken*, an eighth-century blade belonging to the emperor that came from the Shosoin imperial storehouse in Nara. The choice of Natsuo was significant, since he had received his training in the *machibori* ["town carving"] commercial sword-fitting workshops, rather than the *iebori* ["house carving"] workshops of the Goto family, which had the exclusive right to manufacture formal ornaments for swords worn on official duty in the capital. It seems that a decision had been taken to turn away from traditional sources of luxury goods in favor of artists like Natsuo and Zeshin who were unconnected with the discredited regime of the shoguns. Even at the very beginning of the Meiji Era, then, artistic commissions could have political significance.

364
BOX
About 1905
Musen and cloisonné enamels worked in
gold and silver wire; silver mounts
14.2 × 26.1 × 21.7 cm.
With the silver wire seal of Ando Jubei
Made by the Ando Jubei Workshop

Most Imperial Presentation document boxes
were made of lacquer and this appears to
be the only published example of a cloisonné
Imperial Presentation document box of this
size. The decoration of trailing wisteria is
treated as it would be on lacquer.

365
VASE
About 1905
Moriage enamels; silver rim
Height 44.4 cm.
With the silver wire seal of Ando Jubei
Made by the Ando Jubei Workshop

This vase was originally presented by the
Meiji Emperor to Sir Abdul Karim Abdul
Shakur Jamal (1862–1924), who was
founder and half-owner of the Indo-Burma
Petroleum Co. Ltd. and a Member of the
Burma Legislative Council.

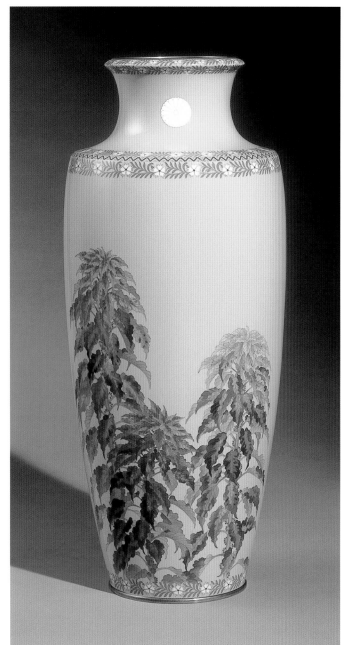

366
PAIR OF VASES
1910 or later
Cloisonné enamels worked in silver wire;
silver rim and foot
Height 44.0 cm.
With the seal of Ando Jubei
Made by the Ando Jubei Workshop

This shape seems to have standard for
Imperial Presentation wares, being found
both in the work of other cloisonné artists
working for the court, such as Namikawa
Sosuke and Hattori Tadasaburo, and
in other media, especially silver (see
numbers 378–80).

367
PAIR OF VASES
About 1915
Moriage enamels worked in gold and silver
wire; silver rims and feet
Height 43.8 cm.
Sealed *Hattori kinsei* [respectfully made by
Hattori]
Probably by Hattori Tadasaburo (dates
unknown)

This pair was presented on June 2, 1915,
by the Taisho Emperor to General Dimitri
Leonidovich Horvath, who served under
Tsar Nicholas II and was president of the
Far Eastern Railway in Harbin, Manchuria.

368
VASE
About 1910
Cloisonné enamels worked in silver wire;
silver rim and foot
Height 25.2 cm.
With the seal of Ando Jubei
Made by the Ando Jubei Workshop

369
BOX
About 1900–10
Wood, lacquered in *takamaki-e* and *hiramaki-e*
on a textured *kinji* and *nashiji*; silver edgings
16.8 × 30.5 × 25.7 cm.
Attributed to Akatsuka Jitoku (1871–1936)

The characteristic granular ground and
arrangement of the design is associated
with the work of the lacquer artist Akatsuka
Jitoku, who made several Imperial
Presentation boxes.[1]

1. Jan Dees, "Imperial Lacquer Boxes by Akatsuka
   Jitoku", *Andon*, vol. 8, no. 2 (1988), pp. 103–110.

370

BOX

About 1900–10

Wood, lacquered in *takamaki-e* and
hiramaki-e on a *kinji* ground with shell;
silver edgings

14.3 × 23.0 × 29.0 cm.

This box depicts flower rafts floating
downstream, a favorite theme in Edo-
Period lacquers.

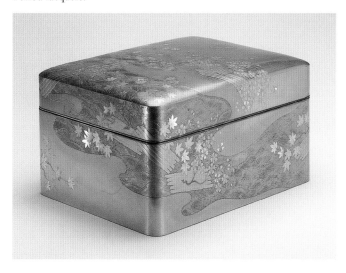

371

BOX

About 1900–10

Wood, lacquered in *takamaki-e* and *hiramaki-e*
on a *kinji* ground; silver edgings

15.0 × 21.5 × 26.5 cm.

372
BOX
About 1910–20
Wood, lacquered in *takamaki-e* on a *kinji*
ground; silver edgings
10.8 × 16.5 × 20.8 cm.
Signed *Yanagisawa Ippo kinsei* [respectfully
made by Yanagisawa Ippo]
By Yanagisawa Ippo (dates unknown)

A cabinet by this little-known artist was
presented as a wedding gift by the Empress
in 1922.[1]

1. E. A. Wrangham, *The Index of Inro Artists*
   (Harehope, Northumberland, 1995), p.91.

373
BOX FOR WRITING PAPER
About 1900–10
Wood, lacquered in *takamaki-e* and
hiramaki-e on a *roiro* ground
17.4 × 32.2 × 62.3 cm.

The *shochikubai* grouping of pine, bamboo,
and plum is first mentioned in Chinese
poetry of the Tang Dynasty (618–906) and
occurs as a subject of Chinese painting
from the fourteenth century. In Japan, the
shochikubai is especially associated with
the New Year, and it may be that this box
was presented by a member of the Imperial
family at a New Year ceremony.

374
BOX FOR WRITING UTENSILS
About 1900–10
Wood, lacquered in *takamaki-e*, *hiramaki-e*,
and *kirikane* on a black lacquer ground;
silver-gilt water-dropper; silver edgings
5.3 × 25.5 × 28.1 cm.

375
BOX
1911 or earlier
Wood, lacquered in *nashiji*, *takamaki-e*,
hiramaki-e, and *hirame*; silver edgings
12.7 × 19.8 × 24.6 cm.

An inscription on the accompanying
storage box reads: *on-montsuke nashiji
tebako Togu no daibu gomen ni tsuki
Kotaishi dohi ryodenka yori onshi Meiji
yonjuyonnen rokugatsu Masayoshi kinshiki*
[a *nashiji* box with the Imperial *mon* [crest],
presented with the permission of the Grand
Chamberlain of the Crown Prince by their
majesties the Crown Prince and Princess on
the sixth month of the forty-fourth year of
Meiji (1911). Respectfully recorded by
Masayoshi].

376
BOX
About 1900–10
Wood, lacquered in *hiramaki-e* on a *kinji*
ground; silver edgings
14.3 × 21.5 × 26.0 cm
Signed *Shumin*
By Funabashi Shumin (*b.* 1859)

A handwritten label accompanying this
box reads: *kin maki-e tebako onshi Shoken
Kotaigo yonjuninen taikan no sai senko*
[gold *maki-e* box presented to my late
father by the Empress Mother Shoken on
his retirement from forty-two years in
office]. The arrangement of the flowering
clematis motif is similar to that seen in the
work of Akatsuka Jitoku (see number 369).

377
CABINET
Made between and 1904 and 1911
Wood decorated in *takamaki-e*, *hiramaki-e*,
hirame, *kirikane*, *nashiji*, and other techniques; silver fittings
110 x 51.5 x 103 cm.
By Harui Komin (1869–after 1922)

The exact circumstances of the manufacture
of this remarkable cabinet, a masterpiece of
late Meiji-Era classical lacquerwork, are
revealed in the English translation, recently
discovered in the Victoria and Albert
Museum, of a letter from Baron Sumitomo
dated April 12, 1922:

> Tokyo, 12th April, 1922. Explanation to
> the Offering to His Royal Highness the
> Prince of Wales from Baron K.
> Sumitomo.
>
> The manufacture of relief lacquer wares
> is a complicated affair. The master mind
> that conceives the whole thing and not
> only superintends the processes but per-
> sonally conducts the most important
> part thereof, is the "makieshi". The
> word maki-e-shi means one that makes
> relief lacquer wares. The laying of relief
> lacquer in gold or silver is the most
> important part of the process, and is,
> consequently, personally attended to by
> the directing artist himself. But the rest
> of the operations is delegated to a series
> of artists and specialists.
>
> Taking, for instance, the present spec-
> imen made to Baron Sumitomo's special
> order, it passed through the hands of
> nine men besides the directing maki-e-shi,
> Komin Harui.
>
> In the first place, the frame-work was
> prepared by Kenjiro Inaba, the wood
> used being old hinoki (Japanese cypress)
> of the well-known Kumado variety pro-
> duced in the province of Owari.
>
> It was next coated with cloth, over
> which plain lacquer was laid in three
> successive operations. The surface was
> then carefully smoothed and polished.
> This part of the process was taken in
> hand by two specialists, Gennosuke
> Iwamura and Kosuke Taura.
>
> The book-case was now ready for per-
> sonal treatment by the directing artist,
> Komin Harui. But even here he had to
> call in the service of a painter to draw
> pictures and decorations, the artist
> employed for this purpose being Gokyo
> Miyake.
>
> In putting on gold lacquer, Komin
> Harui was assisted by four experts,
> namely, Ikkyusai Matsumoto, Chosai

> Yoshizumi, Shunkei Kurokawa, and
> Shumin Shimizu.
>
> The gold used in relief lacquer work is
> generally in the form of dust. But in this
> piece there are parts that are of gold
> plates inlaid. They are the patterns
> enclosed in tiny squares on the corner
> pieces. The pictures marked out in relief
> gold-lacquer on door-leaves represent
> the eight classic views in the regions
> south of Heng-Shan in China. The inside
> faces of the doors bear pictures of
> phoenixes on paulownia trees and of
> peonies, lions and waterfalls.
>
> Lastly there remain metal works in sil-
> ver which adorn various important
> places. They were made by the metal
> decorator, Kansuke Teramoto.
>
> Work was commenced in September
> 1904 and completed in December 1911,
> four out of the seven years being spent
> on the laying of relief gold lacquer.
>
> Komin Harui to whose conception and
> workmanship is due the credit for this
> beautiful piece of work, is one of the few
> living masters whose names will be
> handed down to unborn ages. Next to
> Shosai Shiroyama of Tokyo, he is proba-
> bly the greatest of the living artists in
> this line of work.
>
> He was born to a makieshi family in
> Osaka in 1869. Losing his father while a
> boy, he learned the art under his father's
> old pupil, Gyokushu Nakagawa, who
> was one of the best masters of the day.
>
> By the invitation of the well-known
> dealer in art objects in Kyoto, the late
> Seisuke Ikeda, with whom his father had
> had some dealings, Komin Harui removed
> to Kyoto while still young. Here he at
> once applied himself with his character-
> istic ardour to the study of the superb
> specimens of old makie wares which
> happened to be in the possession of the
> dealer. The result was a marked improve-
> ment in his style of workmanship.

> He meanwhile continued to work for
> his friend Ikeda who derived much prof-
> its by exporting art objects. Very few of
> his best productions remain at home,
> having mostly gone to adorn museums
> and private collections in foreign coun-
> tries. Severing his connections with
> Ikeda in 1914, he removed to Suma near
> Kobe, where he continues to live and
> work in quiet seclusion. A devout
> Buddhist, he despises money and world-
> ly honours. He is widely held in high
> esteem for his noble character no less
> than for his prominence in art.
>
> The present book-case is the largest
> piece of work he has ever produced.

Other sources give a slightly different
account of Harui Komin's career, recording
that he was a pupil of the fifth generation
of Yamamoto Rihei and worked for Ikeda
Seisuke in the Meiji Era. In 1912, after
the closure of Ikeda's business, he moved
to Kyoto and later, for health reasons, to
Suma.[1] Nothing is known of the collabora-
tors listed, with the exception of Miyake
Gogyo (1864–1919), a minor Kyoto
painter who exhibited from 1907.

In 1921, the Crown Prince of Japan,
Hirohito, visited England. To symbolize the
significance of the trip and to cement peace
and good will, this lacquer cabinet was
presented to the Prince of Wales, later for a
brief period, King Edward VIII. The cabinet
was apparently commissioned by Baron
Sumitomo, presented by him to the Emperor,
and subsequently selected as an appropriate
gift for the royal visit.

1. Kyoto Shikki Kogei Kyodo Kumiai [Kyoto
   Association of Lacquer Craftsmen], *Kyoshikki:
   Kindai no bi to dento shiryohen* [The Beauty
   and Tradition of Kyoto Lacquer in Recent
   Times: A Collection of Research Material],
   s.v. Harui Komin.

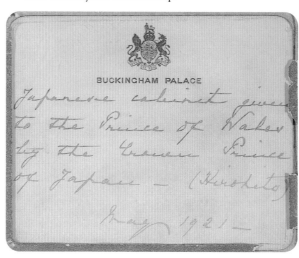

Handwritten label on
Buckingham Palace notepaper,
dated May 1921.

378

PAIR OF VASES

About 1915
Silver, with *shibuichi*, copper, and gilding;
wood stands
Height 35.2 cm.
Signed *Kazuteru koku* [carved by Kazuteru]
By Yamaguchi Kazuteru (1876–*c*.1930)

The accompanying storage box is inscribed
ginsei kabin gyoson no zu [silver vases
with design of fishing village] and *Yosai
Yamaguchi Kazuteru kinkoku* [respectfully
carved by Yosai Yamaguchi Kazuteru], with
a seal *Kazuteru no in* [seal of Kazuteru].

 Yamaguchi Kazuteru was born in Gifu
and moved to Tokyo with his father in
1888. He studied with Sato Kazuhide and
Kagawa Katsuhiro (see number 397).

379

PAIR OF VASES

Before 1922
Silver; with *shakudo*, bronze, and gold
Height 33.5 cm.
Signed *Shin'ya koku* [carved by Shin'ya]
and *Chitokusai*, sealed *Koka* and *Shin'ya*
By Sekiguchi Shin'ya (1877–*c*.1932)

The original wood box is inscribed
*Kogoheika onkashi ginkabin kujakubori
ittsui* [a pair of silver vases carved with
peacocks, graciously presented by the
Empress]. The interior is inscribed *Taisho
juichinen shigatsu Fukuoka onbettei gyokei
no setsu onkashi hin* [graciously presented
on her visit to Fukuoka Villa in April, 1922].

 Sekiguchi Shin'ya was born in Tokyo,
and from the age of fourteen studied under
his father. The vase decorated with the
peacock bears a striking similarity to the
one exhibited by his father in 1910 at the
Japan-British Exhibition.[1]

1. Office of the Imperial Japanese Government
 Commission to the Japan-British Exhibition,
 *An Illustrated Catalogue of Japanese Modern
 Fine Arts Displayed at the Japan-British
 Exhibition, London, 1910* (Tokyo, 1910),
 no. 189 (the English version ascribes it to
 Seishukwan, but the Japanese version has the
 correct name).

380
PAIR OF VASES
About 1910
Silver with *shakudo* and gold; wood stands
Height 36.4 cm.
Signed and sealed *Masami*, and signed
Miyamoto kinsei, jungin [respectfully made
by Miyamoto, pure silver]
By Ito Masami (dates unknown)

The accompanying storage box is
inscribed *Ginsei kabin menka no zu ittsui*
[a pair of silver vases with cotton-flowers].
Ito Masami lived in Tokyo and was a
member of the Tokyo Chukinkai [Tokyo
Cast Metalworkers Association].

381
VASE
About 1905
Silver; with *shakudo*, *shibuichi*, gold,
and copper
Height 33.5 cm.
Signed *Ichiya koku* [carved by Ichiya],
Ichiya no in [seal of Ichiya], *Kazuhiro to*
[carved by Kazuhiro], *Dai Nihon Tenshodo
sei* [made by Tenshodo of great Japan];
sealed *Eisho* and *Kurokawa* and marked
jungin [pure silver]
By Sekiguchi Ichiya (1850–1932 or later)

This vase is inscribed on the reverse *zotei
Dai Eikoku Kotei Heika no Shina kantai
shirei chokan Noeru taisho kakka kinpyo
kangei no bii ni soro, Meiji sanjuhachinen
juichigatsu mikka, Dai Nihon teikoku
Hiroshima-shi* [respectfully presented as a
small token of welcome to Admiral [Sir]
Nowell [Salmon], Commander of the
British Imperial Chinese Fleet. November,
Meiji 38 (1905), Hiroshima City, Empire
of Japan].
   Sekiguchi Ichiya was a member of the
Nihon Bijutsu Kyokai [Japanese Art
Association] and the Tokyo Chokokai
[Tokyo Association of Carvers and
Sculptors]. His son Sekiguchi Shin'ya was
also a metalwork artist (see number 379).
The Tenshodo Company, whose name also
appears on the vase, was located in Ginza,
Tokyo. Founded around 1879, it became
one of the largest shops in Ginza, specializing
in high-quality works of art, watches,
clocks, and metalwork, and commissioning
some of the most important metalwork
artists of the period. The company is still
flourishing, dealing in jewelry.
   Kurokawa Eisho, who made the silver
body, worked in Tokyo in the Meiji and
Taisho Eras.

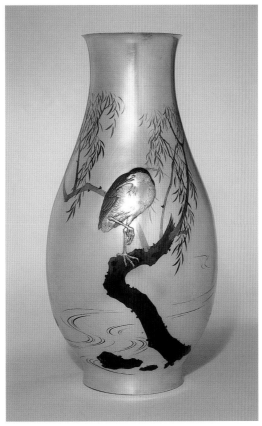

IMPERIAL ARTISTS

This last section features works by artists who were appointed to the rank of *Teishitsu Gigeiin* [Artist to the Imperial Household], an order established in 1889. Where possible, the pieces illustrated here date from late in the artist's career and were made after his appointment. So as to emphasize the collaborative nature of much craft production in the Meiji Era, even at the very highest level, throughout this catalogue many signed pieces have been described as products of the workshop operated by the artist whose name they bear. The masterworks selected for this section, by contrast, have been assigned to individual artists as a tribute to the individual creativity, as well as the commercial acumen, which brought about such a flowering of the decorative arts in the years from 1868 to 1912.

382
VASE
Late 1890s
Porcelain; painted in underglaze blue,
blue-gray, green, and copper-red and white
enamels on a yellow enamel ground
Height 49.5 cm.
Signed *Makuzu-gama Kozan sei* [made by
Kozan at the Makuzu kiln]
By Miyagawa Kozan (1842–1916)

Kozan, who was appointed in 1896, was
the second of only five potters to be named
Teishitsu Gigeiin [Artist to the Imperial
Household]. This example of his work is
outstanding both for its bold design and for
its mastery of an exceptionally wide range
of underglaze colors. Although he operated
a large workshop, Kozan appears to have
been very much a hands-on entrepreneur,
and it is reasonable to suppose that he may
have played a direct part in the creation of
the best works bearing his name.

383
VASE
About 1890
Earthenware with a crackled orange glaze
Height 28.0 cm.
Signed *Dai Nihon Seifu zo* [made by Seifu
of great Japan]
By Seifu Yohei III (1851–1914)

Seifu Yohei III was, in Japan, universally
acclaimed the finest ceramic artist of his
generation; in the West it was Kozan who
was usually preferred. He was born in
1851, the second son of the Maruyama-
school painter Okada Ryohei, entering
the studio of the painter Tanomura
Chokunyu (1814–1907) in 1866. He was
then adopted by Seifu Yohei II (Gokei) and
married Gokei's sister. He became Seifu
Yohei III on the death of Gokei in 1878.
The first international exhibition to which
he contributed was in Philadelphia in 1876.
At the third Naikoku Kangyo Hakurankai
[National Industrial Exposition] in 1890,
he won the *itto myogi shohai* [first prize
for technical excellence] for a water jug
and a gourd-shaped jar, which were highly
praised by the judges. He exhibited three
pieces in Chicago in 1893, and was
appointed *Teishitsu Gigeiin* [Artist to the
Imperial Household] in the same year. He
was awarded the Green Ribbon, another
Imperial honor, in 1895.

384
JAR
About 1920
Porcelain with a celadon glaze, modeled in
low relief and painted in underglaze red
and gray
Height 17.7 cm.
Signed *Sozan*
By Suwa Sozan (1851–1922)

Suwa Sozan came from a military family.
He worked in porcelain, first in Tokyo from
1875, then from 1879 to 1900 in Ishikawa
Prefecture. After moving to Kyoto he
worked with Kinkozan (see numbers
114–5, 117, 206, and 330) until 1906,
when he set up his own workshop. He
seems to have specialized in ceramic carving
and the making of celadon. He exhibited a
model of a Chinese-style celadon *shishi* at
the second Naikoku Kangyo Hakurankai
[National Industrial Exposition] in 1881,
and showed at several other exhibitions in
Japan. In 1914, he was commissioned by
the colonial government in Korea to assist
with the revival of the celadon industry. He
was named *Teishitsu Gigeiin* [Artist to the
Imperial Household] in 1917.

385
INCENSE BURNER
About 1910
Cloisonné enamels worked in *shakudo*,
silver and gold; *shakudo* rim
Height 11.8 cm.
Signed *Kyoto Namikawa*
By Namikawa Yasuyuki (1845–1927)

Namikawa Yasuyuki was one of a group of
craftsmen appointed *Teishitsu Gigeiin* [Artist
to the Imperial Household] in 1896. This
masterly incense burner, with its subtly
understated bravura effects, seems a summary of all Namikawa had learnt and
achieved in the previous thirty-odd years.
He made a somewhat similar incense burner
in 1912,[1] when all the *Teishitsu Gigeiin*
were engaged, each in their own metier, on
a work to be presented to the Emperor
Meiji on his sixty-first birthday, as a token
of appreciation for the encouragement he
had so consistently given to the arts. The
presentation was to have been on November
3, 1912, but was canceled owing to the
Emperor's untimely death. The works
were, however, completed and presented
in the Emperor's memory to his successor,
eventually finding their way into the
Imperial Household Museum.

1. Suzuki Norio and Sakakibara Satoru, *Nihon
   no shippo* [Japanese Cloisonné Enamels]
   (Kyoto, 1979), no. 182.

386
INCENSE BURNER
About 1910
Cloisonné enamels worked in gold and
silver wire; silver rims and foot
Height 12.6 cm.
Signed *Kyoto Namikawa*
By Namikawa Yasuyuki (1845–1927)

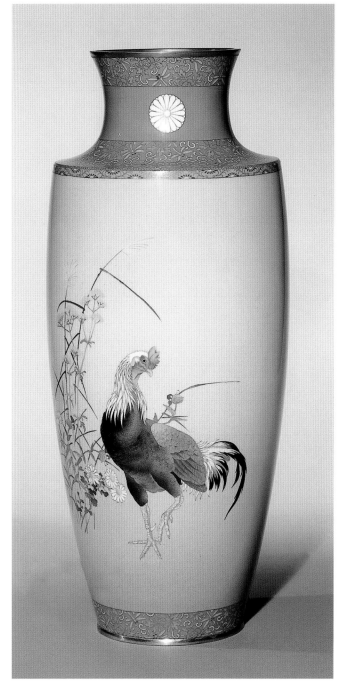

387

PAIR OF VASES
About 1890–1900
Musen and cloisonné enamels worked in
gold and silver wire; gilt copper rims and
feet; wood stands
Height 42.7 cm.
Signed with the *Sakigake* seal of Namikawa
Sosuke
By Namikawa Sosuke (1847–1910)

These vases are an example of an Imperial
Presentation piece made by a *Teishitsu
Gigeiin* [Artist to the Imperial Household],
Namikawa Sosuke having been appointed
to the order in 1896. The lid of the outer
storage box accompanying the vases is
inscribed *Tenshi musen shippo akikusa tori*

kabin [*Musen shippo* flower vases with
autumn grasses and fowl, presented by the
Emperor], and a long inscription inside the
inner lid can be translated as follows:

At the army maneuvers of November
1902, Duke Naganari welcomed the
Emperor at Fukuoka and went with him
to Kumamoto, where he presented a
tachi [sword] and made a paper presentation of a Takatori-ware vase to the
Emperor on November 12. When the
Emperor visited the grave of Prince
Takako on November 15, the Governor
of Fukuoka Prefecture was given the

rank of *jusanmi*. The pair of *musen*
enamel vases with the Imperial *mon*
[crest] was given by the Imperial Household Agency on December 12. Made by
Namikawa Sosuke.

Although the date of presentation of these
vases is recorded as 1902, they were clearly
made considerably earlier; the Imperial
Household Agency not only favored somewhat conservative tastes, using this shape
with some frequency and also in other
materials (see catalogue numbers 378–80),
but also held such presentation wares in
reserve, awaiting the appropriate occasion.

388
TRAY
About 1900
Musen and cloisonné enamels worked in
silver wire; *shakudo* rim
19.0 × 14.2 cm.
Signed and sealed *Seitei* and signed on
the reverse with the *Sakigake* seal of
Namikawa Sosuke
By Namikawa Sosuke (1847–1910), from a
design by Watanabe Seitei (1851–1918)

389
TRAY
About 1905–10
Musen enamels with details in silver wire
28.5 × 28.5 cm.
Signed with the *Sakigake* seal of
Namikawa Sosuke
By Namikawa Sosuke (1847–1910)

The unobtrusive delicacy of these late
masterpieces by Sosuke demonstrates
how far he, like his namesake Namikawa
Yasuyuki, was able to pick and choose
what technique was best suited to what
area of decoration, without feeling the
need to show off his skill. The overall
effect is reminiscent of the oval panels
Sosuke made in 1909 for the newly
built Akasaka Detached Palace.

390
BOX FOR WRITING UTENSILS AND BOX FOR WRITING PAPER
1904 or earlier
Wood, lacquered in *takamaki-e*, *hiramaki-e*, and *kirikane* on a *nashiji* ground; silver and gold water-dropper; silver fittings
5.5 × 24.5 × 26.0 cm. (box for writing utensils); 13.0 × 36.0 × 61.0 cm. (box for writing paper)
Signed *Shosai* with a *kao* [cursive monogram]
By Shirayama Shosai (1853–1923)

Shirayama Shosai, one of the leading lacquerers of the Meiji and Taisho Eras, was named *Teishitsu Gigeiin* [Artist to the Imperial Household] in 1906, not long after this set of boxes was displayed at the Louisiana Purchase Exhibition (1904). He started his career by studying metal sword decoration before switching to lacquer. He worked for the Kiritsu Kosho Kaisha [First Industrial Manufacturing Company] from 1880 and in 1892 became a professor at Tokyo School of Art.

391

BOX FOR WRITING UTENSILS AND BOX FOR WRITING PAPER

About 1870

Wood, lacquered in *takamaki-e*, *hiramaki-e*, and several other techniques; with coral and shell details, on a polished orange-red ground

5.0 x 22.5 x 27.0 cm. (box for writing utensils); 10.0 x 30.1 x 39.5 cm. (box for writing paper)

Both boxes signed *Zeshin*

By Shibata Zeshin (1807–1891)

Perhaps the greatest of all Japanese lacquerers, Shibata Zeshin was the only lacquerer named as *Teishitsu Gigeiin* [Artist to the Imperial Household] in 1890, the first year that the honor was conferred. A panel exhibited by Zeshin at the second Naikoku Kangyo Hakurankai [National Industrial Exposition] in 1881 is described in the first section of this catalogue (number 34); that was a conscious imitation of the framed Western canvas and was in the more formal, almost academic, style adopted by Zeshin for such great occasions. This set of boxes, by contrast, is a masterpiece in his more usual manner, with its seemingly artless and yet always perfect positioning of motifs, its vast range of techniques, many of them invented by Zeshin himself, and its constant

allusion to popular customs and beliefs. The decoration here consists mostly of the *takaramono* [auspicious motifs associated with the Seven Gods of Good Fortune, (see number 126)], including the *kakuregasa* [hat] and *kakuremino* [cloak] of invisibility, weights symbolizing trade and prosperity, the *hanabishi* floral motif within a rhomboid

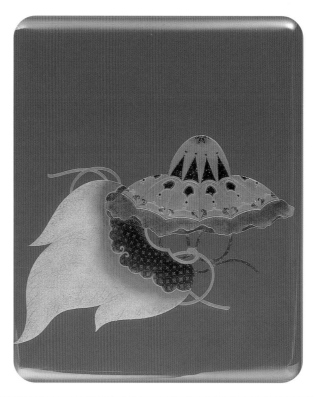

formed of arcs of a circle, and a stylized clove. The wealth-bestowing mallet of Daikoku, a god of wealth, appears on one of the sides of the larger box and continues underneath. These designs are continued inside both boxes so that the viewer's eye is drawn across their every surface.

392
DISH
About 1875–1900
Wood; lacquered in *roiro*, *seigaiha-nuri* (see
below), *hiramaki-e*, and shell
Diameter 23.5 cm.
Signed and sealed *Taishin*
By Ikeda Taishin (1825–1903)

This tray with its design of *chidori* (see
number 212) in shell inlay flying over
waves was made by Ikeda Taishin, the
first and best pupil of Shibata Zeshin (see
number 391). Taishin was named *Teishitsu
Gigeiin* [Artist to the Imperial Household]
in 1896, only five years after his master,
who had died in 1891. The *seigaiha-nuri*
technique, in which specially treated lacquer
is worked with a comb-like tool to gain an
effect resembling the waves of the sea, is
one of several methods invented by Zeshin
and carried on by Taishin. Although Taishin
was a frequent exhibitor at domestic and
foreign exhibitions and had his own school
of followers, the Yagenbori-ha, none of
them matched up to his skill and artistry,
and the Zeshin manner died with him.

393
GROUP
About 1900
Bronze with *shakudo* details; wood stand
Height 70.0 cm. (overall)
Attributed to Suzuki Chokichi (1848–1919)

Suzuki Chokichi, whose work for the early
domestic and international expositions
was introduced in the first section of this
catalogue, was one of a group of metalworkers, enamelers, potters and lacquerers
who were named *Teishitsu Gigeiin* [Artist
to the Imperial Household] in 1896. This
group is attributed to him on the basis of a
bronze plaque inscribed:

> Bronze group by Suzuki-Chokichi, a
> famous art worker now retained by and
> working exclusively for the Emperor of
> Japan. It illustrates two famous Samarai
> [sic] viz Kawuyzu Sammuro and Mataro
> Goro, the originators of the art of
> wrestling, hence the gods of all the
> wrestlers of Japan.

Although the work is unsigned, the attribution on the plaque seems quite likely. The
plaque itself certainly appears original to
the group. The high quality of the casting
conforms with the attribution, while the
more naturalistic Western style would
indicate a somewhat late date, certainly
well after the period when Chokichi was
producing work for the Kiritsu Kosho
Kaisha [First Industrial Manufacturing
Company] (see number 31).

394
TABLE SCREEN
About 1890
Shibuichi with *shakudo*, the reverse lacquered
in *togidashi-e*; zelkova-wood stand
16.4 x 18.0 cm.
Sealed *Natsuo*
By Kano Natsuo (1828–98)

This plaque with a view of the Kiyomizu
temple in Kyoto, one of the most famous
sights of both traditional and modern
Japan, is by Kano Natsuo, who was named
Teishitsu Gigeiin [Artist to the Imperial
Household] in 1890, the first year that the
honor was conferred. The son of a rice
merchant, Natsuo was adopted by the
sword-dealer Kano Chisuke at the age of
six and given the name Kano Jisaburo. He
started his own business in Kyoto in 1846,
changing his name to Natsuo at some time
between 1848 and 1854. Like many of the
most outstanding artists introduced in this
catalogue, Natsuo's training was not confined to the acquisition of craft skills; he
also studied painting with the leading artist
Nakajima Raisho, as well as calligraphy
and classical poetry. In 1854 he moved to
Tokyo and by the early 1860s he was producing about fifty pieces a year. In 1869, he
started to work for the newly-established
Imperial Mint in Osaka; Shibata Zeshin
(see number 391) was one of the first of his
friends to welcome him back to Tokyo
after eight years working there. He was a
judge for the second, third, and fourth
Naikoku Kangyo Hakurankai [National
Industrial Expositions] and a professor at
Tokyo Art School.

Natsuo is universally acknowledged as
the finest metalworker of his day; indeed,
many would claim he was the finest metalworker of Japan, a country justly famous
for its creations in this genre. He consistently
won the highest prizes available to metalworkers at the Naikoku Kangyo Hakurankai,
against the stiff competition of Unno
Shomin (see number 395), Namekawa
Sadakatsu (see number 228), Unno Bisei,
and others.

This screen is accompanied by two
preparatory drawings mounted as *kakemono*
[hanging scrolls]. One is in ink on silk and
is sealed *Nihon kinko* [Japanese metalwork]
and *Natsuo*; the copper *jiku* [scroll ends]
are signed *Natsuo* with a seal *Koi* [in the
ancient manner]. The other scroll is a sketch
on paper, sealed *Kano Natsuo saikusho*
[Kano Natsuo's workshop].

The wooden storage box is inscribed by
Natsuo's third son, Akio, *rogin usunikubori*

*Kiyomizu no zu, migi senko Hokujakuen
Natsuo kaishin saku, tsunezune jiai seshi-
mono nari, kinoto-i nenji yayoi Akio shirusu*
[design of Kiyomizu in *shibuichi* carved in
low relief, a work of the heart by Hokujakuen Natsuo, always cherished by him,
written by Akio in March of the *kinoto-i*
year (1935)].

395
PLAQUE
About 1910
Copper, with gold and *shakudo*; silver
border, mulberry-wood frame
25.7 × 19.2 cm.
Signed *Kaitekian Shomin teppitsu* [the iron
brush of Kaitekian Shomin] and sealed
Shomin
By Unno Shomin (1844–1915)

This plaque, with a half-length figure of the
ferocious demon-queller Shoki (see number
137), is worked in relief in *uchidashi* [raised
designs achieved by hammering sheet metal
from the front against a shape applied to
the reverse] and finely carved in *katakiri-bori*
[carving with an angled chisel that can
create a V-shaped groove of varied width
that emulates the thick and thin strokes
of ink painting]. It is the use of this latter
technique that led Unno Shomin to add the
word *teppitsu* [iron brush] when he signed
this masterpiece.

   Shomin was one of the two most
renowned Meiji metalworkers (the other
being Kano Natsuo, see number 394). He

trained under his uncle Unno Yoshimori I,
and later under Hagiya Katsuhira (1804-
86) in Mito, the homeland of so many of
the best Meiji-Era metal artists. He also
learned painting, drawing, and calligraphy
before moving to Tokyo in 1871 and
changing his name from Kihei to Shomin.
The character *sho* means "superior", and in
this case he intended to be superior to the
renowned metalworker Yokoya Somin
(1671–1733) who is said to have invented
the *katakiri-bori* technique. Shomin's figure
of a dancer, made for the third Naikoku
Kangyo Hakurankai [National Industrial
Exposition] in 1890, for which he won the
myogi [technical excellence] prize, is now in
the Imperial Collection. He also exhibited
in other domestic and international exhibitions, receiving many honors. In 1890, he
joined the Tokyo Art School as a teacher

under Kano Natsuo and in 1894 became
professor; he was named *Teishitsu Gigeiin*
[Artist to the Imperial Household] in 1896.
He acted as one of the judges at the fourth
and fifth Naikoku Kangyo Hakurankai of
1895 and 1903.

   The accompanying inner and an outer
storage boxes bear inscriptions by Unno
Kiyoshi, Shomin's son. The outer box is
inscribed *Senko Shomin saku suaka
usuniku Shoki gaku Taisho mizunoto-i
Unno Kiyoshi* [made by my father Shomin,
copper panel of Shoki in low-relief carving,
mizunoto-i year (1923) Unno Kiyoshi]. The
inner box is inscribed *Senko Shomin saku
Shoki suakaji chokoku Taisho mizunoe-inu
Unno Kiyoshi* [made by my father Shomin,
Shoki carved on copper ground, *mizunoe-
inu* year of Taisho (1922), Unno Kiyoshi].

396
PLAQUE
About 1910
Copper, with gold, silver, and *shakudo*; gilt
border; wood frame with gilt fittings
Diameter 36.0 cm.
Signed *Hoshu Shomin koku* [carved by
Hoshu Shomin]; with a partially unread
seal, *Koi* ... [in the ancient manner ...]
By Unno Shomin (1844–1915)

For Unno Shomin, see opposite. This
plaque is executed in the same techniques
and shows Kanzan and Jittoku (see number
58). The use of the word *koi* [ancient
manner] in the signature refers to Shomin's
debt to fourteenth- and fifteenth-century
Japanese paintings of this subject and
their earlier Chinese antecedents.

397
BOX
1913
Silver; with *shibuichi*, gold, and copper
4.9 × 15.2 × 11.3 cm.
Signed *Katsuhiro koku* [carved by
Katsuhiro], *Mitsuharu*, and *Ka*[tsura]
By Katsura Mitsuharu (1871–1962) and
Kagawa Katsuhiro (1853–1917)

This box combines many of the decorative
metalworking techniques, originally devised
for sword-fittings, that were developed
with such success during the Meiji Era,
including *takazogan* [relief inlay], *honzogan*
[flat inlay], *katakiri-bori* (see number 395),
and *nikubori* [relief carving].

Katsura Mitsuharu was born in Tokyo,
becoming independent in 1898, and starting
his own business at Asakusa, in Tokyo.
Kagawa Katsuhiro, who was appointed
Teishitsu Gigeiin [Artist to the Imperial
Household] in 1906, was born in the
working-class district of Shitaya, Edo
(Tokyo). He learned wood-carving from a
No-mask carver, drawing from Shibata
Zeshin (see number 391), and metalwork
from Nomura Katsumori and Kano Natsuo
(see number 394), with whom he worked
on a sword for the Meiji Emperor. He
exhibited extensively at both national and
international exhibitions, including
Nuremberg (1885), Chicago (1893), Venice
(1898), Paris (1900), and London (1910).

The accompanying storage box is
inscribed *gin rogin sei makitabako-bako*
[cigarette box made of silver and *shibuichi*].
A paper label on the side is inscribed
*Katsuhiro Mitsuharu gassaku, makitabako-
ire* [cigarette box made in collaboration by
Katsuhiro and Mitsuharu]. The interior is
inscribed *Bokusui hyakkaen no zu Taisho
ninen mizunoto-ushi shoka Katsura
Mitsuharu saku Kagawa Katsuhiro saku*
[design of the Hundred-Flower Garden in
Sumida, April of the second year of Taisho,
mizunoto-ushi (1913), made by Katsura
Mitsuharu and Kagawa Katsuhiro].

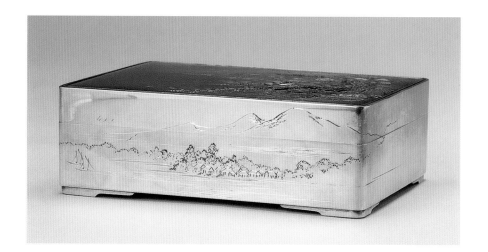